WHO WROTE THE MODERN CLASSICS?

Other John Day Books by Nora Stirling:

WHO WROTE THE CLASSICS? Volume I

(Shakespeare, Austen, Hawthorne, Verne, Kipling, Poe, Twain, The Brontës, Dickens, Stevenson)

WHO WROTE THE CLASSICS? Volume II

(George Eliot, Melville, James, Edith Wharton, Stephen Crane, Scott, Hardy, Shaw, Conrad)

WHO WROTE
THE
MODERN CLASSICS?

Nora Stirling

THE JOHN DAY COMPANY
NEW YORK

To Leslie and Margaret Pearl

The John Day Company, 257 Park Avenue South, New York, N.Y. 10010

An **Intext** Publisher

Published on the same day in Canada by Longmans Canada Limited.

Library of Congress Catalogue
Card Number: 77-124156
Printed in the United States of America

Portions of *O'Neill: A Biography,* by Barbara and Arthur Gelb, are reprinted here with the kind permission of Harper & Row, Publishers.

Photograph of W. Somerset Maugham used with permission of United Press International Photos. Photograph of Eugene O'Neill used with permission of Culver Pictures, Inc. Photograph of F. Scott Fitzgerald courtesy Charles Scribner's Sons. Photographs of Thomas Wolfe and Sinclair Lewis used with permission of Wide World Photos.

Contents

W. Somerset Maugham
(1874-1965)

W. Somerset Maugham
(1874=1965)

LIKE SEVERAL well-known writers—notably Bernard Shaw and Thomas Hardy—Somerset Maugham lived to a very great age. He was ninety-one when he died. But his latter years, unlike those others', were not marked by either serenity or humor. The Maugham face of late photographs, with its disillusioned eyes and mouth like a down-turned crescent, is so twisted by bitterness that one cannot accept it as just the face of a tired old man. Laying it alongside a picture of the thirty-year-old man—or, even more startling still, that of the lovely, sensitive child of ten—one is forced to wonder what evil spirit was present at his birth to cancel out all the bountiful gifts bestowed on him by nature.

Even the searing love affair described in *Of Human Bondage* surely alone did not work such havoc. Noel Coward has written that the only important facts about Maugham's life are the literary ones, and that his unhappy marriage and his "sexual inclinations" are irrelevant. But nothing is irrelevant to a man's face, and that bitterness had to come from more than the normal wear and tear of the literary life.

Maugham's first years were extraordinarily happy. His father, one of a line of prominent Maugham lawyers, solid, respectable and upper middle class, had married a beautiful girl sixteen years his junior. Edith Snell brought not only charm and sparkling social gifts into the family circle but introduced a blood line running proudly back through baronets and earls and dukes to a brace of kings. Her charm and his brains together made them a social success in Paris, where Robert Maugham was lawyer to the British Embassy.

The Maughams were a conspicuous couple, for her grace and beauty were a startling contrast to his ugliness, which was almost terrifying at first glance. But even more startling to the sophisticated habitués of Edith Snell's salon was her devotion to her husband. Asked why she, who could have had any man in Paris, was so perfectly content with her little monster, she replied simply, "Not once in my entire married life has he ever hurt my feelings."

The Maugham home was a place of luxury and comfort, an apartment just off the Champs Elysées to which came the nobility and intelligentsia of Paris. But Edith Maugham suffered from tuberculosis, and as pregnancy at this time was considered beneficial for tuberculosis patients, she bore up under a schedule of childbearing that must have shortened her life rather than lengthened it.

Six little boys made up the brood, though two died in infancy. There were Charles, whom Maugham later described as "the saint," and Henry, whom he called "the bore"; these made small impact on his life. But Frederick, "the great one," was an overbearing, supercilious older brother whom in time he regarded as "the most odious man he had ever met." This Frederick was brilliant, haughty, and inflexibly righteous. He became Lord Chancellor of England and First Viscount Maugham of Hartfield, and he made no bones about his disapproval of his notorious brother. (In his autobiography he gave him exactly three lines.) There was between them a mutual dislike that erupted in cold flame whenever they met, and since he lived to be ninety-two Maugham did not have many years of freedom from him.

William Somerset Maugham was born in Paris in 1874, younger than all the others by several years, and thus was especially cherished. When he was only three the older boys were sent away to an English school, and for the next five years he reigned as undisputed center of the home.

These were the only completely happy years of his life. He was surrounded by every physical comfort, including beautiful art objects in the home and in the nearby Luxembourg and Louvre museums. He had French playmates of his own age, a loving governess-nurse, and a father so kind and indulgent his ugliness somehow disappeared. Best of all, he had the lovely mother, even then, though he could not know it, fading away. These early memories were to haunt him, ghostlike with their lost perfection—the mornings when he visited her where she lay in bed, her hair spread out on her pillow, her complexion translucent like a magnolia blossom; the afternoons when she played softly with him, her large brown eyes wistful with a foreknowledge of death.

Toward the end of 1881, once more pregnant, she was struck by the dreadful thought that she was going to die and that her children, too young to remember clearly, would never know how she had looked. She called her maid and had herself dressed in a white satin evening gown, with long earrings and a locket on a black velvet ribbon. The coachman drove her to a photographer's, and there the picture was taken that eighty-four years later stood on her son Willie's bedside table when he died. Shortly thereafter the new baby was born, to live but a few days, and on January 31, 1882, his mother died. It was one of the most important dates of Maugham's life, the cut-off date for heaven.

The bereft father did his best for the next two years. But he himself was dying, and the pain of his illness made him irritable. The older boys were in England. So Willie's mainstay and comfort was his nurse, who tenderly tried to fill the child's emptiness. When he lay sobbing at night, when he went into his mother's closet and, taking her dresses into his arms, buried his face in her delicious scent, the nurse understood and consoled him.

Then in 1884 all links with his past were cut; his father died, and in accordance with his will, Willie was left in the care of an uncle in England. So the ten-year-old child with the poignantly sweet face was dressed as became a young traveling gentleman, in Little Lord Fauntleroy velvets, and put on the boat train in care of his nurse. All the way across the Channel he clung to her hand; when the cliffs of Dover appeared, she said, "There's your new home," and he nodded reluctantly, still clinging.

At Dover he discovered how utterly strange this new world was. The nurse spoke no English at all. And though he understood English, French had been the family language in that chic Paris house, and when they stood on the dock waving for a cab, all the English he knew left his terrified brain and he stood there piping helplessly, *"Porteur! Cabriolet!"*

Whitstable was a small town on the south coast of England, whose All Saints' Church, seven centuries old, was its religious center. The Vicarage nearby was a large house with dark silent rooms where reigned his uncle, a shortish, roundish, self-important man with hair plastered across his bald spot and a laugh that tried to be hearty. The Vicar's wife, German and childless, had been taught that wives lived to serve their husbands, and all her attention was given to serving hers.

The night Willie arrived the Reverend Henry Maugham took him onto his knee and explained the present situation: contrary to expectations, contrary to the manner in which his father and mother had lived, there was actually little money in his father's estate, barely one hundred and fifty pounds a year for each of the four boys. His brothers would have to continue their education on scholarships, and he himself would always have to be very careful. And of course his nurse could not stay on with him; they couldn't possibly afford such a luxury.

Eighty years later, telling his nephew of the events of that evening, Somerset Maugham's eyes filled with tears. "After both my mother and my father had died my nurse was the only person in the world I loved. She was my one link with all the happiness and affection I'd known in the Avenue d'Antain. She was the only real friend I had. You see, my brothers were older than I was. But my nurse had been with me constantly since my mother died. . . . I think she was as fond of me as I was of her. . . . My last link with my mother . . . and they took her away from me that very night."

It is not hard to appreciate the shock to a sensitive child already shaken by two deaths, to be suddenly cut off from all the safety he had ever known. Had he been less protected before, less enwrapped in love and warmth, the abrupt change in his life might not have been so traumatic. But not only had he lost mother and father and nurse—as far as his eyes could see not a friendly face or friendly French tongue existed; all was harsh and strange and forbidding. A child's psyche would have to be rugged indeed to endure such a shock without casualty.

Whether he did or not is a question. But one thing is certain, that whatever the cause, Maugham was forever racked by one terrible affliction, though whether his famous stammer was a direct result cannot be determined. His early playmates in France, interviewed late in life, had no recollection of an impediment in his speech, and apparently no one in Paris had ever mentioned it, for he himself was not then conscious of having such an affliction. Only after he came to England did it begin to plague him. So one wonders whether the happy little boy in Paris ever had a stammer at all, or whether it only followed the later miseries in England.

These miseries were undoubtedly harrowing. The Vicarage atmosphere was heavy with long prayers instructing the Lord how to run His business; the empty Sundays were a grim foretaste of eternity, for games and all reading matter but the Bible were banned; laughter was distrusted as frivolous; ordinary boyish spirits were accounted the Devil emerging, and all contact with the local boys was forbidden as contaminating the family gentility.

The contrast between this bleak atmosphere and that he had left behind was profoundly disorienting. In Paris, the famous and titled in his mother's salon were taken as a matter of course, while here his uncle nearly bent double when a Sir-something stopped in the road for a chat. In Paris every luxury was at hand, while here *The Times* was read in haste because two other houses shared the subscription.

The school he went to added most of all to the confusion and gloom. In later life he wondered that so much architectural beauty could contain so much ugliness, for Canterbury Cathedral, with its Cloisters and adjoining King's School, was one of the visual prides of England. But this ancient school, alma mater of Christopher Marlowe and other illustrious Englishmen, had its crawling underside of meanness and brutality. Small, frenchified, and frightened, Willie Maugham was a natural butt for bullies and his stammer made him the perfect target for the older boys. Even the masters were not above showing their irritation at his annoying habit of speech. In *Of Human Bondage* Maugham gave his prototype, Philip Carey, a club foot instead of a stammer, but the effect was identical, and the book is an unforgettable classic in the realm of childhood suffering.

The early chapters contain the incident which, Maugham said later, destroyed all religious faith for him forever. His uncle had asserted heartily that God always answered prayers if one prayed hard enough, so after much merciless taunting at school the child prayed with all the vehemence of his soul for his stammer to be taken away. Nothing happened. So from then on Maugham dismissed the Deity as a cruel fraud and took every occasion to be sarcastic and witty at His expense. Still, like many another agnostic, he could not dismiss Him entirely from his thoughts and seemed by his very taunts to be trying to elicit some answering sign of life.

He was, then, stuck with his stammer. And though he seldom spoke about it, an essay he wrote many years later about the author Arnold Bennett, who also stammered, is revealing. His description of Bennett's stammer is full of eloquent words—*exhaustion, strain, torture, struggle, humiliation, ridicule, exasperation.* "It tore his nerves to pieces," he wrote. "Few knew the distressing sense it gave rise to of a bar to complete contact with other men. It may be that except for the stammer which forced him to introspection, Arnold would never have become a writer." Many friends thought that with a change of names the essay could have been about himself.

In time he learned to live with his affliction. And as its novelty wore off his schoolmates left him in peace, and his last years at King's were so much more peaceable that in his affluent old age he gave the school many generous gifts, contributing largely to a boathouse and a science building, and donating the manuscripts of his first and last novels and much of his personal library.

In late adolescence he became ill with a lung disorder. By now he was in possession of a small inheritance from his father, and his guardians, remembering that his mother and an aunt had died of tuberculosis, hurried him off to the south of France. There he underwent the usual adolescent experience of falling in love with an older woman, his tutor's wife. Recovering from both maladies simultaneously, he returned to England intact. But the warm French atmosphere and the stories of Maupassant, which he had read there for the first time, had planted the seeds of independence within him. Both his uncle and King's School, which through the centuries had concentrated on turning out clergymen, had expected him to go into the Church. But he was already developing literary ambitions, and as a tentative step away from the fate planned for him, he asked for a year in Germany "to continue his studies and perfect his languages." This request was normal enough not to arouse his guardians' suspicions, and he was sent to Heidelberg with their blessing and many letters to respectable German relatives.

Heidelberg completed his emancipation; he saw plays, heard music, studied philosophy, discussed ethics and religions, listened to fresh and startling ideas. He discovered the irony and cynicism of La Rochefoucauld, whose influence continued to appear in his plays for sixty years. And, thrown among strangers for the first time, he began that lifelong habit of observing people with shrewd, unemotional accuracy that made his fiction a veritable pharmacopoeia of human frailties.

His year abroad also introduced him to the beauties of the earth, the lush Rhine valley, the lofty Swiss Alps, the architectural ecstasies of Italy, and his mild first wanderings set his feet on travel paths that lured him on for the rest of his life.

Returning to Whitstable at eighteen, he grimly set his jaw against the clergy. His guardians' principal concern was that he should enter some similar profession such as the law, but his three brothers were already shining there and he was not of a mind to compete with the supercilious Frederick. So, unable to wedge him into the Church or the bar, they tried him on chartered accountancy. That lasted barely two months. Medicine had by then become respectable, even elegant, so when their tiresome ward suggested that profession they were glad enough to agree and get the matter settled.

The ward's interest in studying medicine was hardly a call to healing; what he wanted was a chance to live alone in London and see life raw as a preparation for authorship. St. Thomas's Hospital, whose school he entered in 1892, was ideal for that purpose, for this enormous mass of five-hundred-year-old buildings stood just across the Thames from the Houses of Parliament and served the Borough of Lambeth with its reeking slums. He took lodgings nearby with a typical Cockney landlady (who later bobbed up amusingly in *Cakes and Ale*) and lived adequately on thirty shillings a week.

His first two years, given to memorizing the names of thousands of muscles and bones, bored him ferociously, and he studied only enough to pass the examinations. Actually he was concentrating on gathering material for the future, noting down ideas for stories and plays, snippets of dialogue, epigrams (he was very fond of epigrams), and caustic observations in the Rochefoucauld manner—all, he said later, very young and ingenuous.

After the two dull years of theory, he was plunged into the excitement of practice, and for the next three he witnessed firsthand most of the situations and emotions of which the human creature is capable. In the Out-Patient Department he did accident duty in the emergency ward; he spent months in obstetrics delivering babies and went, night and day, down foul dark alleys where even the police hesitated to go alone. Here he learned the magic protection of the doctor's little black bag, for the roughest criminals let him pass unharmed. Once inside, he saw human nature naked in all its unimaginable variety; before him there were no reticences; fear and pain loosened every tongue and disclosed every misery and guarded vice. The doctor's business was to listen, and no details were too intimate for his ears.

During this time he saw how men died, how they met suffering and endured despair. He saw hideous poverty and cold cruelty. And from it all he drew certain conclusions: though courage and kindness might occasionally be found in the midst of squalor, the notion that man was ennobled by suffering was a sentimental fallacy. Actually, the fruits of suffering were selfishness, meanness, suspicion, and brutality. The dying became cowardly, the poor dishonest, the sick pettily self-centered. One learned to expect no good from human nature and thus when it did appear one received a pleasant surprise. This was not cynicism; one was merely being realistic.

During these years Maugham's hospital day ran from dawn until six P.M., but his evenings were his own and he made full use of them. Reading French, German, Italian, and Latin, he plunged through world literature with an ardor that never left him. (He confessed once that, when asked the most thrilling moment of his life, only fear of seeming pretentious stopped him from saying, "The moment when I began to read Goethe's *Faust.*") And though writing came as naturally as breathing, he never deceived himself that it was easy to do well. He worked at it like a day laborer, studying other writers and trying out their techniques and tricks. Dissatisfied with an unadorned style, he analyzed the exotic phraseology of Walter Pater, Oscar Wilde, and The Song of Solomon, making lists of peculiar and arresting words and fitting them into sample sentences. Finally, after turning out elaborate passages which, on rereading, bored him to death, he decided against trying for a conspicuous style and settled instead for lucidity, simplicity, and euphony. Later in life he phrased his writing credo even more succinctly—Stick to the point.

It was during these years—somewhere between 1894 and 1897—that more than his philosophy and writing style was being determined. In his autobiography, *The Summing Up,* he writes obliquely, "I entered little into the life of the hospital and made few friends there, for I was occupied with other things." It was these "other things," one feels, that, like a barrier across a road, detoured him into the bypath he might not otherwise have traveled.

All that is known of this period is what he has chosen to tell. And the cryptic sentence above is all he has admitted directly about the "other things." So one has to turn to *Of Human Bondage,* the novel about this period. And thus forced into conjecture and interpretation, one pours that mixture of fact and fiction through a sieve and examines the solid matter that is left behind.

There is a great deal to work with. The first part of the book, the early years, is admittedly close to the truth, and Maugham has even identified many of the characters. The accountant's office and hospital experiences are likewise factual. But the dramatic core of the novel, the feature that makes it burn with an acrid, blinding flame, is the love affair with Mildred.

But actually, love affair it was not, for that phrase implies some sort of mutual attraction. Philip Carey's love for Mildred was totally unrequited; the tawdry, selfish waitress to whom he was drawn by some irrational attraction was incapable of love for anyone. All she did was use him, meanwhile contemptuously mocking his infirmity. Finally, in a rage she swept like a tornado through the lodging he shared with her, ripping and shattering and leaving it a wreck.

In the couple's story there is no redeeming feature. Mildred has not even physical beauty to justify Philip's devotion, and his helplessness before her is disgusting. The remarkable thing about it is its believability. Mildred is inescapably real; she *happened.* So did Philip.

Yet Maugham has denied that Mildred really existed. "A composite impression," he calls her, "largely imaginary."

Quite late in life Maugham, in describing the composition of his novel, said that around 1912, some fifteen or twenty years after the actual events, he began to be haunted by the memory of those early years; ". . . it all came back to me so pressingly, in my sleep, on my walk . . . it became such a burden to me that I made up my mind that I could only regain my peace by writing it all down in the form of a novel." So to ask the reader to believe that the love affair was not real is to demand too much credulity. (But perhaps he had to demand it, being simply ashamed. And in truth the story is so shabby, so embarrassing, that, while he had to get it out of his system by writing it, he might not care to admit it afterward.)

It is remarkable that, with such a powerful emotion to occupy Maugham during his hospital years, he could have thought about anything else. But he did work at his writing. For this was a man who had to write—all his life he had to write, every day and everywhere, in trains, on shipboard, while visiting, while sick or dying of heartbreak. Every morning between breakfast and lunch, whether he had an idea or not, down he sat, and if nothing better came he wrote his name over and over till the obstruction broke.

Three or four hours was his limit, for early in life he read somewhere that Charles Darwin had produced his epoch-making books in three hours a day, and he reasoned that if science and religion and ethics could be overturned on such a schedule, his more modest ambition required no more. But in another sense he was working all day, for everywhere he went he was collecting material, observing, making notes, speculating on this silent and veiled personality, putting that dull bore into an amusing story.

He started with short stories during his internship, sending them out and, like most beginners, monotonously receiving them back. But suddenly something different happened: a publisher, while returning two of his stories, enclosed a letter asking if Mr. Maugham had a full-length novel to submit instead. Mr. Maugham didn't but he sat down and wrote one.

Liza of Lambeth was a bald, harshly unromantic account of the last year of a young factory girl, her pathetic love affair and death. Its setting was the dirty alleys where he had gone to deliver babies, and the language he heard and the sights he saw there were reproduced unsoftened. Critics found its realism startling; some admired it while others thought it disgusting and unhealthy. But when the famous Bishop Wilberforce found the book worthy of a sermon in Westminster Abbey a second printing was called for directly.

The young author, only twenty-three, was so uplifted by his critical success—he did not know how little cash the success was to bring—that he waited only long enough to receive his medical degrees and then renounced the practice of medicine for life. Later he wished he had pursued it longer, for no other occupation, he believed, offered the same wealth of dramatic material. (For a similar reason he deplored the effects of success, which cushioned the author against many of the realities of life and seduced him with softer, more superficial fare.)

The death of Uncle Henry Maugham in 1897 shortly after the publication of his book completed Willie's independence. So now, taking his father's legacy in hand, he made off for Spain to become a writer. A full year passed before he received his first royalty check from *Liza of Lambeth* and then it was only twenty pounds, but he managed well enough, living the life of a handsome young bachelor, growing a moustache, smoking Filipino cigars, wearing a broad-brimmed Spanish grandee's hat, and playing the guitar (not well). After his bleak years life seemed gay and pleasant, for Spanish girls were easy-going and the beauty of the country laid a lasting hold on his soul. He wrote a book about it but it was no good.

Everything he wrote for the next several years was no good. Settling in Paris in a fifth-floor Montparnasse flat, he consorted with other struggling Left Bankers. And here too life was exciting, though somewhat threadbare. However, the legend of extreme poverty that has clung to this period of his career arose less from lack of money than from lack of success. He never really starved, but the enforced scrimping did give him a bitter recognition of the power of money. It was, he said, like a sixth sense without which one could not make the most of the other five.

"Lack of success" does not mean that he could not get his writings published. *Liza of Lambeth* had been sufficiently promising to induce his publisher to ride along with his failures, and indeed, one novel, *Mrs. Craddock,* did receive fair reviews, rising just above the failure level. Otherwise, he seemed to labor in vain. But still labor he must, because his financial needs were pressing.

Not only must he support himself but, on occasion, there were others he wished to support—in particular one young lady with uncomfortably expensive tastes. His rivals in that quarter were very rich and he had to keep writing hard to hold his own against them. But even a bad book takes a month or so to write and a month or so to get published and a few more to get paid for. So by the time he was in a position to court her really effectively his passion had faded and he used the money to take a trip to Egypt instead.

He was living in London by this time. All during this period he had been trying to write plays as well, hoping they would be easier, and finally he did get a gloomy tragedy in the Ibsen manner produced by the Stage Society for two performances. *A Man of Honour* was hailed as "artistic" and "important," and he thought now the way was clear ahead. But there were still hurdles to negotiate. The play's lighter scenes having convinced him that he had a comedy touch, he wrote a play making fun of a clergyman. But this was twenty years before *Rain,* in which he scalped a clergyman, and his irreverence was considered as shocking as the gutter talk in *Liza.* No one would touch it.

Next he essayed a "strong" play with a big scene to attract a big woman star. The scene was big enough—the heroine, in order to disillusion a young lover, decides to let him see her without makeup and her hair in a mess. But what star would consider a scene like that?

So then he tried a thoroughly harmless little piece which he believed no one could possibly object to. This was unfortunately *so* slight, *so* placid, that no producer could summon up the energy to put it on. Time was going on; he was over thirty.

Discouraged with women stars, he turned to men. But *Jack Straw* left the male stars as cold as clams. It seemed that his one produced play had given the impression that he was a gloomy playwright; and while one couldn't call his comedies exactly gloomy, they were vaguely unpleasant and misanthropic—certainly not the cheerful kind of thing the public wanted. They were left lying about on managers' desks month after month and he was almost losing heart.

At the last moment a perceptive agent came to the rescue. Something told him these plays were good, that they were even —that magic word—commercial, and he kept shoving them into managers' hands. Finally, one with enough glue on it stuck. *Lady Frederick,* the play with the strong female part, was announced for the Court Theatre.

Lady Frederick was his final test. He had been writing for ten years, with dazzling lack of success. He had run through his father's legacy and seemed unable to earn a living, having tried journalism and failed at it and then play reviewing and been told he lacked theater sense. By 1907, almost penniless, he had left London for cheaper living elsewhere, and so on October 26 it was a desperate man who faced the opening of his new play; if this one failed, there was nothing to do but go back to the hospital for a refresher course and become a ship's surgeon.

But *Lady Frederick* pulled him through. Maugham's sister-in-law, whom he liked as much as he hated his brother Frederick, wrote in her diary that October night: "To dine at the Berkeley and then on to Willie's play *Lady Frederick.* Willie very pale and silent. He sat at the back of the box. The play was an enormous success. It is very witty and interesting. I believe it will prove a success with the public."

Mrs. Maugham was prophetic. It was a smash. And suddenly, in a tidal wave, managers began beating at his door begging for plays. The harmless *Mrs. Dot* was produced within three months, and *Jack Straw,* whom no man had wanted, a few weeks after that. A still earlier reject, *The Explorer,* came along in the spring—all of them successes. Nothing like the Maugham avalanche had ever been seen, and *Punch* ran a cartoon—a billboard advertising William Somerset Maugham's four hits with William Shakespeare standing aside biting his nails.

The external change in his way of life was dramatic. Barely able, before *Lady Frederick*'s opening, to raise the price of a ticket to London, he was overnight rich, famous, sought after, quoted, and envied. Some people called him conceited because they thought he must be. But the truth was that, internally, success had made no difference. He had always, he admitted, expected it, and had only been discouraged by how long it took. He did note one difference, however. Walking along a London street one evening, he looked up and saw the clouds painted pink by the setting sun. Stopping to admire, he heaved a sigh of relief. Thank God, he reflected, I can look at a sunset now without having to think how to describe it. Novels, he thought, were behind him forever.

Ahead, he thought, was a lifetime of writing plays, all bringing him riches and acclaim. The first part of the dream was working out; during the next seven years he turned out ten plays which rewarded him handsomely. But the second one rather failed. At one time he told his agent, "I seek distinction rather than lucre," but despite the crowded houses the critics were cool. The more frivolous periodicals praised his epigrammatic wit (asked once by a director for a few more epigrams, he sat down in a corner and dashed off twenty-four), but these critics disapproved of his cynicism. The serious ones, on the other hand, found him merely cheap and artificial. All he could do was pocket his pounds and vow to show them all later.

Meanwhile he would enjoy life. A handsome bachelor in his middle thirties, with a good crop of hair and a crisp military moustache, with an upper-class accent, a mansion in Mayfair and a bulging bank account—what cannot such a man do? What cannot he have?

Well . . . love. Sex he could have in plenty, for dazzling young women were throwing themselves in his path, ladies of title and ladies with names up in lights. The stars of his plays were linked with him in all the better columns. And there was one important affair, about which he was discreetly vague in his own reminiscences but which was common knowledge in society at the time. This "Nan" was connected in some way with the stage—according to some biographers she was an actress, to others the wife of a producer and later married to a titled personage. All biographers agree that she moved in his own smart circles, and after the affair had a long and happy life.

Maugham never forgot her. He put her in *Cakes and Ale,* enough disguised to protect her and her family, but he acknowledged in his preface that the book's Rosie was someone very close to him. As an old man he told his friend Garson Kanin that she had been his one great love affair, an enchanting creature with the most beautiful smile he had ever seen on a human being. He also said that with her he had known love for the first time.

She was, it seems, intelligent, good-humored, and unaffected, an expert bridge player (which to Maugham was a prime requisite), and a lady. She was also utterly and unashamedly promiscuous. For the eight years of their affair Maugham knew that she went from man to man, even from one friend of his to another, with simple directness, making no apologies. He resented her faithlessness but eventually accepted it as a quirk of temperament and decided to marry her anyway. But by a wry twist of fate, at the exact moment when he approached her with a ring, a casual affair had tricked her into pregnancy. So the magic moment passed —the moment, he implied to Kanin with tears in his eyes, that by giving him a happy marriage might have altered the whole course of his life.

Maugham often referred affectionately to this Nan. But there is an oddly elusive quality in the story, for he could never quite make up his mind how to end it. In one place he wrote that she had died before 1930, in another that she lived until 1948. To Kanin he said it was 1951 or 1952.

Is this one date all that was questionable in Maugham's statement to Kanin? When he said the affair with Nan was the first time he had ever known love, was he pretending that no such person as Mildred had existed? Or had he so desperately wished to forget her that he had actually succeeded? (By then, of course, he had purged himself of her by writing *Of Human Bondage,* and so perhaps he really had.)

In 1913 Maugham met his future wife. And if ever there was an ill-starred marriage this was it—ill-starred because artificial from the start. Syrie Wellcome, as she was then, was small, dainty, vivacious, and quite lovely to look at. Her father was a wealthy and famous philanthropist named Barnado, her husband an equally wealthy industrialist. Uninhibited by her married state, she made it clear that she was irresistibly attracted to Maugham, and as she was smart and amusing they made a generally accepted duo for a year or more. "In the circles in which we moved," he wrote in his reminiscences, "it was understood that I was Syrie's lover."

All these women ... all these so very public affairs ... it sounds almost as if he were bragging. Only Mildred was never allowed even to have existed.

This anomaly could not help but be noticed, and his silence on the point naturally started some rumors. In Hollywood, while Leslie Howard and Bette Davis were making *Bondage,* the gossip was current that the character had really been not a girl at all, but a boy. This belief, in view of other gossip, was widely accepted.

Other people, however, do not accept this theory. They think there was in fact such a girl but that she left him so emotionally crippled that in spite of his struggles to whip up the proper emotion so as to present an acceptable front to the world—and in spite of his near-hit with Nan—it was impossible for him to love any woman.

When he met Syrie perhaps he thought once more that he could. Certainly she believed it, and continued to believe it for years. She even got a divorce and persuaded him to marry her. There was one child, a daughter named Liza after his first book.

But this was at a time when the world was breaking up, when old patterns of behavior, of traditions and appearances preserved at all costs, were cracking and coming apart. World War I had begun. Maugham was forty. Too old for front-line fighting, he volunteered as a Red Cross ambulance driver. And there, in the mud and bursting shells, his old pattern of struggle and failure was shattered and he adopted a new one.

Gerald Haxton was a young American adventurer twenty years old, conspicuously handsome, spoiled, but brave and reckless. Gifted with a disarmingly ingenuous smile, he had the high spirits, the charm and social genius that for the next twenty-five years were to be expended in return for a luxurious and glamorous life. Irresistible when sober, when drunk he was foul and unmanageable, and was finally barred from ever reentering Great Britain for outrageously obscene behavior. As by that time he had become indispensable to Maugham, he was one of the chief reasons for their eventually settling in France.

The friendship was an intermittent one at first, for this was wartime and Maugham's services were much in demand. His War Office friends had decided that his brains, his five languages, and his international fame as a writer were being wasted in a Red Cross ambulance, and they recruited him for Intelligence.

That work, he related, "appealed both to my sense of romance and my sense of the ridiculous. The methods I was instructed to use in order to foil persons who were following me; the secret interviews with agents in unlikely places; the conveying of messages in a mysterious fashion; the reports smuggled over a frontier; it was all doubtless very necessary ... but I could not but look upon it as little more than material that might one day be of use to me." It was, in fact, very useful one day; he got the main character and the plots for the *Ashenden* spy stories from it. (But Ashenden's exploits had unfortunate repercussions during the Second World War.)

After nearly ruining his health carrying out secret orders in the harsh Swiss winters he was transferred to the Pacific on an equally secret mission. Passing through Chicago, he found Gerald Haxton and invited him to join him in his travels. And here Gerald revealed his real value. Maugham's nerves were tense and raw over his personal problems involving the insistent Syrie, and Gerald's high spirits were an antidote to his depression. Gerald's handiness with steamship tickets, schedules, and suitcases were also a boon, as was his resourcefulness in emergencies, in particular one occasion when their sailboat capsized and he saved Maugham's life. Most useful of all, however, was his function as liaison between Maugham and the world at large.

In *The Summing Up* Maugham says, "I have been attached, deeply attached, to a few people; but I have been interested in men in general not for their own sakes but ... as material that might be useful to me as a writer." Again, "Though I have never much liked men I have found them so interesting that I am almost incapable of being bored by them." And, "I could not spend an hour in anyone's company without getting the material to write at least a readable story about him." But his stammer and consequent shyness made first contacts difficult. So on their travels about the world Gerald's conviviality was invaluable.

"I was fortunate enough," Maugham writes in one of his few references to Gerald, "to have on my journeys a companion who had an inestimable social gift. He had an amiability of disposition that enabled him in a very short time to make friends with people in ships, clubs, barrooms, and hotels, so that through him I was able to get into easy contact with an immense number of persons whom otherwise I should have known only from a distance."

Gerald brought him back gossip like a friendly retriever, sometimes raw snatches, sometimes whole stories ready to be written. And in the exotic Far East, at this time largely untraveled by Europeans, he found that which he had not enjoyed in such abundance since his St. Thomas's Hospital days. Among the London poor, the desperate, and the unlettered he had been permitted to see straight through clothing, skin, and muscles to the guts, ugly but essential. Later, in the polite world of Mayfair the person was cloaked in so many layers of well-bred manners that a writer had to wait and watch for a glimpse of the real man. But in the East he found plenty of exciting new types. "Here," he wrote, "people showed themselves bare. . . . Their peculiarities had been given opportunity to develop unchecked. . . . These men had never had their jagged corners rubbed away. They seemed to me nearer to the elementals of human nature." Here he found many characters and plots for later use and here he returned periodically until his eighty-sixth year.

After this 1916 Pacific trip with Gerald, Maugham was recalled and sent on another highly secret mission to Russia. Given vast sums of money by British and United States Intelligence, he was asked to stop the Russian revolution, no less, a task that not unnaturally gave him pause. His cover-up was his visible occupation as correspondent for *The Daily Telegraph,* though actually his job was to rearm the forces opposing the revolution and support anti-Bolshevik propaganda. Obviously, he failed to put an end to Communism, and he came back to Britain discouraged. He was, furthermore, ill with tuberculosis, and he spent two years in a Scottish sanatorium lying peacefully in bed. He had earned a rest and he enjoyed it, for the past thirteen years had been excessively full.

The success of *Lady Frederick* in 1907, followed by that string of other successes, had been intoxicating at first. The fame (modestly he called it notoriety), the balls, the weekends in great houses, the hobnobbing with famous writers, artists, and members of Parliament—all had tasted very sweet. But like a steady diet of marshmallow, it had finally turned his stomach.

Beyond that, the necessities of playwriting had begun to irk him—having to expand or contract an idea to fit the allotted time, to reach carefully spaced climaxes, to provide vehicles for stars' favorite tricks, to be wittier and smarter than life—that too made him feel as if he were standing up to his knees in glue. By 1912 the freedom and the mobility of the novel had come to seem, by contrast, like heaven.

Concurrently, for some reason, the tedium of this life began calling up early painful memories that demanded to be written out. "The writer," he said, "is the only free man. Whenever he has anything on his mind... grief... unrequited love... wounded pride ... anger ... he has only to put it down in black and white ... to forget all about it." So, longing to forget all about it, he had written *Of Human Bondage.* The proofs of the book were corrected by candlelight in a French billet within the sound of German guns. It was published in 1915. But Britain was suffering through a long and unhappy war, and not many readers wanted to suffer through a long, unhappy story. It languished in the British bookstores, and perhaps it might never have penetrated overseas had not a copy fallen into the hands of a New York publisher's wife, who wanted something to while away a bout of influenza. Her enthusiasm activated her husband; when it came out, Theodore Dreiser reviewed it with cheers, and gradually it caught fire. Fifty years afterward, it still sells thousands of copies every year.

Though the acrid power of the Mildred episode dominates *Of Human Bondage,* Maugham had another motive besides freeing himself of that evil memory for writing it, a philosophic one. He had originally chosen as the book's title a phrase from Isaiah 61: "... to appoint unto them that mourn in Zion, to give unto them beauty for ashes, the oil of joy for mourning, the garment of praise for the spirit of heaviness." But "Beauty for Ashes" had already been used so he had to find another. Both the old and the new, however, refer to the need to slough off old burdens and be free of old bonds.

All through his youth Maugham, like many another of his generation, had been tormented by the great philosophic questions posed by Darwin's overturning of fundamentalist beliefs. He read numerous scientific and theological treatises to answer the question, What is the meaning of life? but found no answer he could accept, always rejecting any suggestion of the goodness of

God with the sardonic, "I have seen a child die of meningitis." Commenting on such a death, he said, "You felt that God at the Judgement Day would have to account for such things as this." To him, it was obviously just another case of the Almighty's callous cruelty, in line with his own unanswered prayer over his stammer.

By the time he wrote *Bondage* he had arrived at an answer that, curiously enough, satisfied him: life had no meaning; it had no purpose; it just *was*. Today and its events were simply the inevitable result of a yesterday that could not be changed because it had passed.

This discovery was for him a kind of "beauty for ashes," for it brought him a welcome relaxation of tension. If things were as they were, unchangeable, then nobody could do anything about them and one might as well stop trying. One simply accepted everything as it was—including himself.

Looked at analytically, there is something a little pathetic in his eager grasping at this solution, for it reflects the years of miserable self-condemnation that had gone before. He had become profoundly dissatisfied with himself and his way of life, the superficiality, the forced, empty sex, the inability to give himself in a cleansing, whole-hearted love. He once wrote of his longing for "peace and a settled and dignified way of life"; and Philip Carey's engagement at the end of *Bondage* to the unsoiled, unsophisticated Sallie exemplifies this longing.

Thus one may read in his fatalistic philosophy the giving up of an agonizing struggle, a sort of throwing in of the sponge. Powerless to alter the forces that had shaped him, he was powerless to alter himself. Therefore he would just take things as they were. Not very long after this he more or less gave up trying to lead a normal sex life and settled for that with Gerald.

This he did not acknowledge openly. But in less intimate areas he was brutally frank and honest about himself. He was, he said, weak and sensual and cold. He had only a second-rate intellect, though he did believe himself to stand in the first rank of the second-raters. He had no gift for friendliness, having never in his life liked a person at first sight. He could never forget himself for a moment, and he was so jealous of his independence that he was incapable of complete surrender. Therefore he lacked, would always lack, the broad human touch of the really great writer. He did grant himself a clear and logical brain, great discipline and capacity for hard work, and a fair degree of inventiveness.

He also made a few alibis for himself: his lack of friendliness was to be blamed on shyness, springing from his stammer. His self-consciousness was due to his height ("the world is a very different place to a man five foot seven from what it is to a man six foot two"); and the sardonic set of his mouth was caused by the lack of proper attention to his teeth in childhood.

His nephew Robin, Lord Frederick Maugham's son and himself a novelist, has written that his uncle was crippled and maimed by his early experiences. "As a cloak to protect an abnormally sensitive and shy person from the frosts of an indifferent world, he adopted a pose of cynicism and worldliness. Gradually the pose became a part of the man. But imprisoned behind the seemingly impassive, ruthless, world-famous, world-weary author was a lonely person who still craved for affection." Things having turned out as they had, Gerald's affection—or what passed for it—had to serve, and having found him a useful companion and secretary, Maugham traveled with him almost constantly for a full decade after the World War.

During his Scottish sanatorium years he had written several plays that were produced in London and New York during the twenties, some of which—*The Circle, Our Betters, The Constant Wife*—even exceeded his former popularity.

But so completely had he used up familiar people and places that by now he needed new scenes, new types. On his 1916 visit to the East he had seen English expatriates, government officials, doctors, businessmen, adventurers, acting under the stress of strange environments in ways that enthralled him. So back he went, to China, Malaya, Borneo, Java, Tahiti, Australia—later to South America and Africa. Traveling by ship, train, car, chair, foot, or horseback, sleeping in anything from grass huts to palaces, he observed his compatriots with cool objectivity. After five or six months of absorbing impressions he would find himself satiated and have to return home to think and sort out his findings.

During Maugham's early years in Paris he had heard his artist friends discuss the strange French broker who had thrown up business and family life to go to Tahiti and paint. Ever since, the life of Paul Gauguin had held him fascinated, and at the first opportunity he made for the Islands to investigate it. (There, besides copious information, he picked up an actual memento, a door taken from Gauguin's cabin, on which was painted a picture in rich warm colors. Removing it from its hinges, he took it back to England, later installing it in his French studio.)

The Moon and Sixpence flowed through his pen like oil. So thoroughly had he absorbed and organized his material that, once started, it went without a hitch, and he simply corrected the pages and sent them off to the publisher, a miraculous first-and-only draft. In 1955 this manuscript was sold at auction for 2,800 pounds, whether to a regular collector or to an envious writer is not known.

Often regarded as a biography of Paul Gauguin, the book was in fact merely suggested by the painter's life, and it contains almost as much of Maugham as of Gauguin. Here Maugham appears as Ashenden, a man with a background similar to his own, and while the real Gauguin was always on good terms with his wife, even after he opted for Tahiti, Maugham made Strickland a woman-hater, possibly as a means of working in some acid remarks about women in general.

The rest of this decade was occupied with plays and short stories. And it was during this time that, having made a mark as a novelist with *Bondage,* he chipped away another niche for himself as a storyteller. The four volumes of stories that came out of these itinerant years have been called by many critics the greatest in our language.

Then, in 1928, he changed his way of life. After seven long

journeys about the world, he found his powers of assimilation dwindling. When he met new people he found them no longer new but always falling into one or another familiar category, and he could not shape them into fresh characters. He had, furthermore, grown weary of the ordeals of travel. Having twice nearly died of fever, having nearly drowned and nearly been killed by bandits, he decided he had had enough of movement. He would now take his ease in one place.

After considering all the delightful places of the earth he plumped for the Riviera, warm, beautiful, and removed from but convenient to all the European centers of culture. Cap Ferrat, a point of land jutting out into the Mediterranean between Nice and Monte Carlo, had once been owned by King Leopold II of Belgium, who, being old and full of sin, had built there a villa for a favorite bishop in order, it was said, to have him handy for absolution in case of a quick demise.

The house, when Maugham found it, was hideously ornate and ugly, but its fourteen acres on a hillside overlooking the sea recommended it to him, and he spent thousands of dollars altering the interior and trimming off the external junk. He laid out around it terraced gardens with tropical plantings, including the first avocado tree in Europe and, in the kitchen section, sweet corn from California seeds. Into a terrace high above the house he sunk a blue-tiled swimming pool. Into the house itself, with its large central patio, he introduced every creature comfort. And about the whole, upstairs and down, he distributed one of the most famous private collections of French Impressionist paintings in the world. Each purchase had been an exciting personal adventure; he sought an atypical example of each painter's work, and for a time he amused himself by offering five pounds to any guest able to identify an obscure Toulouse-Lautrec.

Onto the mansion's roof this workman, this sweating day laborer, built a room to accommodate the engine that powered the place—his studio. There, shut off from all guests, he daily put in his three or four hours of hard work. The room had no comforts, no furnishings save an eight-foot table built low to match his height, at which he wrote wearing his *corset digital,* a specially knitted glove to ease his writer's cramp. He neither typed nor dictated but used a fountain pen with a thick collar for a better hold. Though the whole beauty of the Mediterranean lay outside, he could not see it, for the south window had been blocked off. "This room," he said, "is for working, not looking." Left inside was nothing but the Gauguin painted door and one picture on the wall, a portrait of Nan.

This, then, was the Villa Mauresque, where he settled with Gerald in 1928. On every possible spot—front doorway, stationery, ashtrays, matchboxes, fireplaces, radiator grillwork—he had engraved the cabalistic symbol that always appeared on the covers of his books, a Moorish design found by his father in Algeria and said to protect its possessor from all harm. "It must work," he told a visitor. "This is a happy house."

Certainly it was an active one. Almost immediately it had become the mecca of the chic, the brilliant, the important, even the scandalous if they were amusing enough. A visit to "Willie's Villa" was a must. And truly, life there was like nothing so much as a scene in a Maugham play. During the morning hours the guests amused themselves while the host, having risen at seven no matter how late up the night before, labored alone. They used the tennis court or the swimming pool, drove in the Rolls-Royce to the harbor at Villefranche, where they boarded the yacht *Sara,* registered in Gerald's name, and sailed to a nearby golf course. At twelve-thirty the host joined them for cocktails and a luncheon party. After his afternoon nap there was bridge, walking, riding, more swimming, or plain loafing, all done in the most casual of attires. But for dinner, dress was another matter. Then the black tie prevailed, and the bare back; served at nine or ten, every dish was a gourmet's delight and was brought to the terrace dining table by footmen in livery. The staff was twelve strong, and to each house guest a maid or a valet was assigned on arrival.

Maugham liked his guests to contribute something to the

party. Charm or excitement served as a rule; unusual wit carried in people otherwise impossible—ugly, or common or disgraceful. Greatness such as Churchill's was a sure passkey, and of course royal blood helped. The Duchess of Windsor might have rated entrance on her own, for her conversation was outstanding, but the Duke's credentials were doubtful. "I can't say too much for his intelligence," Maugham observed drily. "But of course he was certainly well brought up."

Maugham's contentment in this new home spilled over into his work, and just at this time he produced his sunniest book. Sitting in the studio looking all day at the round perky face, the red hair and mischievous expression of "the one real love of his life," he was impelled to put her down on paper. *Cakes and Ale* is a portrait of Nan's real personality, though far from her real history. "Rosie" was a former barmaid and a slut; Nan was a society lady and a slut; both were adorable. But their futures went different ways, for while Nan went on to marry a title, Maugham's Rosie went on to a tasteless flat in Yonkers.

Critics agree that Rosie is Maugham's most attractive female character, and they seem to regard her portrait as a sort of valentine to Nan, taking it to mean that despite Nan's refusal to marry him he bore her no ill will. They disregard the fact that in a sort of postscript the narrator looks up Rosie after many years and finds her living in a cheaply ornate flat, a coarse, red-faced caricature of her former self, still flirting kittenishly at seventy.

This book does have a less bitter flavor than most Maugham novels. But to many readers who saw below its surface it had a bitter aftertaste. For two of its characters were seen as satires on the writers Thomas Hardy and Hugh Walpole. Accusations and denials flew about like angry birds pecking at each other, Maugham's accusers pointing out all the resemblances and he pointing out all the differences. There were plenty of both.

The resemblance to Hardy may have been accidental, for stranger coincidences have occurred and Maugham had no personal reason for taking pot shots at Hardy. But in 1930 Walpole was a serious rival. There Maugham's disclaimers were not very convincing, and the book left some bad feeling in literary circles. The town of Whitstable's feelings were likewise upset, for he had used well-known local names for certain shady characters, and when he visited the town many friends of the respectable Ganns and Kemps turned a cold shoulder. There was some talk of libel suits but nothing came of it.

The question of the ethics of using real persons in fiction undisguised comes up often. There have been many lawsuits and many more hurt feelings. Such use as Maugham's is certainly unkind, and there has been endless discussion in writing circles about its permissibility. Actually, the practice is as old as writing itself. H.G. Wells, Aldous Huxley, Ernest Hemingway, Thomas Wolfe, Bernard Shaw—all were tempted and fell. And among the older writers it was even commoner. Sometimes, as in the case of the Mother Goose rhymes and Gilbert and Sullivan operettas, the original is forgotten. But in others, the original is remembered to his glory. Who now would know of Beatrice if Dante had not named her? Authorship, it may be, has an ethic of its own.

The decade of Maugham's *Cakes and Ale* contained three other novels as well, *The Narrow Corner, Theatre,* and *Christmas Holiday;* his last two plays, *Sheppey* and *For Services Rendered;* three books of short stories; and *The Summing Up,* in which, thinking that at sixty-five he was almost finished, he attempted to add up the pluses and minuses of his life. This however was a gross miscalculation; he still had twenty-six years to go. And the next few were some of his most eventful.

Although World War II broke out officially in the fall of 1939, that winter was known as the Phony War—Hitler just breathing heavily before jumping on Europe in the spring. The British government asked Maugham to write some propaganda pieces, which he dutifully did. But in the main, life was not disturbed; the Riviera was as pretty and comfortable as ever. Many guests came and went, and Maugham's daughter Liza, now a grown woman, came to stay with her husband.

Maugham had scarcely known Liza as a child, for during her early years he had spent most of his time traveling with Gerald, while she lived with her mother. Syrie in the meantime had become one of the best-known interior decorators both in London and New York, especially celebrated for her all-white rooms. She and Maugham were officially divorced after ten years of a nonexistent marriage.

Maugham always contended that his wife was a trivial, unintelligent woman interested solely in clothes and society, and had been a poor influence on their daughter. (Asked if he had been a good father, he admitted with reluctant honesty that he doubted it. Throughout her childhood he had supported her and taken her to lunch at Claridge's once a year, but that, he supposed, was probably not enough.)

The girl had grown up torn between opposing loyalties, but by 1936, when she married the son of a Swiss diplomat, Maugham and she were on good terms, and in 1940, when the real war broke out, she was staying at the Villa Mauresque with her two small children. (While her husband served in the British army she took them to the United States. Later, after she was divorced, she married Lord John Hope, and ended up with the imposing title of Lady Glendevon.)

Hitler's sudden attack on Holland, Belgium, and then France took Maugham as much by surprise as the rest of Europe. But once it came, he knew that his own position was perilous and he must leave at once, for Goebbels, Hitler's Minister of Propaganda, had discerned from his *Ashenden* stories that he knew a great deal about spying. Nazi broadcasts announced that he was slated for capture.

The British government had ordered all nationals out of France and it sent a collier to pick up those on the Riviera. Built to accommodate a cargo of coal and a crew of thirty-eight, it was now expected, Maugham learned, to take on an additional five hundred frightened refugees. Since the captain must dodge enemy submarines and airplanes the voyage would be long and circuitous. Furthermore, with heavy seas and an overloaded ship, capsizing was a distinct possibility. Maugham considered his options gravely.

He could go with the others and take his chance of getting through. Or he could stay at the Villa and take a chance with Hitler. But a Nazi concentration camp, he decided, was definitely the poorer choice, so Gerald, who was no prize to the Nazis, offered to stay behind and hide the most valuable of the paintings while Maugham made his escape. (Having had to slip out with very little money on him, Maugham developed such a horror of being caught short that from then on he never traveled without an attaché case containing a hundred thousand dollars in cash.)

After spending some months in London under the bombing, Maugham was again put into government service, this time in the United States, on an assignment never entirely spelled out. His publisher, Nelson Doubleday, met him at the airport and after the greetings Maugham asked for a bourbon old-fashioned. At the bar he drank it carefully and then took a vial of poison out of his pocket. "I shan't be needing this now," he said, and dropping it to the floor, crushed it under his heel. He disliked death, but there had been other things he dreaded more.

After being a famous host for a number of years, he was now a guest. The Doubledays built a house for him on their South Carolina plantation and for the duration of the war Parker's Ferry was his home. Here he wrote *The Razor's Edge,* for which he had prepared himself by a long visit to India in 1938. In point of sales, it was his most successful novel though not, probably, what he will be best remembered by.

Gerald Haxton, after hiding the Villa Mauresque valuables, had followed Maugham to New York and eventually to Parker's Ferry. While the quiet life appealed to Maugham, who was nearing seventy, Haxton was only fifty, full of vigor and anxious, under the spur of war, to prove himself before the world. For over twenty years he had been Maugham's appendage, accepted for the famous man's sake but sometimes with open contempt. Now he rebelled and to Maugham's distress took himself to Washington and a clerical war job.

Alcohol had always been a sore point between them. Early in life Maugham had learned that he could not drink—"It is my good fortune," he said, "that after two drinks I become violently sick. I wish everyone had that safety valve." Haxton's drinking was a perpetual embarrassment to Maugham and he did his best to restrain it. But alone in Washington Haxton was free of restraint and in the next two years seemed to be determined to drink himself to death. He developed pleurisy, which in his undermined condition easily went into tuberculosis. Maugham took him to Saranac for treatment but recovery was not in him. He died there in November, 1944.

Maugham retreated to South Carolina and refused to see anyone for months. But finally the worried Doubledays sent to Europe for his nephew Robin, himself a war casualty, and gradually the two helped each other get well.

After the war Maugham went back to see what was left of the Villa. It was known, of course, that the Germans had plundered it, but it seemed that everyone else too had taken a shot. The Italians had come first and confiscated his automobile and furniture. When the Germans came they cleaned out his wine cellar and turned the house into an observation post. A British warship shelled it by mistake, and finally, hungry neighbors roasted and ate his pet dogs.

At the end of the war the house was used as a rest home for British and American troops, and any wrecking that had not yet been done was completed at that time. Maugham was in despair when he looked at it. Still, he decided to have it repaired. The art objects hidden by Gerald were disinterred and the whole was restored to its original lovely state. Guests again filled the rooms. Only Gerald was not there.

But his loneliness had appealed to a man with a kindly disposition and once again he had a companion-secretary. Alan Searle has more than once been called a saint, a man as different from Gerald as night from day. During these last years he was more companion than secretary, and more nurse than both. He was patient and gentle with Maugham's every whim, traveling with him when he felt restless and staying still when he felt lazy.

Maugham wrote little after his return—some collections of essays and criticism—and in the late fifties he held a series of bonfires. Evening after evening he and Alan sat before the sitting-room fire and dropped onto it letters, documents, unfinished acts of plays, the whole written skeleton of his life. Much there was of value to biographers, but that was the reason for the bonfire: he wished no biography, though he knew well enough many would be written anyway. But at least his own papers would not be there to help them. And Alan was not to help them either. Alan acceded to his wishes, as always.

In return for Alan's loyalty, Maugham made him his heir. And, sadly, the last years of his life were marred by contests between his daughter and himself over his property. The suits were accompanied by allegations unbecoming a father and daughter. And during these same last years (surely Alan tried to prevent it) he published two scurrilous articles about his former wife, who was dead by this time. Everyone wondered how he could have done it.

So shocking were the articles, indeed, that many wondered about his sanity. And Garson Kanin, a deeply loving friend, has suggested a possible explanation. Ten years before, Maugham had begun taking a cure in Switzerland which other famous old men were said to be taking. Describing its effect, he said it made him feel "strange . . . not myself. Not ill, just strange." After that, Kanin had noticed him becoming increasingly jumpy, irrational, unstable. Was it, he wondered, the cure that caused it? It would be kindest to think so.

On the surface, his interest in the cure seems inconsistent, since for years he had been loudly wishing for death. In interviews he talked about it grimly or at times humourously. He called himself an old party on the brink of the grave. He said to his nephew, "Dying is a very dull, dreary affair," and added with a smile, "and

my advice to you is to have nothing to do with it." To Alan, however, he said that every night when he went to bed he prayed
never to wake up.

Yet at the very time that he seemed to be courting death he
was undergoing this cure, which was described as violent and
dangerous, in the hope of a few more years. That is not the act of
a man wishing to die.

The conclusion must be that, after all, he loved living, that in
spite of his bitter face he had found it well worth doing. He once
told a friend that there was only one drawback to a writer's life:
"When you have finished the day's work and you have to take your
leisure and wait for your creative gift to be restored next morning,
anything you can do in the remaining hours seems a little pale and
flat."

Before his death all his lawsuits were settled. The faithful Alan
Searle was with him till the end, and he died on December 16,
1965. At his own wish he was buried at King's School, Canterbury,
evidently having forgiven its cruelty for the sake of its beauty.

Sinclair Lewis
(1885-1951)

Sinclair Lewis
(1885=1951)

"ALWAYS GROPING . . . always dissatisfied . . . always restlessly straining. . . ." The words are a description of a Sinclair Lewis character but the picture is of Sinclair Lewis himself. Superlative success though he was, Nobel Prize winner and chronicler of a nation and an age, still his greatest genius seemed to be for making disastrous mistakes. One can only guess how much his tragedy stemmed from the chill of his early years and how much from the fortuitous fact of a miserable complexion, but the final result is clear—a brilliant man compulsively destroying himself and those around him. With all the mayhem he committed, indeed, it is a wonder he survived as long as he did.

Sinclair Lewis was born in 1885, the third son of Dr. E. J. Lewis of Sauk Centre, Minnesota. Of Welsh and English stock, the elder Lewis had taught school in Pennsylvania briefly and then, after taking a two-year course in medicine, moved west and hung out his shingle in this tiny village huddled in the snow. He and his wife had three sons, Fred and Claude close together, and then, after a six-year wait, little carrot-top Harry Sinclair. The young mother died soon thereafter of tuberculosis, and a year later Dr. Lewis took another wife, a kindly, practical woman who did her duty and a little more by the boys but seems to have left no deep impression on any of them. It was the father whose mark went so deep.

In that white clapboard house the doctor's word was law. Not exactly cruel but dictatorial and harsh, Dr. Lewis was apparently without feeling. He believed in himself and in good hard work, in that order; *his* views, *his* wishes, dominated the family. Even the dullest minutiae of his days were sacred: for years he left his office at exactly eleven thirty, went home for dinner, hung his hat on one of three pegs in the dining room and put on another of three hats hanging there; then he crossed the street with a large water pail and filled it at a well. Not once in many years did he change the whole routine, though the reason for it the family never discovered. (Perhaps no one ever dared ask.)

A strictly upright man, he expected perfection of both himself and his sons, and while he was never disappointed in himself, two of his sons failed him badly. Fred, the eldest, early crumpled under the weight of his father's expectations; after a few fruitless months at a dental school he retreated sadly into a flour mill and almost disappears from the record.

Claude, the second son, was very different. He had all the graces and talents Fred lacked; he was handsome and popular, steady, industrious and, eventually, a brilliant doctor.

From the beginning the brattish third son was left far out in the cold. With no endearing qualities, this skinny, freckled, pop-eyed little boy was forever rushing about hysterically trying to attract attention. As a five-year-old he embarrassed his stepmother by crawling across the lawn on all fours shouting to her guests, "Look at me, I eat grass like a cow," and proceeding to do so. He played unfunny practical jokes and made a general spectacle of himself, all in the attempt to win the approval of his two gods, Father and Claude.

He never won it. Tagging along after Claude and his friends, he was invariably told to "go off and chase yourself"; and his father's usual reaction to his oafish capers was an irritable, "Harry, why can't you do like other boys do?" Many years later he confessed that for sixty years he had tried to impress his brother Claude and, more especially, his father. And until his father's death in 1927 he doggedly wrote the doctor weekly letters retailing any triumph he could muster. But to the end his only success

with his father was a sardonic, "It is certainly marvelous how such
a bundle of nerves can pull in the money."

This bundle of nerves was endowed with an active brain and
an iron determination to make his mark somehow, anyhow. Inept
at all sports, he was scorned by the other boys in high school, and
the girls were merely irritated by his sudden grabs and labored
compliments, so that he had to depend entirely on his brain. But
this saved him; being a good student and a brilliant debater, he
won an occasional part in a play, and early he developed that
pathological craze for dressing up and giving imitations that was
first to delight his friends and then weary them to death.

Not surprisingly, he felt happiest when alone—or, if not exactly happy, then at least safe. He filled his leisure with reading,
walking, and studying languages and religion, and already, at sixteen, the future author was emerging—a very elegant author
named H. Sinclayre Lewys, Poet.

When considering a choice of colleges, Harry dreamed of
Oxford, Cambridge, and Edinburgh universities, but since Dr.
Lewis' father had once lived in New Haven, the doctor looked on
this as reason enough to pick Yale for his son. In the meantime,
Oberlin Academy was chosen for a six-month brush-up course in
algebra and Latin, and so, in September, 1902, behold H. Sinclayre
Lewys, in a three-dollar derby hat, entraining for the wide, wide
world.

Oberlin was supposed to yield him that peculiar joy of college
life, companionship. In his diary he wrote of his wistful yearning
for a friend, someone who would understand and share his every
thought and mood. But, immediately he arrived, his roommate
took one disgusted look and wrote home describing him: ". . . a
long, lank, redheaded freckled face chap from some crossroads up
in Minn., and such a fresh youngster you never saw. . . . He thinks
he knows more than anyone else on earth." His lack of social graces
tried the roommate sorely: "When I received that box of fudge
from Sis I told him she said to divide up between we four fellows.
He took nearly his whole share that first time. Twice afterwards he

came over and helped himself to another piece ... I cannot repri-
mand the fellow for he simply goes up in the air."

The other youths liked him no better, and the girls found his
complexion "repulsive." During the weekly drawing for seats in
the dining hall everyone prayed not to sit beside him. The first
roommate lasted only until Christmas, the second barely a week.
Thenceforth he lived alone.

His only consolation was his interest in religion. Attending a
YMCA meeting soon after arrival, he was impressed by the pre-
vailing sincerity, and one eventful day he stood up to profess
himself a true Christian. This day he regarded as one of the most
crucial of his life, and soon decided to become a foreign missionary. To that end he volunteered to teach a Sunday school class of
eight little girls in the next town, and weekly pumped his way
thither and back on a railway handcar. "I pray to God that I may
teach them some of His word," he wrote in his diary.

This public zeal may have been partly a bid for attention. But
the emotion back of it was real. He disliked prayers at assembly
because he thought prayer too precious and sacred to be dragged
into every trivial issue. "Of course an inward mental petition to
God for strength and purity is always necessary when starting
anything, but not verbal, vocal long prayer." He read the Bible
hungrily and sampled the services of all denominations, but even
at the Y he made no friends and his loneliness became an almost
physical pain.

In December he confided to his diary, "I have been fighting
a hard fight ... I almost decided to give up and go back home and
implore Father to let me try it over again, somewhere else. But I
have won! I *will* stay here and fight to the end." Here already is
the Sinclair Lewis of all the years to come, the Lewis trying the
somewhere else because the here was unbearable. Despite the
brave words, he did not stay. A convenient lack of geometry in-
struction provided him with the excuse he craved, and in March
he persuaded his father to let him leave. So much for Oberlin.

So now for Yale. And since Yale was somewhere else it would

surely be better. But the boy who went there was, unfortunately, not someone else, and he began spoiling things even before he arrived. Meeting a young man on the journey east, he told him proudly that he was "a Yale man." Later he met this same youth on campus and learned that bragging of being a Yale man was the unforgivable Yale sin, branding one a boor and an outsider. From this blunder he went stumbling on to others, until his senior advisor told him a few facts of life. Then he noted, "I've been doing a lot of things wrong . . . I have been fresh—dreadfully so. I owe Rankin an unbounded debt."

Another man was equally candid with him about the necessity of being "a gentleman (tactful, quiet, etc.)." Here, in this humble eagerness to improve himself, is the Sinclair Lewis whom one acquaintance recalled as "the only man I ever knew who *learned* how to be charming."

Even so, life continued utterly friendless. During Christmas vacation he hung about New Haven with a few other strays too poor to go home, and one evening he did have a spread with one of them, hot dogs, rolls, sugar wafers, nuts, and dates. They sat and talked till nearly eleven exchanging views on scholarship, girls, and dating, and he recalled it happily: "Long discussion—at last." At last a glimpse of real college life, the heart-to-heart talks, the baring of one's soul that led to lifelong friendships. He pictured himself and this other as David and Jonathan united against the world and ready to die for each other. But after the holidays the stray youth faded into the mists and he was alone again.

Failing charm, as at Oberlin he fell back on his brain. The goal of all the literary minded was the Yale *Literary Magazine*, the president of whose board was Frederick Pierce, top man in the senior class, Phi Beta Kappa, Skull and Bones, etc. Lewis did everything he could think of to win this man's friendship, but while many of his contributions were accepted, the editors ignored their author coldly. Indeed, they took fewer stories and articles than they might have, for by tradition those lower classmen scoring most acceptances became the future board. It came to his ears that it was being said, "God forbid that Lewis should ever make the *Lit.*," and nearly in tears he went to one of the editors. Was even this recognition to be denied him? The embarrassed editor spoke soothingly, and in due course the honor did come his way.

The one consolation during these desolate years was the kindness of one or two professors. The older men could see through the surface braggart to the brilliance within, through the windbag to his creativity, through, perhaps, the show-off to his desperate loneliness. Understanding him, they found him endurable, and the encounters with his sympathetic English professor, Chauncey B. Tinker, were his only moments of real happiness. He recorded one glorious walk during which the teacher praised his work, saying that he was sorry to see the valedictory abolished, for he had hoped to see Lewis hold it. "What a wonderful, talented man Dr. Tinker is!" he wrote, exulting.

His second and third years were almost as barren as the first, for though he mooned wistfully after a number of girls the interest was always one-sided. Reading became a kind of opiate. And he began noting in his diary that he was smoking and drinking too much.

Finally he made a friend. Allen Updegraff was a nonconformist who ignored usual Yale standards and respected him for his intellect, so at last he had someone to share interests with. Together "Up" and "Bonfire" flooded the *Lit.* and *Courant* with stories. Up, who had sold some poems to a commercial magazine, prepared some of Bonfire's for him to send out. Bonfire helped Up with his Greek, and Up introduced Bonfire to abstruse philosophers. One night they even picked up two girls; what happened on that occasion is not known, except that it made little impression.

Lewis' restless mind was ever seeking new means of expression—plays, fantasies, stories of his boyhood, even children's verses. Finally, thanks to his omnivorous reading he made a sale. Spotting a similarity between a current best seller and a novel of some years before, he made out such an impressive case of plagiarism that *The Critic* bought his article for twenty dollars. He was now a professional author with a byline.

During his first summer vacation he went to Harvard to wait on tables (Harvard was somewhere else and he was considering switching to it), but he became bored in two weeks and shipped out on a cattle boat for England. This was to have been a romantic adventure supplying material for literary labors later, but the work was back-breaking, the food loathsome, the living conditions unspeakable, and the only compensation was the fact that now he was a traveled man.

The next summer he spent in Sauk Centre. And now, for the first time, he enjoyed a faint glow of superiority. A sophisticated Easterner, he carried a cane and wore a silk cord on his eyeglasses and, having had X-ray treatment for his skin, he was even acceptable to Sauk Centre girls.

But now Sauk Centre girls were no longer desirable to him. They were "typical villagers, without a thought outside of S.C." Moreover, the young men's smutty stories disgusted him (he was always offended by smut). There was nothing to do but drink and play poker, and after a few weeks of the dry heat and local gossip boredom settled down like smog.

He could not even think. He tried to write a story describing the town's debilitating dullness; "The Village Virus," he called it. But he could not get started; the virus had done its work even on him, and soddenly he drank the summer away.

In his third year he made both the *Lit.* and *Courant* boards. But now this exalted society appeared in a very different light. Where before he had bowed reverently when passing one of the editors on the sidewalk, now he appraised them coolly and wrote a few editorials pointed right at their hearts. Always he had pretended not to notice his ostracism, but now, under the heading "Unknown Undergraduates," he lambasted the "typical Yale man" for his neglect of that *other* Yale man, the outsider, the heretic who dared to be different. "You may dislike him because he does not think and act as the 'typical Yale man.' . . . [But] remember that he may have too big and too important a personality to permit it to be crushed in the mold you worship." Rising to heights of defiance, he went on, "Incidentally, the heretics of each age, the men with outlandish ideas and customs, have often become the heroes of the next."

In other ways, too, he defied the Establishment. Traditionally the *Lit.* board set aside an hour a week when writers of rejected manuscripts could call and get helpful criticism. Actually, the beginners were more often brushed off with a word, but one struggling youth found Lewis warm, friendly, and helpful, and later declared, "I don't think I ever received any other criticism as conscientious and discerning as his." (Lewis' generosity toward other writers was unstinting all through his life, not only toward the neophyte who threatened no competition but to his most powerful rivals. Disliking a man with his whole heart, he could still accord his work high and public praise.)

By his senior year Yale had lost so much glamour that a month after enrolling Lewis walked out. He and Updegraff took jobs as janitors at Upton Sinclair's socialist colony in Englewood, New Jersey, for $35 a month. But boredom pursued them to Englewood, and after a month they wrote a gaudy description of life at Helicon Hall for which the New York *Sun* paid them $23.35. Armed with these riches, they decamped and took a furnished room in New York, where Up clerked in a store and Bonfire peddled his children's verses. A sample: "The pussy and the puppy and my darling doll and me / We often go a-fishing in the depths of Wash-tub Sea . . ." There were miles more of the same, but respect for Lewis' memory forbids further disclosure.

During this time a female interest entered his life—a very mild interest, apparently, but officially the first. He and Up met a girl they called Cherub at Helicon Hall, a spectacled little redhead with faintly literary leanings. Later they all forgathered in New York, where they and the Cherub formed a cosy relationship of undetermined intensity. Up for a while worked as a stock boy while Bonfire wrote and did the housework, but then Up fell ill and went west. Cherub and Bonfire were left to fight the battle of New York alone.

Lewis planned to marry the girl and take a $26-a-month flat where they could write together, but when Up returned the Cherub transferred her affections to him and Lewis was left alone again. He seems to have been more distressed by his loneliness and Up's neglect than by the Cherub's loss, and after their marriage he continued to be friendly with both.

In 1907 the United States was in the midst of a financial depression and Lewis, unable to find work or sell his pieces, lay around the flat "mad with melancholy." Finally he took his usual cure and went somewhere else. But the steerage voyage to Panama solved nothing and suddenly, in December, he decided to return to Yale.

By pulling strings his friends Professor Tinker and William Lyon Phelps, another faculty member, got him into his old class. This meant doing a year's work in half a year, but the Lewis brain, once cleared for action, was capable of miracles, and he graduated in 1907, though loftily refusing to attend commencement exercises.

Before graduating he had called on Tinker to discuss future careers. The Oberlin missionary phase had long before been discarded in favor of medicine, the profession of his father, grandfather, uncle, and Claude, but by now it was writing or nothing. When he told the professor of his plan, however, he was taken aback by the instant reaction, "You'll starve."

Tinker's response may have been the result of having received some of Lewis' letters. At this time the apprentice's ear for various styles of expression was developing ahead of his judgment, and his ventures into the colloquial were as embarrassing as his child verse. "Gettin' some of my make-up work out of the way, and writing a dramar in verse . . . careful mixture of liquid and high-church vowels . . . Now if this dramar had a surenuff Aglyvaine (Hoonell cares how its spelled?) . . . it might be set to music by Debussy. And wot music my son." He signed himself variously HSL, Hal, Red, Sink. Lewis Esq.

Tinker may also have been reacting to his impulsive abandonment of Yale and equally impulsive return. And, in truth, this young man was as unstable as the wind. For several years after graduation he floated aimlessly from job to job—the Waterloo, Iowa *Daily Courier* ($18 weekly), eight weeks; a charity organization with an unpronounceable 42-syllable name ($75 monthly), seven weeks; the San Francisco *Evening Bulletin* ($30 weekly), nine weeks; the Associated Press ($25 weekly), ten weeks; the Washington, D.C. *Volta Review* ($15 weekly), six months. There were long hiatuses between jobs, when his carefully kept accounts would list, Grub, .45. Fare, .05. Candy, .05. There was an occasional movie, .05, and Booze was a regular item, up to .50.

But neither firing nor lack of encouragement could daunt this restless mind. It was like a goat, able to swallow and digest anything in the way of facts, dialogue, experience, suggestion. The most indigestible material went down whole, to be chewed internally like a cud and regurgitated later in story form. For a time he supported himself by selling plots to Jack London, who could *write* stories but had trouble thinking them up. He charged about five dollars a plot, and one account reads, "14 sh. st. pl. sold to Jack London—$70." At another time London appealed to him in a hurry and he shot along twenty-three. Producing ideas was as easy as breathing, and it may have been this exuberant fertility that had caused Professor Tinker's further comment during their interview.

To the teacher's "You'll starve," Lewis had replied instantly, "I don't care if I do." With the wisdom of a man who had seen sheer drive take a man farther than undirected genius he had smiled and answered, "Then you'll succeed."

It is pleasant to report that this forlorn outsider finally received a gesture of friendship. The son of the publisher Stokes had been a *Lit.* contributor during Lewis' time on the board. Now, remembering his editorial kindness and acuity, young Stokes brought him into the firm as reader. The salary was $12.50 a week.

This time Lewis stuck for two years. From screening out impossible manuscripts he graduated to editing possible ones and thence to the publicity department. As editor he came to know what editors wanted and as publicity man how novels were best promoted. The result was that when he became a successful author he was a publisher's dream, workmanlike, punctual, accurate, and so full of promotion ideas that he was actually invited to sit in on publicity conferences.

During this time he never let the work of editing others' stories interfere with writing his own. "There are few people who can hold a job and do creative work on the side," said Mary Heaton Vorse, a well-known writer of the day. "Sinclair Lewis is one of the few people I have ever known who had the necessary vitality." So now, after selling about seventy stories, articles, and poems, he sat down in his Greenwich Village room and wrote *Our Mr. Wrenn.*

Elizabeth Jordan, then an editor at Harper's, looked up one day to see a tall, thin, redhaired youth bearing a manuscript. "No one could have called him handsome, but he had the widest and most engaging grin I had ever seen," she recalled. After accepting the novel, she made many editorial suggestions, some of which, she said, "were the kind that break an author's heart. He took them all with entire good humor and he never lost his grin. . . . He always wrote and revised with extraordinary ease. I can still see him standing beside my desk, changing sentences and even whole paragraphs . . . without even sitting down to it." After he had taken all the criticism he could stand in one day, he would suddenly stop, grin at her, and say, "Now praise me." And duly she would praise him, saying what she really believed, that he was going to be one of America's outstanding authors.

He was still much in need of praise. Except to a few older women like Elizabeth Jordan and Mary Vorse he was appallingly unattractive. One of his contemporaries wrote, "On every [ship's cruise] a moron is sure to pop up, early during the voyage, known as The Life of the Party. . . . That's what Red has tried to be ever since he hit the Village." He could not control his wildly thrashing energy. Gifted—or cursed—with total recall, he would burst into a gathering and deliver, unasked, parodies of conversations he had overheard, the longer and duller and stupider the better. And at publishers' meetings he would be overly self-confident, repelling the very men he respected and admired, whose friendship he craved the most.

Nor had he learned how to win a girl. There had been several he had chased and proposed to jestingly, braced for a rebuff, but not until 1912 could he make any girl take him seriously. And then it was the most unlikely of girls, no Greenwich Village intellectual but a proper miss from a world he had only read about.

Grace Hegger worked at, of all places, *Vogue.* She had English parents, and though born in New York City she stubbornly maintained an English accent and an air combining innocence and sophistication. Very pretty and very conscious of her "fine golden hair, naturally curly but not fuzzy," she had a tall lithe figure and an exquisite clothes sense, all assets in her particular job.

Her widowed mother, elegant but helpless before the task of bringing up a son and daughter on a minuscule income, had early abdicated to Grace as head of the house, and the girl carried on competently, bringing home her fifteen dollars a week and making herself chic by keeping an eye out for sales. The apartment might be small, the food ill-cooked and skimpy, but the family silver and candlelit dinner table helped Mrs. Hegger and Frank and Grace remember who they were.

It was this girl who, working late at her office in September, 1912, rode down in the freight elevator at 443 Fourth Avenue and saw, without noticing, a man step in at a lower floor. The man, gawky in a shiny blue serge suit with sleeves too short, grabbed off his old derby and said, "I beg your pardon, but haven't I met you before—Miss Hegger?"

Actually he had, though she did not remember it. He had even followed her into a lunchroom a few times just to watch her eat. Now, dithering with excitement as he held open the door, he accidentally knocked her package out of her hand. In picking it up he accidentally dropped his hat, and in retrieving the hat he kicked an empty garbage pail, sending it over with a clatter. The meeting was typical, almost symbolical—his awkward humility, his eagerness to please, his fumbling gallantry—and her laughter.

His courtship began at once; before he left her at the subway station he had asked for a date, confessed he could not dance, inquired her background history, told her his own, mentioned Yale and the *Lit.,* boasted of an unpublished novel and sworn she was the most exciting person he had seen in New York. This too was typical, the frantic grab for friendship and premature assumption of intimacy.

It took him more than a year to win her. But the very elements that eventually separated them were the original attractions. He had a juvenile yearning after the glamorous and unattainable; his early poems had sung of Lancelot and Guinevere, of golden galleons in the setting sun and glorious playfellows skipping hand in hand. Now Grace was his Silver Maid, his Faraway Princess, his Highborn Demoiselle, the Lady Grace Livingstone Hegger of Provence and he her liege servant. She, living in the fantasy world of *Vogue* and impoverished English gentility, swallowed it all whole.

His poverty was touching, and the extremes it drove him to could not help but be flattering; he bought her expensive violets and shivered beside her, overcoatless, in the Easter Parade. When she was ill he composed a four-page daily newspaper, "The Dream Vendor," and peppered her with doggerel verse. Sometimes they were "Toby and Issa," two children eating bread and milk from little blue bowls, at others they were mother and son. Thus was the courtship rooted and grounded in unreality.

More practically, she coached away the harshness of his Midwestern speech; and as she exchanged his ill-made serge for good rough tweeds his ugliness took on a distinguished Scottish look. She read *Our Mr. Wrenn* and made helpful suggestions. And finally, when he showed her its dedication, "To Grace Livingstone Hegger," she found herself in love. The book was published in February, 1914, and they became man and wife two months later.

This spring of 1914 was a turning point for Sinclair Lewis. Behind it lay obscurity, poverty, and loneliness; after it came marriage, fatherhood, fame, wealth—and loneliness. There were to be five years yet of assembling the material for his books, and then a decade when he hung like a flare in the sky, illuminating every detail of American life with disconcerting clarity.

The publication of *Our Mr. Wrenn* announced the emergence of a new kind of writer combining romance with realism. Something of H. G. Wells and Dickens was seen in the pathetic little clerk seeking escape to a more glamorous life, but the pitilessly accurate scenes of ordinary life, the colloquial speech, the social satire, were his own contribution. The book did not make him rich, but it helped to make possible the small house on Long Island where, being very modern, they had separate bedrooms and, being very European, a French housemaid.

Still laboring at his editorial-publicity job, Lewis wrote his own stuff at night, on weekends, in the early morning on the kitchen drainboard, and on the commuting train. *The Trail of the Hawk,* exploring the new field of aviation, was the result of this driving pace, and then, while they waited for its publication, Grace suggested he try short stories. Somewhat doubtfully he looked in his old idea notebook, tossed off one about a back-to-nature colony and, starting at the top, sent it off to the august *Saturday Evening Post.*

"Five hundred smackers!" he shouted some weeks later as a check fell out of an envelope. "That's nearly two months' salary." The accompanying letter was equally gratifying: "This is an exceedingly entertaining story. Now that you have made a start with us . . . I hope you will . . . start in to become a household word." He immediately began talking of leaving the hated office and going "adventuring" somewhere.

Grace managed to subdue this dangerous talk, but it kept up, sometimes strident, sometimes piteous. "Sweetheart," he wrote her once, "I am so tired today. . . . I am so glad that we plan not for a lifetime of this strain, of fame mixed with duplex apartments and motor cars ... but plan instead for queer little colors and fresh breezes and the right to lie on our tummies on a cliff and look at Fujiyama or—Sauk Centre!" Sinclair Lewis' problem was that he wanted both fame-plus-duplexes *and* Fujiyama-plus-Sauk Centre. Wherever he was, the other place was always the siren calling.

The call of fame and duplexes was the loudest at the moment. Hypnotized by the $500 check for a few days' work, he reached again and again into his notebook and began thus a long series of sales at ever-larger fees. At last in December, 1915, he told his boss off and fired himself with a flourish. Then, with Grace beside him, he drove off shouting, "I'm a free man, I've escaped from bondage."

So now came the fresh breezes and Sauk Centre. Rootless, they drifted south to Florida, then west; visiting and sightseeing, quarreling and making up in baby talk, they arrived at Sauk Centre in April for a three months' stay.

So there was Lewis, returning nervously with a double job to do. The dry, revered father and the successful adored brother had to be shown his choice of a wife, had to be impressed, won over, made to accept her. At the same time the airy Eastern wife had to be shown the Midwestern village that had spawned him. Both elements were part of himself but they were not naturally compatible.

Dr. Lewis looked over his son and daughter-in-law critically, while Mrs. Lewis dutifully planned a dinner party, with all the spare leaves let into the dining table. Grace, sleek and chic, greeted the guests with every English syllable ringing out crisply and surveyed the overloaded, overdecorated table in silent wonder. She concealed a slight shudder when the town's "mortician" was presented to her; only the day before she had laughed with delight when she saw the new word on a sign, but she had hardly expected to have to sit next to one at dinner. Lewis defended the guests: "These are the most important people in town, coming to welcome you," he said. "You should be honored."

After an hour of dinner-table conversation heavy with prices on the grain market and recipes for tomato pickle, the talk picked up when a magazine was brought out containing Lewis' latest serial. The banker, told that he had received $1,500 for it and written it in two weeks flat, did a quick sum in his head and whistled. "A hundred and seven dollars a day! Gee whiz! Writing's a better racket than I thought!" Lewis, embarrassed for Sauk Centre's crassness, glanced at Grace. She smiled forgivingly.

Still, despite the place's limitations, they were not unhappy there. Grace claimed sturdily that she *loved* the town, loved Dr. Lewis and Mrs. Lewis to death, and was happy to stay there just as long as Sinclair wanted. And they still played games together— glorious playfellows rolling silver dollars down Main Street hill to see whose would roll the farthest. He took a tiny room over a hardware store and pounded away on *The Job*, while from the window he could watch all Main Street passing under his eyes. But his eyes were more and more the eyes of Grace, and into his notebook went many new observations on the town and its inhabitants.

Then suddenly restlessness broke out again. Suddenly he had to escape this stifling Midwestern trap. So they bought a Model-T Ford and vagabonded for months on end, camping out with an improvised tent and stopping and starting as the whim dictated.

Then Grace discovered she was pregnant. Lewis was aghast —was this the end of freedom, of playmating, of taking off at a moment's notice? There was still so much he wanted to see, to feel. She reassured him. Though she secretly longed for roots she swore that the baby would make no difference.

And in truth the baby made very little difference. Born in July, 1917, the little boy, named Wells for H.G. Wells, Lewis' current idol, spent much of his babyhood being *sat* by Mrs. Hegger. His boyhood he spent in boarding schools. Among his many talents Lewis did not number fatherhood, and it took Wells eighteen years or so to learn to feel like his son. Meanwhile the parents were scarcely ever still. In the next three years they moved ten times —to homes in St. Croix, St. Paul, and Mankato in Minnesota; to two different Cape Cod houses; to New York City; to West Chester, Pennsylvania; and to three different addresses in Washington, D.C.

The move into a new domicile was always the same. The moment the trunks were set down Sinclair would look around briskly and ask, "Now where do I write?" Feeling for the sturdiest table, he would bring out an old suitcase containing yellow and white and carbon papers, pencils, fountain pen, erasers, clips, green eyeshade, and cigarettes. Then, with the typewriter settled firmly, he would say, "Great! Scrumptious! Now kiss me, my love, and beat it."

In time he took to renting a room outside, anywhere that had a good light, a strong table, and enough room to pace in. (Disorganized as was his own life, his workroom was contrastingly neat and prim—an office strangely like that of the methodical old man who had dominated him in so many unlikely ways.)

During these years Lewis drove himself in a kind of frenzy. Holding a firmly pacifist view, he ignored the war in Europe—as, indeed, he almost succeeded in doing again twenty-five years later —and concentrated on his personal concerns. Between 1916 and 1919 he produced forty-three stories, the play *Hobohemia,* and three more novels. Two of these explored new fields: *The Trail of the Hawk,* the budding field of aviation; and *The Job,* the world of the new white-collar girl. *Free Air* was simply the love story of a garage mechanic's son and a daughter of wealth.

In Lewis' books one theme recurs over and over, the outsider trying to get in. Likewise one other personality, the insider, appears over and over. *Free Air* was his vision of himself and Grace the English lady. And, less explicitly, *The Trail of the Hawk* and *The Job* also owed their existence to her. Even later, when Grace was superseded by another glamorous insider, he was still the forlorn one on the outside looking wistfully in.

Since *Free Air,* published in 1919, drew only mild reviews, he had to keep feverishly at work, for the young Sinclair Lewises' expenses were expanding fast. The family, including Mrs. Hegger and Wells, had alighted momentarily in a smart Washington house with a marble bathtub, satin upholstery, and four servants, and Lewis himself, with his English tweeds, his cutaways, and his monocle, was a match for the house. Though he was still plagued by the skin condition that made a stranger's first five minutes with him a painful exercise in not looking at it, the embarrassment was soon dispelled and forgotten. For by now he had learned how to be charming. His conversation was lively and exhilarating, dancing from subject to subject with wit and exhaustive knowledge, while at the same time his interest in others was gracious and flattering, and he could be a ravenous and inspiring listener.

Successful though not yet famous, he was invited to join a smart Washington club, and through it he moved into a circle including ambassadors, congressmen, and future secretaries of state. Prohibition was rapidly promoting getting drunk as the foremost national pastime and Lewis was an enthusiastic participator, but he never entirely forgot the job in hand. Early in 1920 he completed the first draft of a book that had actually been begun in that claustrophobic summer in Sauk Centre when he struggled with a story then called "The Village Virus." Now he had it mastered. Working twelve hours a day in his sweltering little office, he delivered it in July to his publisher. One moment he thought it great, the next he was sunk in despair.

Main Street hit America like a bomb—one of the landmark events of twentieth-century publishing history. Not one of its readers but had a violent reaction—city people were delighted, small-town people infuriated. The story of a city girl who marries a doctor in Midwest Gopher Prairie, rebels against the town's provincialism and tries vainly to infuse it with "culture," it gave Americans a new view of themselves as "a savorless people, gulping tasteless food, and sitting afterward, coatless and thoughtless . . .listening to mechanical music, saying mechanical things."

Small towns everywhere denounced the picture of themselves indignantly; many changed the name of their own Main Streets, and for five months the embarrassed Sauk Centre refused even to recognize the book's existence. Later, however, it found national fame quite soothing to the nerves, and when a few other towns claimed to be the original Gopher Prairie, Sauk Centre reacted huffily by renaming *its* street The *Original* Main Street.

Finally the country came around to embracing its unflattering portrait with almost masochistic glee; it seemed to actually *enjoy* being scolded, to *want* punishment. And for a whole decade, while Lewis went on denouncing and satirizing, pointing out to the people their crassness and hypocrisy and cultural barrenness, the nation blushed and hung its head and asked for more.

It has been said that if *Main Street* had been written ten years later it would have made little stir. But its appearance at this precise moment illustrates one of Sinclair Lewis' greatest gifts, his sense of the national mood. That ear for speech that made his monologues so deadeningly accurate could also catch the murmurings of a whole people and a whole era. As *Main Street* had anticipated America's awaking consciousness of its own provincialism, so *The Trail of the Hawk* before it had anticipated the coming aviation industry with its hero Charles Lindbergh, and *The Job* the emergence of women as business executives. And so it went for many years, Sinclair Lewis putting his finger on one new facet of the American character after another.

Main Street appeared on the surface to be the story of a woman. When he had brought Grace to Sauk Centre in 1916 he had seen the town freshly, from her viewpoint. If, he had asked himself, Grace had married a solid citizen like his brother Claude, could she have stood life in Sauk Centre? What would she have done? The book was his answer to his own question.

He really believed at first that his restless, dissatisfied protagonist was Grace. But actually, he came to see later, much of himself had slipped into the frame. He it was who was unable to take root, who was always groping, dissatisfied, restlessly straining to be somewhere else, without knowing what it was he was seeking.

For a while the mass acceptance of *Main Street* shook his faith in his book—it couldn't be a real work of art if the common herd loved it so much. But he soon recovered from this mood, even so far as to ask his father to prepare notes on the Lewis genealogy for use sometime by a possible biographer. Confidently expecting the Pulitzer Prize, he was somewhat miffed when it went to Edith Wharton's *The Age of Innocence,* but he reminded his publisher to be sure to have *Main Street* translated into Swedish, for after all there was still the Nobel Prize and *that* one really mattered.

At the same time that he was expanding so grandly, this curious man was viewing himself dispassionately, and one of the things he saw was the probable effect success would have on his marriage. "It will change everything," he moaned, "it will spoil us." But actually it did not so much change as magnify. Now he drank *more,* showed off *more.* And Grace grew ever more elegant and airy. Having started signing herself Grace Sinclair Lewis, she was quoted (perhaps apocryphally) as saying, "Even my dentist says to me, 'Mrs. *Sinclair* Lewis, please spit.'" Some of their friends had so much fun over Gracie's airs that one of them stuck up a sign in his house: "It is forbidden to gossip about Grace more than three minutes."

After a year, running true to form, Sinclair Lewis became restless in Washington. This was the era of the American expatriate painting and writing on Paris' Left Bank, so this expatriate from everywhere moved to Europe, taking wife, son, and the mother-in-law he affectionately dubbed The Pride of the British Realm.

The first stop overseas was London, where he could not resist indulging in spats, silver-headed canes, and plus fours for sports (without the sports, which he detested). In London he met titles and great English literary names. And in London, for a while, he found friendship, real male companionship with an American foreign correspondent, Frazier Hunt. "We mixed like Bourbon and water," said Hunt, with unfortunate aptness.

Interestingly, this lionizing, these boosts to his ego, enabled him for the first time to speak about his miserable past. Hour after hour he relived for Hunt the bitter humiliations of his childhood, the brilliant brother always outdoing him, the tyrannical father always putting him down, the bullying older boys and the excruciating loneliness. He described for Hunt the snubs at Oberlin and Yale, dwelling masochistically on each hideous detail. And a few months later he gave himself a grim treat: attending his class reunion at Yale, he found himself the star of it by acclamation. In response to a speech he stood up and looked his classmates over.

"When I was in college here," he told them slowly and clearly, "you fellows didn't give a damn about me. Now I'm here to say that I don't give a damn about you." They thought he was joking and laughed uproariously. Old Red Lewis the card.

After London came Paris and more drinking and high living, and then Rome. But with Rome entered a new element. Since he had learned the trick of being charming, Grace had grown accustomed to seeing him surrounded by a twittering but harmless flock of young women. But now there was a real blond complication.

The affair was mild enough, and it did not last long, for the girl soon got tired of him and begged Grace to take him off her hands. So Lewis returned to London. But Gracie's ego, if not her heart, had been hurt, and she stayed behind to salve it with three Italian beaux, twenty, thirty-five and sixty, all of them more useful than dangerous. He wrote her, noting the new situation: "There is for me no one a bit like you...Oh, my little Issa, I do love you so much. If romance comes to you this winter, I hope it will stay only an episode, that it will not lose me your love." Thus, recognizing the breach but struggling not to see its depth, papering it over and pretending it was solid and durable, they were to go on with the marriage for five more years.

Returning to New York together in May, 1922, they took a house, oddly enough, in Hartford, Connecticut—oddly, because this was a center of big businesses and he had just finished a book skinning businessmen alive. Earlier that year he had described it to H. L. Mencken, whose acid pen had made the *boobus Americanus* the laughing stock of the intelligentsia: "All our friends are in it—the Rotary Club, the popular preacher, the Chamber of Com-

merce...2000 % American, as well as forward-looking, right-think-
ing, optimistic. . . .The central character is a Solid Citizen, one
George F. Babbitt, real estate man, who has a Dutch Colonial
house on Floral Heights."

He had told his publishers that in two years all America would
be talking of Babbittry, and true enough, after *Babbitt* was published, any dull, prosperous booster was a Babbitt, while Zenith,
Babbitt's home town, was variously and positively identified as
Cincinnati, Duluth, Kansas City, Milwaukee, and Minneapolis.

Again Sinclair Lewis had hit America on a soft spot and made
it like it. The book sold enormously, even outselling *Main Street.*
And again he had done it by sensing the mood of the moment. The
country was just becoming aware of the businessman as a type, not
the robber baron of an earlier period but the ordinary, average
go-getter, who in his thousands joined, boosted, lived by the glad
hand and the sharp deal.

By now the novelist Sinclair Lewis had developed a well-
defined *modus operandi.* He started a new book not, like many
authors, with a character or a plot, but with a "field"—aviation,
women at work, smalltown provincialism, businessmen—and to
get to know his field he did exhaustive research. To create Babbitt
the "realtor" (a term he put into the language as he did "Main
Street" and "Babbitt") he became an authority on real estate and
advertising. He drew up a full dossier on the man Babbitt and the
other leading characters, with their backgrounds from babyhood
on; drew plans of their offices and homes complete with furnishings; laid out the town of Zenith—even to the names of its streets
and the names of the trees and the dogs on them—and the surrounding countryside and railway system.

Grace had formerly helped him with his research, but after
Babbitt he took on a series of male secretaries, generally aspiring
young writers like John Hersey. These young men rarely stayed
very long, but Louis Florey, a professional secretary, was with him
through nine novels and two plays and became as well his valet,

traveling companion, bootlegger, and buffer between Lewis and his public.

During the research period Lewis would dictate notes running to hundreds of thousands of words on the characters and scenes in his book. Sometimes going as long as two days without stopping, he would fall asleep in his clothes and after a short nap wake up refreshed to start again at any hour of the day or night. His subject thus absorbed, he would sit down at the typewriter, forefingers wrapped in adhesive tape and eyeshade in place, and bang out a thirty- to forty-page outline. Then, only then, did he start his actual writing. And even this was only a first draft. He overwrote enormously at first, putting down everything he could think of, and then cut and revised through several more drafts.

After real estate the next field to catch his attention was medical research. Dr. Morris Fishbein of the American Medical Association had invited him to dinner with Paul de Kruif, late teacher of bacteriology, captain in the U.S. Army Sanitary Corps, and associate in pathology at Rockefeller Institute, who had himself written extensively on medical subjects. Lewis listened all evening while the two men argued about medical institutions and the difficulties of young doctors trying to do pure research.

For months Lewis had been trying to pull together a novel about labor (he tried off and on for years and never succeeded), but now out of this conversation came a new idea—the conquest of a plague on a Caribbean island. De Kruif, a great booming man with vast vision and enthusiasm, was easily talked into collaborating with him, and a contract was drawn up including an advance to De Kruif large enough to permit him to leave his other work and to get married. His pretty, good-natured wife gave the book its heroine, Leora, since Gracie by this time was no longer serving this purpose.

In January, 1923, the two men sailed for a two-month cruise through the West Indies absorbing people and places—drinking, and talking around the clock. "Every morning," De Kruif wrote later, "Red would sit down at his typewriter and put down what we had talked. He had a terrific brain. He got himself into the swing of what scientific experimentation really meant. It was fantastic how he picked it up and how he picked it out of me; he picked my eyes out about it. Same about epidemiology—the field study of infectious disease. Weird the way he could fictionalize it yet make it probable. . . . By the time we had reached London the framework had been constructed, and the hundreds of thousands of words had been organized into notes which already made a story, with many highly developed characters."

The writing took place all over Europe and the United States, a frenzy of work and then of play. Rebecca West has said that Lewis' deterioration really began on this cruise; De Kruif, a man with the strength of a tiger and the capacity of a camel, had been implored to keep Lewis sober, but he was the wrong man for the job. At a certain stage in a drinker's life drinking becomes a vocation in itself, with all of a vocation's competitions and jealousies, and Lewis, trying to compete with a master, became ugly and offensive.

Though *Arrowsmith* was no autobiographical sketch, there were revealing glimpses of the author in it. "He found," Lewis wrote of young Martin Arrowsmith, "that whisky relieved him from the frenzy of work, from the terror of loneliness . . . then betrayed him and left him the more weary, the more lonely." Here was Lewis writing his whole life in a sentence.

With his public relations expertise, Lewis had selected *Arrowsmith*'s "pub day" cannily. March 4, 1925, was the date of Calvin Coolidge's inauguration, with all its attending brouhaha. So *Arrowsmith* was published on March 5, when the excitement had died down and America had nothing to talk about but Sinclair Lewis' new book.

America reacted as prescribed. Martin Arrowsmith was a new kind of fiction hero, a dedicated research scientist fighting for his integrity. And for a change he and his Leora were characters in a Lewis novel the public could like and even admire. The book was an enormous success, eventually his favorite among all his works, and it brought him the double thrill of being offered the Pulitzer prize and haughtily refusing it.

After *Arrowsmith* Lewis' mind took a holiday, absently grinding out what he called (surely in a drunken moment) "a swell piece of cheese to grab off some easy gravy." *Mantrap* was an adventure story of the north woods and as a movie served Clara Bow, the It Girl, with a suitable vehicle. It did little else for the world.

Several years before this time Lewis had met the Reverend William Stidger of Kansas City, a flamboyant preacher, large and exuberant, with techniques borrowed from the advertising and theatrical professions. Stidger had demanded that Lewis do for the clergy what he had done for medical research and, on hearing that he was indeed planning such a novel, went about Kansas City boasting that he was to be the hero of Sinclair Lewis' new novel.

But Lewis' research was never that narrow. He attended every church in Kansas City many times. After reading over two hundred works on philosophy and religious practices, he gathered fifteen theologians, including a priest and a rabbi, and two agnostics, and held weekly seminars. As they sat at lunch he threw searching questions at his guests, "picking the very eyes out of them": what had their churches accomplished for the community, what were their *official* beliefs and what did they truthfully and honestly believe?

One of them, a liberal Presbyterian, describes these sessions: "Soul-shaking moments come when Lewis speaks with the passion of an Old Testament prophet, demanding 'What sacrifices do you make? What risks will you take? Who will literally follow Jesus into loneliness, ridicule and death?' Lewis has been reading the New Testament and its iron and flame have gotten into his blood. . . . There is a sophistry in the ministerial attitude that he scorns, and to which he attributes the fading distinction between the church and the world. . . . There is nothing flippant about him now." After these polemics, this minister said, there would be an uneasy hush while the theologians glanced sidelong at each other and Lewis glared at them all. It was as if he had pulled a curtain back and been infuriated by what he found.

Unsuspected by the men, Lewis had been doing some research into their private lives, and had they known of it they would have blanched when he made his farewell speech. With a twenty-thousand-word story outline and twenty-four character sketches safely in his suitcase, he embraced each man at the last meeting. "Boys," he said, "I'm going up to Minnesota and write a novel about you. I'm going to give you hell, but I love every one of you."

At the end of the summer he returned to New York. There his publisher met him at Grand Central Station and was handed a mysterious black bag. "What's in it? the publisher asked.

"Dynamite," Lewis grinned.

Elmer Gantry has been called a work of almost pure revulsion, a long shudder of loathing of what it describes. While *Main Street*'s people were at least human and George Babbitt had his pathos, Gantry is a monster, a target erected only to be spat at. In researching the Kansas City clergy, Lewis had pulled each man into small pieces, selecting here a weakness and there a grossness and, putting all these bits together, constructed a mosaic of unrelieved beastliness.

Each of Gantry's traits had of course existed somewhere among his models; Lewis could point to this man's secret adultery and that one's noisy ranting as proof. But the sum total was loaded evidence, and his very selections inspire a basic question about himself: what had the church, all churches, done to Sinclair Lewis to arouse such antipathy?

Any answer can be only speculation, based on a few scattered clues. It would seem that, contrary to the testimony of his book, Lewis had a deeply religious core which he carefully concealed from such atheistic cronies as H. L. Mencken and George Jean Nathan. There is for evidence his active interest in religion at Oberlin; there are revealing slips into reverence such as the lovely and moving prayers he wrote for a minister friend; his agonized search for sincerity among the Kansas City clergy and the almost irrational bitterness of his disappointment. There is the evidence contained in the rucksack he took on a walking tour—nothing but a toilet kit, a heavily annotated Bible, and *The Imitation of Christ.* Last, there is the little pile of belongings assembled after his death as his most personal and typical: fountain pen, soft hat, walking stick, cigarette case, eyeshade, chess set, and Bible.

Why then *Elmer Gantry?* Why the constant outpouring of ribald blasphemy to Mencken and others, the deliberate shaking of his fist in the face of God? Was this loathing simply the darker side of longing? When one has loved in early youth, has expected all life's problems to melt away in that rosy haze and then been disappointed, one may turn in childish rage on his betrayer.

Only an adolescent blames his disappointments on another. But then Lewis always *was* an adolescent. One can finally feel only compassion for a soul so torn.

Lewis had gleefully called his book dynamite. And judging by the explosions in the pulpits of America, he named it well. In expectation of the uproar his publisher had ordered the largest first printing in publishing history, and Boston, Kansas City, and many other cities at once cooperated by obligingly banning the book. The commotion lasted for a year. All those ministers who saw a trace of Elmer in themselves called the book a cowardly insult, but one or two quietly remarked that at least it made a man take a look at himself.

Lewis, exhausted by months of exceptionally heavy drinking, went off to Europe, only to continue drinking even more heavily there. As he wandered aimlessly about, a friend, studying him, remarked that he seemed to be in flight from himself. "He seemed to have no inner certainty, no balance, no serenity, nothing between heaven and earth to which he could withdraw for quietude and healing."

He stayed in Europe for a long time. And after a while it seemed that he had actually found something to cling to, for when he came back he brought with him not only a new novel but a new wife.

The novel was *Dodsworth*. And because it was about himself, and he himself had changed, the book's viewpoint had changed. In *Main Street* and *Babbitt* he had satirized the Midwest and the big businessman. Now he approved of them, drew them kindly. In *Main Street* Carol Kennicott represented his ideal woman, but now, in *Dodsworth*, he depicted her as a well-groomed female American monster.

By the time he wrote *Dodsworth* his marriage had long been disintegrating. He and Grace were quarreling regularly, often in public. His fortieth birthday, a frightening landmark date, had set him off on a frantic chase not only of blondes in Rome but of unimportant, fleeting affairs everywhere. Each episode was followed by repentance and renewed declarations of devotion to Gracie. "G. and I have never been so serene," he reported at one time to his poor publisher, who spent much of his time listening sympathetically to one or the other or both of them at once. But the serenity was always short-lived.

Their last Christmas together was spent in Washington. The gathering included, besides Grace and himself, Mrs. Hegger, Dr. Claude's son Freeman, nine-year-old Wells (who, in growing up, had fortunately ignored his father's looks and taken his own exclusively from his beautiful mother), a young musical protégé of Lewis', and a distinguished if impoverished Spanish gentleman named Casanova. This last had fallen in love with Grace and Lewis was encouraging him hopefully.

With a large and fashionable dinner party in the offing, Grace, hard and bright in shining satin, went to Lewis' room, where she found him sitting undressed on the edge of his bed muttering, "I won't go." She flung out angrily and Mr. Sinclair Lewis' place at his wife's side at the party was taken by Señor Casanova, a prophetic gesture. Mr. Sinclair Lewis himself flung out to join his bibulous chum Mencken in New York. It was the end, though the actual divorce came only in 1928. (At that time he was feeling very generous toward her. She and Casanova between them had lost $50,000 of his money but when his publisher sympathized with him he only shrugged: "After all, I haven't been very good to Grace, and after all, all she lost was money. Let's forget it.")

His eagerness to get rid of his first wife was due to his eagerness to acquire his second. This trio of characters formed the cast of the drama he called *Dodsworth*—rich American businessman wandering through Europe; babied female monster-wife; and wise, great-hearted other woman. ("Oh, he was lonely, this big friendly man, Sam Dodsworth, and he wanted a man to whom he could talk and boast and lie, he wanted a woman with whom he could be childish and hurt and comforted, and so successful and rich was he that he had neither, and he sought them, helpless, his raw nerves exposed.")

This Sam Dodsworth had found his woman at a Berlin tea party given for the press. This was the period of the great foreign correspondent—Gunther, Beaverbrook, Knickerbocker, Mann, Mowrer, Seldes, Sheean—and among them there was one handsome and brilliant woman, the undisputed queen of the hive. Dorothy Thompson was forceful and highly emotional, with a round baby face that utterly belied her businesslike attitude toward life and her job. On meeting Lewis she immediately invited him to a dinner party the following night, when she was celebrating both her thirty-third birthday and a newly acquired divorce.

Their attraction was mutual and instantaneous. She looked at his haggard face and thought, "My God, how he suffers." Having suffered herself in her short marriage, she wanted to say to him, "Let's stop suffering, let's help each other."

He, knowing nothing of her thoughts, stood up at her dinner table and made a five-word speech: "Dorothy, will you marry me?"

The courtship was a year's frenetic race all over Europe as she chased after stories and he chased after her. Finally there was a London wedding in May, 1928, with the minister adjuring the groom to write books that men would "go to for strength when they were in despair" (what made the good man think he could?) and then a honeymoon with a car and trailer, a few cooking utensils and two typewriters. So began what Dorothy called fourteen years of "intense pleasure and blackest pain."

Asked, once, why she had married this man so known for instability, she answered simply that she had loved him. And besides, there was his agonized need. A born nurse does what she can for a sick man, even if she knows he is dying; and though Dorothy Thompson could not know just how sick this man was, for he was to be twenty-five years a-dying, the process was already showing in his death's-head face.

Dodsworth was a fine book and a successful one, but it was the end of the great decade of Sinclair Lewis, and after that his flare began to sputter out. For four years after the marriage there was no novel at all, and then came *Ann Vickers,* which by baldly satirizing himself and Dorothy showed what those four years had already done to the marriage. The book made money, however, and that was a miracle in the Depression year of 1933. Following that there was a long string, tending always downward: *Work of Art,* about the hotel business; *It Can't Happen Here,* about home-grown fascism; and then books that were about hardly anything except himself and his problems.

As he repeated this literary theme with sad insistence, so he repeated it in his life. The story of the second marriage is almost a replay of the first, only with a change of cast. Sinclair Lewis is there still, but now the wife is a different personality, with consequent differences in emphasis and effect. The story, however, moves in the same groove to the same bitter end.

While the dissimilarities between Grace and Dorothy were many, as wives of Sinclair Lewis they had many things in common. Grace, when he met her, was a glamorous being from a strange and distant world, his faraway princess. He worshiped her and felt glamorized by her touch. So with Dorothy Thompson, queen of another new and fascinating world. Wanting, like Sam Dodsworth, a woman with whom he could be childish and hurt and comforted —a woman, that is, stronger than himself—Lewis seized on her, clung to her, and for a long time worshiped her. When they returned to America and bought a place in Vermont, he even believed that he wanted to settle down on a farm with her forever.

Grace's virtues had turned into faults, her society manner becoming in his eyes a simpering affectation and her way of taking over when he was drunk a deliberate emasculation. Her insistence on doing "the correct thing" was bully tactics calculated to reduce him to a cipher, and therefore nothing would revive his creative powers but freedom and independence. So, again, with Dorothy. Proud of her at first, he encouraged her to take on assignments and lecture tours, but when she was absent on those assignments he became irritated and filled the vacuum with liquor. As her anti-Nazi activities multiplied and she was spectacularly ejected from Germany, arms full of flowers from the other correspondents, he resented her growing fame. He was terrified of becoming Mr. Dorothy Thompson. And when groups gathered around to hear her views on the international situation, he fumed and sulked. In 1932 he exploded, "I love Dorothy. But I get so damn tired of hearing about This Situation! If I ever divorce her, I'll name Hitler as co-respondent."

In the area of fatherhood also, he repeated himself. On his first time around he had greeted Wells nervously, fearing to be tied down. That he never was is evidenced by some notes Wells made when he was twenty-five and himself a budding author: "Article on myself, born in big city, in cosmopolitan society, among big names, seeking. . .background for myself as an individual. . .a 'home,' as I really have no home. . . .Tragedy of lack of roots." (Two years after making these notes Lieutenant Wells Lewis was killed in France. He had written a novel and some stories and, more remarkably, had matured into such understanding and compassion that he could write to his mother, "Father's a bit difficult at times, but I love the old bastard.")

Lewis' second marriage also produced a son, Michael, who was greeted in much the same way as his half-brother had been. Dorothy and Lewis were traveling at the time of her pregnancy and, being thirty-six and nervous, she wanted to be at home near her doctor. So Lewis sent her off alone. (It was then, she said later, that she felt the first hint of trouble, like the warning twinge of a toothache.) Though Lewis was charming with other people's children, he was unable, somehow, to be easy with his own; they bored and irritated him. After he and Dorothy separated she kept begging him to see his son more often, to give him some attention, to *be a father.* But aside from money he had little of anything to give the boy.

This marriage, like the first, died slowly and in pain. The two of them argued, she about his drinking and he about her working —argued and railed and then made up, argued and railed and then did not make up. At times he was very funny at her expense, giving imitations of her "pontificating." At a party he would stand up and put on a wise face, saying, "Now I'm Dorothy Thompson. Ask me anything at all." Ashamed, he would then call her and apologize, declaring that she was his one and only refuge. Frantically, in momentary terror, he made her promise that no matter how hard he begged, she would never divorce him.

But later, fearful for his creative powers, he walked out and insisted that she must give him a divorce. Having given a promise, she wrote him instead, "No. I shall sit at home, in our home, and be there when you come back to it."

When he did come back, it was only to suffer further unendurable indignities: lying in bed one Sunday morning, he answered the telephone, to be told that the White House was calling Miss Thompson. He handed her the phone where she lay beside him, and with the wire stretched taut across his throat, pinning him down, he had to listen to his wife telling the President of the United States how to handle Hitler.

Finally she accepted the inevitable and divorced him. (Happily, she had a few years of peaceful marriage later on with a painter, Maxim Kopf.) So he got what he wanted, freedom. And it brought him what he did not want, more loneliness.

The peculiar tragedy of this man lay not in tragic events, for except for Wells' death there were few of those, and even this seemed not to matter very much. Rather the tragedy was that even the happy events went so sour.

The thing he had wanted most, the Nobel Prize, came in 1930. The first American writer to be so honored, he was intensely proud —so elated indeed that no matter how hard he tried not to boast, he could not keep it out of the conversation. Which made the public's reaction to the award all the more unbearable.

Europe approved of it well enough, for he had been pointing out America's faults for ten years and many who disliked Americans found it signally appropriate. But the writers and critics at home rose up in a body. For God's sake, with all the really fine authors in America, what were the Nobel people *thinking* of, to choose Lewis! This was no great creative artist, this was a mere prophet and recorder of social history—good enough for his own time, of course, but that time had passed and gone and he with it. Reading the papers, Lewis all but wept with anguish.

His misery was so plainly visible that one of the many young writers he had helped and encouraged recorded his tragic figure in his own fiction. In *You Can't Go Home Again* Thomas Wolfe drew such a character: "I met a truly great and honest man who had aspired to Fame and won her, and I saw that it had been an empty victory. . . .Fame was not enough. He needed something more, and he had not found it."

But once again, in 1939, he thought he had. Fascinated by the theater from early youth, he had written several unsuccessful plays and helped dramatize one or two of his books. In 1937, summering alone in Massachusetts, he began hanging around the Stockbridge theater while attempting to write a play. Lonely and unhappy, he was irresistibly drawn to this bustling, gregarious world and its lively, hard-working people. Like Grace's world and then like Dorothy's, this new one had glamour and magic and he stood on the sidelines watching wistfully, the outsider looking in.

To the theater people, however, he was a world-famous figure honoring them by his presence, and it was inevitable, once they discovered his gift for mimicry, that they should invite him to act.

Eagerly he agreed—to get the feel of the theater from inside, he explained to himself.

Excited and humbly anxious to learn, he watched the other actors rehearse and listened to their suggestions, renewing his youth in this glistening company. He made his debut in a dramatization of his *It Can't Happen Here,* performing with a certain amateurish charm, and during the next year or two appeared in several other plays, including his own *Angela Is Twenty-two.* He was not drinking these days. After a frightening spell with delirium tremens, during which he sustained three broken ribs, he had a long happy drying-out period, when he lectured his alcoholic friends earnestly. It was while thus sober that he found the something more he sought.

Not surprisingly, she was only eighteen. A young apprentice actress with the Provincetown Players, Marcella Powers was pretty, desperately poor, and ready to be impressed by any famous man, even a haggard scarecrow of fifty-four with a hand so shaky it could not lift a coffee cup unaided. And while the story is so routine it almost tells itself—fantasy and infatuation on his part, hard-headed realism on hers—she at least did not strip him of his fortune or what dignity he had left. He acted with her in one or two plays, and when she proved to have no future on the stage he got her a job on a magazine. Later he put her in a novel, *Cass Timberlane,* and dedicated it to her. In the story the girl marries her elderly lover, but that was part of his fantasy.

During these last years he was moving about like a hunted man, always looking to that somewhere else for contentment. Hotel suites and houses and apartments were taken and left within a few months—a cavernous duplex penthouse on Central Park, a mansion in Duluth and another in Massachusetts. His son Michael visited occasionally among crowds of other guests, and Marcella came too, but gradually less and less.

Finally Marcella decided to get married. Practical but not merciless as she pulled out, she made him a present of her mother, a stolid, silent, almost invisible woman who became his housekeeper when Marcella left. Souvenir of her daughter, he kept her near as buffer and traveling companion.

During the last shattered phase, when he went back to drinking hard, he dragged this submissive woman all over Italy as long as she could bear it. Then, having taken a villa alone in Florence, he invited a man picked up in a restaurant to be his secretary-companion. This Alexander Manson, of uncertain nationality, moved into the villa for the last year of his life.

Lewis, desperate with loneliness, reached out one last time to his older brother, the solid, handsome man he could never quite impress. He persuaded Dr. Claude to come over and be shown Italy. Michael came too, and the three spent Christmas together. At dinner Dr. Claude, watching him getting drunker and drunker, said sardonically, "Hal, you go on this way, I give you one year to live." He went home after Christmas and Lewis never saw him again.

That year of 1950 was spent being cared for, if that is the phrase, by the slightly sinister Alexander Manson, who kept writing Lewis' publisher for more money, and whose wife over the months became unaccountably well dressed. But he did at least keep Lewis company, and Lewis could afford the money.

Dr. Claude's prognosis was remarkably accurate; on New Year's Eve, 1950, Lewis collapsed from acute delirium tremens. When the gentle Italian doctor came to tend him he looked up vacantly, with a child's stare, and addressed him as "father." Whether he thought he had finally been accepted by that inaccessible man, one cannot say. He died eleven days later without ever fully regaining consciousness.

Willa Cather

(1873-1947)

Willa Cather
(1873=1947)

T O THE CASUAL observer Willa Cather was as hearty and un-complicated as her own windswept Nebraska plains. But this was only the visible surface. Below lay the submerged seven-eighths of the woman, unseen and unknowable save by a selected few.

Rarely has a well-known person kept her private life so screened from view. Not only did Willa Cather refuse all inter-views of a personal nature during her lifetime, but in her will she instructed her executor never, repeat never, to permit the publica-tion "in any form whatsoever of the whole or any part of any letter or letters" written by her; period. This held also for notebooks, diaries, and all other private papers. And unfortunately, the inti-mates who after her death wrote their memoirs of the woman and the writer respected her wishes only too well.

The inevitable effect of this unanimous secretiveness was to raise questions she herself would have no doubt deplored. But since the woman *was* the writer, any study of the writer legiti-mately concerns itself with the whole woman. And where many important facts have been forbidden the public, the student must find them wherever he can.

Some quite routine details of Willa Cather's life can be in-ferred only by dragging them struggling out of her own fiction. But other facts are plainly seen—such facts, for example, as the unusual influence on her of *places*. The places where she lived, indeed, have an identity of their own, becoming, as it were, foreground characters in her stories, so intertwined with the other characters that without them the books could not exist. The ardor with which she responded to places seems almost to have been a sublimation of the ardor other men and women feel for human beings.

The first of these was the place where she spent her eight childhood years and where she returned in her old age to write *Sapphira and the Slave Girl*. Back Creek Valley was a particularly beautiful part of Virginia's Shenandoah Valley. During the Civil War the nearby town of Winchester had been won and lost and won again no less than sixty-eight times, and the Boak and Cather grandparents had lived through turbulent years. Cathers had been farmers in these parts for a hundred years, sturdy, respectable people; and so had Boaks, though the Boaks had a bit the best of it socially. Willowshade Farm, where the young Willa grew up, was a good 304 acres, and the house, not quite a mansion but more than a farmhouse, had a formal front garden with spreading willow trees. It was a damp, cool place, made for easy living, where large flocks of sheep grazed in the fields, their wool providing a comfortable income.

Charles Cather, Willa's father, was a pleasant, kindly man with fair hair and the handsome blue eyes which his daughter was especially proud to have inherited. In gentle Southern style he addressed her all his life as Daughter; his gentleness, indeed, was the bond between them, and she was never to forget how it extended even to the sheepdog Vic, for whom he made little leather shoes to wear when scrambling over the pasture's sharp rocks.

This gentleness ran all the way through Charles Cather. But not so with his wife. She too was soft, but with her the softness stopped halfway in; like the flesh of a peach, sweet and luscious, it had a hard pit at the core. In the story "Old Mrs. Harris" there is a woman unmistakably taken from Virginia Boak Cather, a handsome energetic woman of meticulous grooming and perfect manners but inside vain, self-centered, and imperious—the woman Willa Cather remembered from her childhood. Like many Southern gentlewomen with soft voices, Virginia Boak Cather ruled the

household and children quietly enough. But let a murmured request fail to bring instant action and the steel-gray eyes and
purring soft voice would harden into a threat and the delicate
white hand as like as not reach for a rawhide whip.

Demanding special treatment, Virginia Boak Cather received
it. She never left her room less than perfectly gowned and coiffed,
whatever the domestic emergency; her hands were never soiled
or her complexion marred by the outdoor sun. Her dignity, her
beauty, were the crown of the household and husband and children were ruled by it; her femininity was her most potent weapon.
But, just possibly, the sharpness of this weapon, constantly in contact with another's sensitive skin, may have caused a resistant
thickening and hardening that took a curious shape a few years
hence.

The first child born to Virginia Boak Cather and her husband
Charles was Willa Sibert. The birth date was December 7, 1873
(though in later life she chipped a year or so off her age as she went
along, and at her death *Who's Who* was listing her as born in 1876).
After her came Roscoe and Douglass, the two brothers who were
her lifelong friends, and then Jessica. There would be three more
children later, but that was after a vast change in the Cather
situation.

Sturdy, square little Willa was an oddly positive child from the
beginning. With eyes and ears that missed nothing, neither the
gossip of the old ladies over their quilting frames nor the men's
tales of the war and the slaves' Underground Railroad, she absorbed the Virginia atmosphere like a blotter. Of formal education
there was not a trace; her Grandmother Boak, who lived at Willowshade, read the Bible and *The Pilgrim's Progress* aloud to her, but
where she ever acquired spelling and figuring is a mystery. Perhaps the answer is that she never really did, for they were run by
guesswork till the end.

A life as sparsely documented as this leaves much for the
imagination to chew on, but a few significant early stories survive.
She was, for example, always fiercely independent. At the age of

five she stood one day stolidly enduring the attentions of an old judge, a caller at Willowshade, who patted her curls and cooed patronizingly at the "dainty little doll" at his knee. Suddenly losing all patience, she drew on her somewhat limited store of shocking words and shook off his hand, shouting ferociously, "I'se a dang-'ous nigger, I is!"

By this time, too, she had developed the trait that was to direct her whole life: whenever her parents reached out a hand to assist her in some task she would push it away, crying, "Self-alone, self-alone!" What made her so soon fearful of leaning on others is not in the record; Willowshade existence seems to have been smooth and pleasant enough, with parties and house guests, and parents apparently loving and kind.

But all at once, when she was eight, this serene existence was blasted and she was torn up by the roots, to be dropped down in a strange, forbidding landscape and told to call it home. After the Civil War thousands of acres of Nebraska land had been given away cheap to Easterners brave enough to settle these wild bleak wastes, and one of Willa's uncles had been among the takers. Later her Grandfather and Grandmother Cather had followed him. And now, with the fortuitous burning down of the Willowshade sheep barn by spontaneous combustion, Charles and Virginia Cather were moved to do likewise. Willowshade was sold, the furniture was auctioned off, Vic was given to a neighbor, and the children, Grandmother Boak, and a simple-minded farm girl named Margie were scrubbed, polished, and packed up for traveling.

Willa, yanked thus roughly out of the soil she knew and loved, was bewildered and terrified. The disruption was somehow personified at the railroad station by the sight of Vic, broken loose and dragging her chain behind her, bounding down the tracks after the train as it pulled away. Willa's first change of scene was made in a flood of tears, and ever afterwards she feared and resisted change.

Following several long days of staring at strange scenery through dirty windows and longer nights of sleeping on dirty plush seats, the Cathers arrived at Red Cloud, Nebraska, thence to take a wagon sixteen miles to Grandfather Cather's house out in Webster County.

Willa once said that the years from eight to fifteen were the really vital period in a writer's life, and certainly her next few years yielded the richest ore of her career. Yet her first emotion on seeing these empty prairies stretching out to infinity on every side was pure terror, the helpless sensation of being swallowed up and lost in space. This was a country of almost unbearable loneliness. In contrast with the lush, friendly Virginia woods and gardens, the bleak prairie seemed as bare as the palm of her hand. She visited the few trees in the vicinity as though they were personal friends, and wept over the first wildflowers because they were so lovely and there was no one around to notice them. But in time she came to understand and love the vastness. In it she saw a beauty none had ever seen before, and she lived to picture it through her incomparable prose as no one has ever done since.

The country's inhabitants were equally new and unnoticed by the world. This part of Nebraska had been settled only fourteen years before when one Captain Silas Garber, late of the Union Army, had led a contingent west and built a stockade, naming it Red Cloud after a famous Sioux Indian. Other adventurers followed from New England and Virginia, among them the first Cathers. Soon came a second wave from Germany, Bohemia, Denmark, and Switzerland. They broke soil never before trod by human feet and built houses out of square bricks of sod cut and packed and dried. Both groups led lives hard and rugged, but the Virginians, most of them educated people only recently impoverished by the war, regarded the unlettered foreigners with compassion not untainted by scorn.

All except Willa. In the words of Edith Lewis, a long-time friend, "she gave herself with passion to the country and to the people, the struggling foreigners who inhabited it; became at heart their champion, made their struggle her own—their fight to master the soil, to hold the land in the face of drouths and blizzards, hailstorms and prairie fires." For two years she roamed the countryside on horseback, visiting the Bohemian and Danish and Norwegian neighbors and making friends that stayed her lifetime. Unconsciously she absorbed so much that thirty years later all she had to do was sit down with her pen poised and whole lives flowed effortlessly down onto the paper.

After two years the Cathers moved to Red Cloud, the town of 2,500 people with a real school for the youngsters and an office for farm loans and insurance for the father, who was more suited to writing mortgages than driving a plow. The house was comfortable enough but as crowded as an anthill—mother, father, Grandma Boak, Margie, Willa, Roscoe, Douglass, Jessica, and now three more children, James, Jack, and Elsie. At mealtimes two boarders sat at the table as well.

The attic was the children's domain, and Mrs. Cather solved that part of her housekeeping worries by never going near it. It was one long open space, with beds in a row and, in the wintertime, snow drifting through the roof cracks onto their faces. They were perfectly happy in their private kingdom where no adults imposed neatness or cleanliness, but later, when Willa was deemed too big to share a room with her brothers, she screened off one end, papering it with a large rose design, and reigned alone and grand in her Rose Bower.

Though she had girl playmates, her preferred companions were Roscoe and Douglass, the brothers who occupied always a unique position in her heart. The times spent with them were her "most perfect form of happiness." But she had other less likely friends: elderly teachers and storekeepers and, very particularly, the hired girl next door, loyal, hard-working Annie Sadilek, whom no one would ever have visualized as the heroine of a novel.

There was, too, the couple whom Willa watched with breathless fascination, Captain Silas Garber who later became Governor of Nebraska and, no less fascinating, his lovely Southern wife with her inscrutable charm and unforgettable soft laugh. The Garbers would one day give her one of her best books.

Not surprisingly, as adolescence overtook this forceful girl she sought to expand her world and discover new interests. Two of her best friends were the town's two doctors, with whom she was privileged to visit cases. When, therefore, the will of a deceased relative unexpectedly brought a box of surgical instruments into the house, it was like a sign from heaven. Without more ado she plumped for a medical career. She dissected dogs and cats passionately and, watching her doctor friends administer anesthesia, she absorbed the technique so well that once, in an emergency, she administered chloroform while a boy's leg was amputated. It was one of her proudest moments.

Her eccentricities excited mild amusement at first, no more. Then, when her beautiful mother fell ill and there was no one to comb out the girl's long curly hair, in a wild gesture of independence she went to a barber and had it cropped short like a boy's.

The effect was cataclysmic. Tension had long been tightening as the daughter's strong personality began to assert itself. Her demands for freedom collided with the equally strong personality of her mother, who here, as in every other encounter, wielded her soft-spoken femininity as a weapon. Each was driven into an extreme position. Mrs. Cather wept reproachful female tears and Willa, rebelling against all things female, scraped up the most defiant weapons she could find, a boy's jacket, a starched shirt, and a tie. When the opposition hardened still further, she added a man's watch chain, a derby hat, and a cane. The total effect, with her chubby fourteen-year-old face, produced a somewhat unsettling effect on the town. She had always preferred the "Willie" form of her name; now she answered only to Will or Billie, and from her amused doctor friends she even got an indulgent "Dr. Will."

The town at large was shocked, and deep sympathy flowed to Mr. and Mrs. Cather. But outrage is the food that rebellion feeds on, and during Dr. Will's high school days she stalked about town being a "dangerous nigger" indeed, airing irreligious views and comparing Red Cloud's narrow orthodoxy with the enlightened world without. In 1890, utterly at odds with the "bitter, dead little Western town" she was to love so dearly later on, she made off to Lincoln to enroll in the University of Nebraska. (Always jealous of her privacy, she turned the key in the Rose Bower door and no one was ever allowed to enter while she was away.)

Announcing that she had come to study science and the classics, she adopted a heroic routine, rising at five, studying till midnight, and carrying her own coal scuttle up two flights to her tiny rented room, where she lived on fifteen dollars a month for food, rent, and clothing. With gruff boyish voice and impatient manner she disavowed any interest in male attention, and the impression she made on the student body was considerably less favorable than that on the professors.

One of these was so deeply impressed that he unconsciously helped her toward her destined course in life. He had assigned his English class an essay on the personal characteristics of Thomas Carlyle. The paper she turned in was a dissertation not so much on that Scottish titan's personality as on the problems of the nonconformist in a hostile environment, a subject much closer to her heart, and so brilliantly was it written that the professor showed it to the editor of the Lincoln *State Journal*. He in turn printed it with an accompanying editorial on the "remarkable production of this young girl of sixteen years from Webster County."

In the ensuing excitement she found herself turned sharply about and swept toward a new career. The sight of her work in print, she said later, had an effect on her positively hypnotic, and for the rest of her life she did proceed like one hypnotized, looking neither to right nor left nor heeding any other distraction or noise. In that very schoolgirl essay, in fact, she had laid down her lifetime philosophy: "Art of every kind is an exacting master, more so even than Jehovah—He says only 'Thou shalt have no other gods before me.' Art, Science and Letters cry, 'Thou shalt have no other gods at all.' "

From then on she went crashing through college like a tornado, apparently unimpeded by the emotional entanglements that

trip up most people her age. She had decided, however consciously or unconsciously, that love and marriage were not for her
and that artistic creation was to be her only preoccupation and
religion.

She began her devotions immediately, joining the student
periodical *The Hesperian* and soon becoming its editor. One student later wrote: "My themes were passed on by a rather mannish
young woman with a head that seemed vast under her jungle of
hair. [Willa had dropped her aggressively masculine toggery and
haircut, but the general effect remained.] She did me the great
honor of calling me to her office. 'You write not badly,' she said.
'But you don't *see.* Learn French, a little French, and read Flaub-
ert or even Maupassant. They *see.* ' " Here then was Willa, not yet
twenty but already a writer who did herself see with astonishing
penetration.

In her third year a financial panic overran Nebraska and her
family suffered heavily in a bank failure. By now Willa had won the
confidence of the *State Journal,* and she was offered a dollar a day
for any column she cared to write, and a dollar for each drama
review. With her modest style of living she became thus almost
self-supporting.

The Willa S. Cather reviews were soon well if not always
happily known. A writer on the *Journal* remembered later, "Many
an actor of national reputation wondered on coming to Lincoln
what would appear next morning from the pen of the meat-ax
young girl of whom all of them had heard. Miss Cather did not
stand in awe of the greatest actors, but set each one in his place
with all the authority of a veteran metropolitan critic." Brutal she
often was, and at times sophomoric in displaying her brilliance,
but for one who had never seen a first-rate theatrical performance
until three years before, her reviews were remarkably perceptive.
Of a performance of Julia Marlowe she wrote, "She lives too
beautifully to live very hard, dies too gracefully to die very effectively.... The greatest art in acting is not to please and charm and
delight, but to move and thrill; not to play a part daintily

and delightfully but with power and passion."

Her daily column consisted of verse, dialogues, satirical portrait sketches of friends thinly—but sometimes too thinly—disguised. Later she declared that only once had she put a friend into
a book raw, but these portraits made her some lasting enemies by
their sharp truthfulness. Most important to her columns, however,
and to herself, were the stories they sometimes contained. Some
were very well written, though violent, caustic, and cruel, while
others were awkward and overdone. But almost all interestingly
concerned themselves with the hard-working immigrants who
peopled her later novels. Unprotected by copyright, these stories
were collected for republication during her years of fame, but she
fought the plan with all her force, maintaining that they were
immature and worthless and should be allowed to die decently. (It
was this concern for her literary reputation, she said later somewhat unconvincingly, that moved her to forbid publication of all
of her writings not intended for the public eye.)

Even as a child in Red Cloud, she had been fascinated by the
third-rate touring companies that appeared in the Opera House
over the hardware store. Her position as drama critic in Lincoln
therefore afforded her constant pleasure, permitting her not only
to see performances but to meet actors and actresses backstage
and even to watch them putting their makeup on. In this glamorous world she was an easy touch for the hard-up, and no matter
how careless young actresses might be about repaying her they
were always forgiven; artists were creatures apart, members of a
freemasonry with privileges and laws of their own.

These exhausting college days took their toll—classes in the
morning, the theater at night, thence on to the *Journal* office to
write her review, and home at one or two. Late one night the
famous writer Stephen Crane, who was passing through town and
dropped in at the newspaper office, was galvanized by the unusual
sight of a young girl with fuzzy hair standing up in a corner fast
asleep. After graduation she went home and collapsed.

The following year in Red Cloud was miserable, a time of

enforced conformity and idleness. Under pressure from her style-conscious mother she had worn to the commencement exercises a gown of ivory satin and gold sequins, with long gloves and hair piled high, but her graduation photograph shows no corresponding look of festivity on her sulky face. Another photograph of the time caught her wearing an elaborate cape trimmed in Persian lamb and possibly the ugliest hat ever recorded by a camera. But after six months she kicked over the maternal traces and went back to the tailored suits and severely simple hairdo that were her trademark thenceforth.

This period's finery was more easily disposed of than its idleness. There was nothing for her to do in Red Cloud, yet after her spectacular success in Lincoln she imagined the eyes of the little town on her, skeptical and hostile. Oppressed by the need to prove herself, she felt inept, drained of confidence and resentful of those who made her feel so. Her emotions expressed themselves some years later in a vitriolic tale, "The Sculptor's Funeral," in which an artist, considered a crackpot because he has never conformed to his tight little town, is surrounded by uncomprehending hostility even in death.

Finally, however, she escaped. After a year her editorial experience brought her the offer of a job in Pittsburgh on a new magazine, *The Home Monthly*. Now was her chance to "show" Red Cloud, and she accepted it gratefully. In her book *The Song of the Lark* she wrote of a young singer in a somewhat similar situation that "she had an appointment to meet the rest of herself, sometime, somewhere. It was moving to meet her and she was moving to meet it." Willa's move to Pittsburgh was a step on the way to herself.

Her first five years in that city were spent in writing for *The Home Monthly* and local newspapers, and another five in teaching English and Latin in high schools. Curiously, though places always meant so much to her, Pittsburgh never figured in her writings. Life here had no glow, no sheen, for journalism and teaching were merely routine steps to be taken and then forgotten. Sending much of her pay home, she lived just above the level of squalor and developed a dread of poverty that left her always a little nervous about luxuries like taxis. Nevertheless she was happy, feeling for the first time free of critical eyes and clacking tongues and at liberty to expand in her own way. And to make the kind of friends she wanted.

Here let it be recorded that in spite of a certain paucity of the usual graces there was something unusually winning about Willa Cather. Not beautiful—indeed, short, stocky, unstylish, with only fine eyes to catch the attention; not witty—in fact, somewhat deficient in humor; not gracious—often dogmatic and intolerant—she had a rare charm that inspired and held the devotion of a great many people for a very long time. Tremendous vitality was certainly hers, a brilliant mind and an eager, spontaneous interest in those who attracted her. There was too a passionate appreciation of beauty in nature and art and people, and an unforgetting kindness to those early friends she had seen struggling through bad times. Lastly, she herself had a vast talent for giving friendship, and that is never a one-way street.

Several of her most important associations were made at this time. Dr. Lawrence Litchfield and his wife were a wealthy Pittsburgh couple who entertained a great deal and made Willa welcome at their musical At Homes—Ethel Litchfield was her devoted friend forty years later. Edith Lewis was a Nebraska girl who had admired her dramatic criticisms in the Lincoln *Courier* and became her friend in Pittsburgh—she lived with Willa for many years and became her literary executor after death. Closest of all was the friendship with Isabelle McClung, a bond that neither distance nor any other obstacle could break—at least until the unlooked-for sequel many years later.

Typically, it was in the dressing room of an actress friend in Pittsburgh that Willa Cather met Isabelle McClung. This tall and strikingly beautiful young woman was, like Willa herself, something of a rebel. Daughter of a prominent and wealthy judge and his cultured wife, Isabelle was less interested in Pittsburgh's society than in its painters, musicians, actors, and writers, of whom there was a surprisingly rich supply. Her father, though brilliant, was narrowly conservative, and at the time Isabelle met Willa she felt herself all but smothered in the atmosphere of her home.

Willa had by now acquired something of a reputation through her newspaper work; further, the simplicity of manner, the open face with its flashing smile and intermittent play of dimples, the unaffected sparkle of mind, all contrasted happily with the heavy formality of the McClung circle. She was exactly what Isabelle's restless nature hungered for and the two became friends on the instant.

Isabelle was one of those dynamic women of wealth passionately artistic but lacking any specific talent, who satisfy their creative urge by helping others create. In Willa she saw a shining talent being eroded in an exhausting, profitless job and imperiously carried her off to live in the Murray Hill Avenue mansion. Though her parents liked Willa herself, they were somewhat stunned by this arrangement at first, but with Isabelle it was no Willa, no Isabelle. So a sewing room on the third floor was furnished with a desk and a chair, and for the next five years Willa lived there in quiet luxury. Like a daughter, she was free to join the social doings downstairs or to retire to the third floor whenever the spirit called.

During this time she had her first trip abroad, which was financed by a series of travel letters sent back from Europe to the *State Journal*. There she *saw* the places and people she moved among with ravenous all-absorbing eyes and stored up great memory banks of France to use in her future work. And when the journalistic grind had been exchanged for a teacher's shorter hours she turned to writing freelance stories and poems for her own satisfaction.

Cheered by the publication of a small book of poetry, *April Twilights*, which she dedicated to her two beloved brothers, she decided to collect some of her better stories and try them on a New York publisher.

S. S. McClure, who ran both *McClure's* magazine and a related book house, was one of the most dynamic men in American letters. Excitable, unpredictable, emitting ideas like fireworks, he was forever dashing off somewhere after some author or artist. Fine writers were his particular passion and he paid generously to publish the best of them, English and American, known and unknown. Kipling, Stevenson, Hardy, Bennett, Crane, O'Henry, London, Twain, Doyle—all had added gloss to his pages, while some yet unknown and struggling ones, like Joseph Conrad, had been recognized and almost literally saved from starvation by his generous support. In 1904 he returned from a European trip to find a package lying on his desk, a manuscript read and rejected by a sub-editor and wrapped ready for mailing. On a hunch he reopened the package and read its contents, and within hours a telegram had gone off to Pittsburgh. Within days the man had gone after it, and the result was the appearance in *McClure's* of two of Willa's finest stories. Subsequently a whole collection came out, *The Troll Garden*, and after a year she was offered an editorial job.

Edith Lewis, now working in New York, put her up in her Washington Square apartment when Willa came to discuss the offer. Willa was flattered and excited by this new prospect, but the years of humiliating poverty had made such a deep impression that while the glamour of the position and the dazzling salary were tempting bait, the very importance of the job frightened her. How well could she do it? How long would she last? At least she was sure of the Pittsburgh teaching job. And she did so hate change. Above all, there was Isabelle—how would she like her leaving? And how would *she* feel?

The decision was months in the making, but finally, with Isabelle's concurrence, she took the plunge. In 1906 she rented an apartment near Edith Lewis and started a new life. Within two years she was McClure's managing editor. In the next four she brought the circulation to an all-time high.

"To the end of her stay at *McClure's*," wrote Edith Lewis, "Willa Cather's relationship with Mr. McClure was without a cloud. She never flattered him, never compromised her own judgment in order to please him. At the same time she understood and truly admired him. . . . As for him, I think he trusted Willa Cather as he did few people." Her first assignment, which kept her in Boston most of two years, was a biography of Mary Baker Eddy, during which time she turned out a series of routine magazine stories which she later consigned to the decent grave she kept for inferior work.

Her growing success, and the greater freedom and breadth of her life, gave her a new self-confidence. "But," says Edith Lewis, "working on *McClure's* was like working in a high wind, sometimes of cyclone magnitude. . . . It was too stimulating for one of her temperament. . . . People had always excited Willa Cather; and the continual impact of new personalities, the necessity of talking to and being talked to by so many people, exhausted her nervously."

She was never one to take people casually. Elizabeth Sergeant, who as a young writer called at *McClure's* in 1910 with an article to sell, was surprised to find the august managing editor "a vital being who smiled at me, her face open, direct, honest, blooming with warmth and kindness. Her eyes were sailor-blue, her cheeks were rosy, her hair was red-brown, parted in the middle like a child's. As she shook hands, I felt the freshness and brusqueness, too, of an ocean breeze. Her boyish, enthusiastic manner was disarming, and as she led me through the jostle of the outer office, I was affected by the resonance of her Western voice, and by the informality of her clothes—it was as if she rebelled against urban conformities. Her blouse was bright with stripes, her Irish tweed skirt was chromatic. Though the fashion was for long skirts, hers cut her sturdy legs in half."

As instantaneous as was her sympathy on occasion, antipathy could be just as abrupt. Then her chin would grow hard and grim, her shoulders stiffen, and her voice, which in affection was soft and musical, would become harsh and edgy. Her friends, hearing the tone of it, could tell even without the words how she felt about a person.

The affections outnumbered the disaffections, however, and during these years she was busily making a galaxy of friends. Her months in Boston yielded three of the most important: the editor Ferris Greenslet, who was to ease her into the book world; Mrs. James T. Field, Boston *grande dame* who had entertained Emerson, Dickens, Hawthorne, Henry James, and Thackeray, and who still maintained a distinguished literary salon; and Sarah Orne Jewett, popular author of *The Country of the Pointed Firs* and other gentle New England stories. Both Mrs. Field and Miss Jewett were many years older than Willa; great ladies watching the younger generation with affectionate eyes, they saw here a spirit worth nurturing and took her to their hearts. In their homes Willa breathed the atmosphere of a gentler, quieter age where the raucous present did not intrude, and here she found the serenity she had always sought. As long as they survived she spent as much time with them as possible.

Sarah Orne Jewett's affection for Willa was reinforced by a deep literary concern. Having read her bitter story "The Sculptor's Funeral," so filled with resentment at the "mean, dead country" she had come from, the Maine writer grieved over her alienation and longed to reconcile her with her roots. She realized, too, that her ability to write, the vitality she needed for it, was being sapped by her tiring days at *McClure's*.

Finally she wrote her a letter: "I cannot help saying what I think about your writing and its being hindered by such incessant, important, responsible work as you have in your hands now . . . . Your vivid, exciting companionship in the office must not be your audience, you must find your own quiet center of life and write from that. . . . To work in silence and with all one's heart, that is the writer's lot; he is the only artist who must be solitary, and yet needs the widest outlook upon the world."

This appeal could not have fallen on more receptive and grateful soil. Though unable yet to resign her job, Willa flung herself into her own work every spare minute, and the first fruit of Miss Jewett's seed was a novel published the following year. But

Alexander's Bridge was a mistake all the way around, not at all what Miss Jewett had intended. A story of international high society, it was a superficial imitation of Henry James at his most literary, and Willa later admitted with a grin, "I had been trying to sing a song that did not lie in my own voice."

But the Jewett seed was still gestating in her mind and, taking a leave of absence, she went to Isabelle's country home and spent the autumn of 1911 writing. And this time Miss Jewett, had she lived, would have applauded, for with *The Bohemian Girl* Willa had returned to her Nebraska roots in the spirit she had intended. Here Webster County and its flat open spaces, its Scandinavian and Bohemian farmers, were understood and liked and cherished.

By this time Elizabeth Sergeant had become a close friend, one whose literary opinion Willa valued, and she asked her to read the manuscript. "It's different from anything I've ever written before," Willa told her, "in an entirely new vein. No magazine is going to buy it, but somehow I like it."

Elizabeth's response astonished her: "This is it, this is absolutely *it*!" It was, she said, Willa herself at last. And better still, it introduced a group of people and a setting new to the reading public. She insisted that Willa show it to *McClure's*.

Incredulously Willa reported to her the next day that the editor there had offered her $750. "I told him I knew better than anyone else that *McClure's* couldn't afford $750 for any story. He said I was a goose. But finally we agreed on $500 if I would take $750 for the next." Willa shook her head, laughing helplessly. "How in the world am I ever going to resign from this devoted *McClure's?*"

She was pulling away nonetheless, taking longer and longer leaves. Isabelle's mother in Pittsburgh fell ill and like a loving daughter she rushed there to help Isabelle nurse her. Then on to Red Cloud to the real parents, whom she visited almost every year. And there, back in her old home, she realized that no region and no person one had ever loved could really be left behind, that they clung to one's mind demanding to be reckoned with.

So now she began singing in her own voice. Somewhat later she said, "Whenever I crossed the Missouri River coming in to Nebraska the very smell of the soil tore me to pieces. . . . My deepest feelings were rooted in this country. . . . I had searched for books telling about the beauty of the country I loved, its romance, the heroism and courage of its people. . . . I did not find them, and so I wrote *O Pioneers!*"

This deceptively simple story of a young Swedish immigrant, a farm girl taming a virgin land, was a paean of praise to Nebraska and its people. The country, she said, had insisted on being the hero of the story and she did not interfere, for it came full blown out of the long grasses. Like her heroine she was plowing virgin territory, and through the years this "firstness" gave her tremendous satisfaction. On publication of *O Pioneers!* in 1913 a Philadelphia paper said, "We question whether any man, in the whole course of American literature, has produced as good a book as this about the actual soil of our country." And in England, Bernard Shaw observed wryly that America was "at last producing an art of its own instead of merely boring Europe by returning its exports with all their charm rubbed off."

By this time Willa Cather was forty years old. She and Edith Lewis had taken a comfortable apartment in Greenwich Village at Number Five Bank Street. Willa was extremely sensitive to noise and a slight problem presented itself when the daughter of the family above started practicing the piano every morning. It was always Beethoven's Appassionata Sonata, nothing, for months, but the Appassionata—but in time Willa came to regard it kindly as a sort of obbligato to her work. When the family moved, however, she took the apartment herself, just in case, and kept it empty during the rest of her tenure. Thus in this quiet Village backwater she moored happily for fifteen years.

Edith Lewis, who worked in an advertising agency uptown, has been described as a kind of first officer of the ship at Number Five, while Willa, the captain, set its course. The two led separate lives and had separate circles of friends, but when a forthcoming book required research in France or a summer spent in New York's heat Edith Lewis cheerfully fell in line.

Willa's writing day was a mere three hours long, but so intense and exhilarating were those hours that she often came out panting like a tennis player. Dressed in a denim skirt and middy blouse and surrounded winter and summer by flowers, she lost herself blissfully in the world of her own people. She had at her mind's tip everything that had ever interested her, down to the exact shade of red on a ladybug's wing, and unlike most writers she never needed to go back each morning over yesterday's work but plunged straight ahead till the whole work was done.

Her social activities were simple—opera with Edith once or twice a week, at first in the cheap seats upstairs and then descending in inverse ratio to her literary climb; informal At Homes on Friday, when friends gathered in such numbers that finally the invitations had to be severely rationed; small dinners, with French wines, soup hot hot hot, and melons cold cold cold. For the public record this was her whole personal life.

Willa Cather's private life or, rather, the lack of it, has been the subject of considerable speculation, and the established facts, sparse indeed, fit into a single paragraph: Willa Cather never married. So far as is known she was never even engaged. Published memoirs scarcely mention any men save editors and husbands of friends. Edith Lewis says vaguely that in Pittsburgh a young doctor had once wanted to marry her. "She admitted that it was a good match, but she did not really care for him. Perhaps the real reason was that she loved her freedom—her liberty to do exactly as she pleased. She wanted nothing closer than friendship." (One is reminded of the five-year-old crying "self-alone, self-alone.") But she was a woman passionately alive and passably attractive. If she never loved any man, on what then did she expend her emotions?

At twenty she had written, "An author's only safe course is to cling to the skirts of his art, forsaking all others, and keep unto her as long as they two shall live. An artist should not be vexed by human hobbies or human follies: he should be able to lift himself into the clear firmament of creation where the world is not. He should be among men but not of them, in the world but not of the world."

Obviously she planned even then to love her art alone, rejecting all close human relationships. But why this stern rejection, this conviction that art should only substitute for life rather than express it? Such shrinking from personal involvement suggests nothing so much as fear. But the nature of the fearful experiences that caused it we shall probably never know.

What we have, then, is a woman who seemed to be shielding herself from something she would not, or dared not, face. That she distrusted the very idea of love between men and women is evident throughout her books. In many of them love scarcely appears at all, and when it does unhappiness usually follows. Almost she seems to be arguing against the idea, persuading herself that her own choice in life is the right one.

But whether a woman so vital and spontaneous can shut out all human emotion is the question that has often been asked. And in the interest of honesty one must acknowledge that there are those Cather students who doubt that she altogether did. They point to the preponderance of women associates and especially to the long devotion between herself and Isabelle McClung.

Even the most guarded accounts of her life emphasize this beautiful young woman's part in it. There were the five years they lived in the same house, and the many months she spent back in Pittsburgh after moving away. There were their trips abroad and Isabelle's many visits in New York. And there was the day in 1916 described by Elizabeth Sergeant when "she told me of a major change in her personal life—this rather drily, bluntly. Her friend Isabelle McClung, whom I knew to be an animating force, was getting married. This, after first youth, one did not expect or foresee. But it had happened. Judge McClung, by then an old man, had died in the fall; 1180 Murray Hill Avenue would cease to be—and of course I knew that, even since she'd had a home in Bank Street, she had spent some months of every year writing in Pittsburgh, where Isabelle always protected and quickened her work in her perfect way.

"Isabelle was a musical amateur, and she had married music too: Jan Hambourg was a gifted and scholarly violinist, known on two continents for his concerts with two musician brothers. . . . Isabelle and Jan would not desert America during the war. But Willa felt they might end up in Europe. Her face—I saw how bleak it was, how vacant her eyes. All her natural exuberance had drained away. 'So you will have to find a new remote place to work,' I said, grasping at the aspect of the situation most easy to talk about . . . Red Cloud? She said no to that . . . she would have to be quite on her own."

Quick assumptions are dangerous, however, for nothing here fits any orthodox pattern. The Hambourg marriage, instead of dividing two friends, appeared to have simply added a third. Willa visited the Hambourgs in Toronto and later in Europe. Hambourg traveled with her in France to help in her research, and she even dedicated two books to him. Further, through the years there had always been a disarming openness about the two women's relationship; Isabelle stayed for long periods with Edith and Willa in New York and became part of Willa's circle. Altogether the situation admits no quick interpretation and none can be safely put forth. Only if the Cather private papers were ever made public would it be made clear. Then perhaps this aspect of her life would be understood. Also perhaps her later withdrawal from the world would be more easily explained.

That withdrawal was still some distance in the future. In the decade from 1910 to 1920 Willa was still expanding, book following book like the waves in a rising tide. Always fascinated by stage people, she wrote an article about three opera singers, Louise Homer, Geraldine Farrar, and Olive Fremstad. Homer and Farrar she found interesting enough but in Olive Fremstad, a mezzo-soprano born in Sweden and brought up in Minnesota, she saw a goddess of her own frontier country, with the force and originality of the pioneers fined down by the discipline of art.

She saw in Fremstad's history much of her own youth, and in *The Song of the Lark* the operatic heroine and herself are so intertwined that Fremstad declared she could not distinguish between them. In the person of Thea Kronborg young Willa Cather is seen feeling the stirring within of the genius demanding to be born, that genius she would have to serve henceforth, sacrificing everything and everyone and, most of all, herself.

At the height of her fame Thea is asked a question about her personal life. "Your work becomes your personal life," Thea answers. "You are not much good until it does. It's like being woven into a big web. You can't pull away, because all your little tendrils are woven into the picture. It takes you up and uses you, and spins you out; that is your life. Not much else can happen to you." *The Song of the Lark* was dedicated to Isabelle McClung.

In this book Willa had used her Nebraska background only for the early part. But *My Antonia* is saturated with it, her own childish self appearing as the little boy Jim and the next door neighbor's hired girl Annie Sadilek as the warm earth goddess Antonia. It has a folk-song, yea-saying quality without the downbeat relationships in so many other books, and perhaps, without knowing it, that was why she once said it was the best thing she had ever done.

In these Nebraska novels Willa Cather had been dwelling in the West's happy and vigorous days. But by 1918 her visits home had shown her a new Nebraska, a place of ugly mechanized prosperity, of rattling Fords and roaring reapers, and it was from this new unattractive world that the mistfit hero of *One of Ours* escapes.

This book had been inspired by the death in May, 1918, of a favorite cousin and is her conception of his wartime life and death. The war, she believed, had brought him a stature and maturity impossible of attainment otherwise. And his death, saving him as it did from "the devouring materialism of early 20th century America" had been a blessed one. Had he returned, she believed his sweet faith in his country would have been shattered by the postwar ugliness.

Though *One of Ours* received the 1922 Pulitzer Prize and was her first real financial success, it also marked the emergence of a new sadness and cynicism. So reticent is the record that the reason for this change is unclear. But her wistful cry to a friend—"the world broke in half in 1922 or thereabouts and I belonged to the earlier half"—bespeaks a bitter disappointment in life as it had turned out. Whether she suffered a sudden blow about that time, or a long dull ache had come then to a climax, from then on she cried over and over, "Our present is ruined—but we had a beautiful past."

She began to turn almost angrily from the present. She refused to read Freud—what did he know that Tolstoi hadn't always known? She refused to own a car—misshapen, sullen things trying to push out the horse in all its beauty. And the new writers with their "novels of protest!" What had Sinclair Lewis and his *Main Street* but commonness, cheapness, ignorance? And Eugene O'Neill—why spend an evening in Hades when there were still good comedies of manners?

In time Robert Frost was to say, "With Carl Sandburg it was 'The people, yes.' With Willa Cather it was 'The people, no.' " Her friends watched sadly as she withdrew in distaste from human contacts. Presumably some of them knew or suspected the reason for it, and Elizabeth Sergeant wonders out loud: "Can a free female-creature be shut up only for and with her work without a serious spiritual penalty?" But she is silent on the cause and it may never be clearly identified.

As her success increased so did her distress, for people would not let her alone. At concerts strangers came up and invited her to sit in their boxes; others stopped her on the street demanding her autograph; she was asked to give interviews, to join societies, to work for charities. All such activities depressed her, and her life became a tug-of-war between herself and her importunate public.

A secretary answered all but important mail with form letters. In Red Cloud her father tried to take on the job, saying, "Now, Daughter, these should be answered personally," but she would protest, "Father, I have a standard to maintain. I can't just dash off answers." Her publisher would suggest gently that she make certain concessions to publicity and she would sit to photographers glumly, saving her frank, hearty grin for her own small circle. Even her new affluence was a bother, for while she had learned to cope with critical success, *One of Ours* now initiated her into the wider problem of stocks and bonds.

These financial difficulties were compounded by *A Lost Lady* and *The Professor's House,* for they brought her, in 1923 and 1925, more money, more distractions, more honorary degrees. One from the University of Nebraska in 1917 had been the first and it was followed by nine more, all demanding time and attention.

A Lost Lady was based on the beautiful young wife of Silas Garber, founder of Red Cloud, whose personality had "teased" her ever since as a child she had watched the fascinating creature flirtatiously trying on hats in a mirror.

It was this book that turned her against Hollywood. In all innocence she sold it to one of the big companies and it was made into a satisfactory picture, with a gala premiere in Red Cloud and Willa and all her relatives attending. Good enough. But later it was made again in a vastly inferior version, and when she tried to stop its release she learned to her horror that she had sold the book outright. Appalled, she laid down her famous restriction: so long as her copyright was in effect, not one of her books was ever to be dramatized, filmed, broadcast, televised or used in any other medium then in existence or discoverable in the future.

As *A Lost Lady* and *The Song of the Lark* were about real women, so was *My Mortal Enemy.* Willa had known this older woman when she visited New York in her early twenties and had been hypnotized by her elegant sophistication, the devotion of her husband, and the place she held in a distinguished circle. Like the other lost lady, Myra Henshawe also seems lost, but Willa Cather had felt the strong thrust of religion since writing the first book and the second had a very different ending. Both novels are unusually short, for she was experimenting with the *novel démeublé*, the novel stripped of superfluous furnishings, and the effect is that of a ring set with a single magnificent diamond.

A Lost Lady had been dedicated to Jan Hambourg, and after finishing it Willa went to France to see her two friends. They had built her a study in their new house, urging her to live there permanently. "But," says Edith Lewis, "although the little study was charming and all the surroundings were attractive, and the Hambourgs themselves devoted and solicitous, she found herself unable to work at Ville-d'Avray. She felt, indeed, that she would never be able to work there." (Why, she leaves unsaid.) So Willa came back and wrote *The Professor's House* in the placid Bank Street apartment.

The Professor's House may be indirectly her most autobiographical novel. It reveals her resentment at "the trap of worldly success," her grief at the decline of her most cherished values, and her dis-ease at being fifty-two, the age she shared with her protagonist, the professor.

The meaning of its curious dedication, "For Jan Hambourg because he likes narrative," is a mystery. It is just possible it means precisely what it says, no more and no less. Or it may be a sidelong reference to the book's long center section, a narration which some readers have criticized as irrelevant. But to her, always fascinated by places, this story of a long-dead city in Arizona had deep significance, and the dedication may have been a sort of defense of it. Lastly, it may have been an expression of something intensely personal, a submerged antagonism toward Hambourg himself.

Whatever the intent of the dedication, the novel itself has a new spiritual orientation. Soon after she had seen the world of 1922 break apart at her feet she had begun reaching out for some order and security elsewhere in the fragmented landscape. The Cathers were traditionally Baptists, but back in her Dr. Will Cather days Willa had loftily dropped religion. Now, however, her spirit was crying for a home and in the beauty and dignity of the Episcopalian service she found a modicum of peace. In December,

1922, along with her parents, she was confirmed by the Bishop of Western Nebraska. Henceforth this interest appears increasingly in her work.

As the Arizona cliff-dwellers' village played a character role in *The Professor's House* so another place, New Mexico, had a role in *Death Comes for the Archbishop*. This widely loved book, by far her most popular, has neither love story nor conflict in the conventional sense; what it does have is warm human people of differing viewpoints who can still work together for a common cause, and an uplifting mastery of language now developed to its peak. The love story here is really Willa Cather's own, her love for a place *seen* as even she had never seen anything before. It is not strange that the writing of this book was "a happy vacation from life."

Willa Cather once said she had no personal problems when writing. And for years her life had been reasonably free of the average person's nagging worries. She had more than enough money for herself and could indulge her generous impulses toward her relatives, her friends, and her old Nebraska neighbors. She had success in her art, a family she loved, companionship, and a comfortable home—all serenely unchanged year after year. But in 1927 the smooth turned rocky. During her Christmas visit her father's heart gave notice of trouble and three months later he died.

The blow shook Willa to the soles of her feet. She paced back and forth in the church where he lay, wringing her hands in panic and grief and something resembling rage. The enemy Change had sprung on her unfairly and everything within rose up to fight it back. But even as she fought it closed in further, for now her mother collapsed and had to be taken to her son Douglass, who was living on the West Coast.

After that came two more swift blows—the Red Cloud house, her home, her cherished retreat, had to be closed; and New York City, joining in the conspiracy, gave notice that it was tearing down Five Bank Street. Willa, glaring at life in shocked disbelief, crept numbly to a hotel.

She and Edith Lewis had expected to come to rest in another home at once, but Change, having tasted blood, kept snapping at her heels. Over two years she was kept traipsing back and forth across the continent, for her ailing mother had been reduced by a stroke to a pitiful half-person. Long ago Willa had recognized that the friction between the two of them had been caused not only by her mother's imperious self-will but by her own, and they had come in time to an affectionate understanding. This made her loss seem even harder to bear.

But cruel as was this blow, nothing equaled for cruelty Isabelle McClung Hambourg's illness. Worse than the normal action of passing time, this was an outrageous, personal persecution. That a deadly malignancy should strike this beautiful woman was beyond comprehension, and for almost a year Willa hardly worked at all but kept hovering over her ill friend in Europe and then, when the Hambourgs came to America, making desperate appeals to New York doctors for help. Standing rigid, she took their grim verdict on the chin and refused to believe it. And unexpectedly, her stubbornness seemed to work, for Isabelle revived for a time, and Jan, who had been offered a conductorship in Chicago, bounced back from his misery and accepted it.

Isabelle insisted on going with him. Willa thought it madness but they went anyway, so she went with them, nurse and companion while Jan struggled with a strange place and strange conditions. After an unhappy summer the couple returned to Europe and Willa followed. There were two last agonizing months in Paris and then Willa crept home alone.

At times a gap in a record can be satisfactorily filled with probabilities, but at others it remains a hopeless enigma. The gap here reads sparsely as follows: "Isabelle died three years later in Sorrento, without Willa Cather ever having seen her again."

Three years . . . A thousand days . . . Five thousand miles apart. This incredible separation strains the imagination. It is true that a person can simply lack the courage to watch another die. That

hardly seems in Willa Cather's character, but there had to be
something that kept her away.

One last footnote only deepens the enigma: after Isabelle's
death Jan Hambourg sent back to Willa a bundle of her own letters
written to Isabelle throughout the years. One by one Willa read
them and then tore them up. Every Sunday, over a number of
weeks, Edith Lewis carried a handful of scraps to the incinerator
and dropped them down the chute.

Elizabeth Sergeant, who heard of this from Willa herself, remarks, "There was a kind of finality in this cremation that brought
a chill of regret and dismay. . . . A lifetime of letters, a deep
communication between two friends, cremated? What remained
was surely an essence, something for the heart alone."

During the last years of this slow crucifixion Willa's writing
dropped off noticeably. But before her powers diminished she had
accomplished one more important work, another book based on
her feeling for a place, on her gravitation toward formalized religion, and on her love for France.

Getting away from New York's heat, she and Edith Lewis took
an old cottage on Grand Manan Island off New Brunswick. Later
they built their own Whale Cottage overlooking the sea, with a
large attic where Willa did her writing. It was cool and quiet here
and they were altogether alone, with only deer, hare, birds, and
the sky. Once, in 1928, they went there by way of Quebec and
Willa responded typically to the city's oldness, its Frenchness and
of course its beauty. She used to say, "If only we could have been
born in the year 1850 we would have had all the best of four
civilizations and none of the horrors. We would never have known
of or dreamed of the horrors." In Quebec she was somehow by-
passing the horrors and returning to "the precious, the incom-
municable past."

Remembering her joy while writing *Death Comes for the
Archbishop* and seeing another chance at the same joy, she placed
Shadows on the Rock in early French Canada. It was her last
important book, though there were actually two more novels and

a collection of her stories. But her energy was declining, as had her interest in the present-day world.

Edith Lewis has said that it was the very depth of her emotions that made Willa fight emotions off. Whatever it was, anyone contemplating such emptiness cannot help but sense an infinite pathos in this life, so disciplined on the surface, and inside, surely, so wounded. One wonders what she must have paid for her artistic success. Either, it seems, she had love and it ended tragically, or else she had no love, and that was even more tragic. A sense of barrenness is left, of terrible helplessness in the grip of circumstance. When her world broke apart all those years ago she was stranded in alien country and resentfully she cried out against her fate. But she, whose pioneer heroines had conquered their environment, was trapped in the grip of hers and gradually she gave up the struggle. Her last years saw her nearly a recluse, sitting out life behind a wall.

But, happily, she could not altogether keep it out. The main paths to her heart were closed, but unwatchfully she let love in through a side door, and it turned out to be the one chapter in her life she would have least wanted to erase. It was fresh, it was young and lovely, and it carried with it no sting. Whatever else Jan Hambourg may have done, he made it up to her with this gift.

Willa Cather had always enjoyed her nephews and nieces and what other children came her way, but these contacts were limited. She had also always loved music—opera at first and later the "purer" music of orchestras and string quartets. In 1930, staying in Paris with the Hambourgs, she was introduced by Jan to Moshe and Marutha Menuhin and their children Hephzibah, Yaltah, and Yehudi. This family of remarkable musicians brought her close to childhood at its most enchanting and music at its most sublime. She was utterly captivated by them, and in turn she was loved almost to the point of worship.

Brought up very strictly, the children were both naïve and mature, and their lives in a way paralleled her own. Like her they lived for their art, traveling continually and at the same time secluded from the public while they practiced many hours a day, Hephzibah on the piano, Yehudi on the violin. Like her, too, they were public figures, requiring similar protection. (The great difference was that the god they served was less jealous than hers and permitted them the happiness of marriage and children.)

At a time when Willa was otherwise almost a recluse, the children's arrival in New York turned her winters into a sort of continuous festival, full of concerts and parties. Orange trees and baskets of flowers kept arriving for her in the midst of snowstorms. There were birthday luncheons, with Russian caviar and champagne, excursions to the opera, when she introduced Yehudi and Yaltah to *Parsifal,* and long walks around the Central Park reservoir, when the three children all wanted to walk beside her and had to take turnabout.

Worried lest the children, living all over Europe with its mélange of languages, might miss some of the richness of English, Willa organized a "Shakespeare Club," with Yaltah and Hephzibah as its only members. To their proud delight Yehudi, older brother and already a famous violinist, asked to join, and together they studied *Richard II, Macbeth,* and *Henry IV,* each with a treasured copy of the original Temple Edition.

The annual reunions continued for fifteen years, when the cavernous Park Avenue apartment where the two women had settled was suddenly filled with laughter and love. In 1947 Hephzibah and Yehudi gave a concert at the Metropolitan Opera House with Willa Cather, struggling against fragility, occupying an honor seat. A day or two later Hephzibah telephoned—might she bring her husband and two children to meet her beloved Aunt Willa? Soon Yehudi followed with his little son and daughter. Thus, in this last year of her life, Willa sat surrounded by the richness of a family life she had feared to take for herself.

Whatever vacuums there were in Willa Cather's personal life, her professional one was satisfying beyond the ordinary. She never sought to write love stories; rather she wrote about people pitting their native strength against the environment, in some sense plowing new ground. Her passion was for pioneering, for conquering, and for preserving against destruction. With a few limitations, she knew people well; and she handled words as if they were jewels, making each one shine.

And whatever other tragedy she suffered, she escaped the tragedy of eclipse. Her popularity held up during her lifetime, and even after her death, which occurred in April, 1947, it continued to grow. She who had resisted any form of popularization, fending off films and plays and broadcasts to protect the integrity of her written word, would surely have been pleased to see how that word survived, read always and only in its own clean prose.

Eugene O'Neill

(1888=1953)

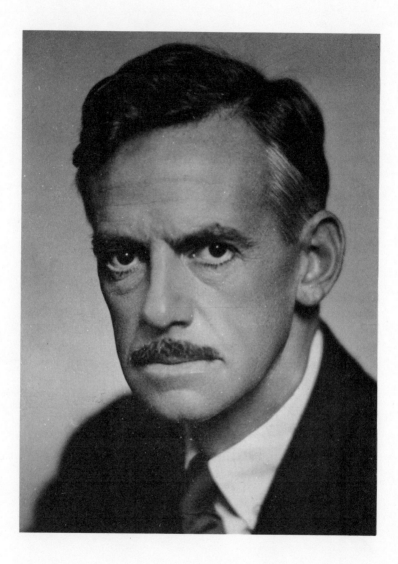

Eugene O'Neill
(1888–1953)

WHEN EUGENE O'NEILL was arranging a divorce from his wife Agnes, who was herself a writer, he insisted that the settlement include the proviso that never, in any memoir, article, or autobiography, was she to use their life together as literary material.

His cautiousness is understandable, for well he knew what a writer can do with the private lives of those around him. In no fewer than twelve plays did he lay bare the tortured relationships of his own mother, father, brother, and himself, while several more dissected his love affairs and three marriages. (Agnes kept her silence until his death, but then apparently all bets were off and she published her version of their first years together.)

O'Neill's family was admittedly tempting material for a writer. Handsome and brilliant, they had an Irish flair that turned their every move into melodrama. O'Neill once said that the critics had failed to notice the most important thing about him, his Irishness, but what the critics missed the O'Neills never forgot; they were eternally haunted by their own concept of the Black Irish personality and subconsciously lived up to it with all the force of their being.

Eugene's grandfather had left Ireland during the terrible potato famine of 1849 and emigrated with his brood to Cleveland, Ohio. However, he soon went back home and at ten the eldest boy, James, found himself the head of the family and working twelve hours a day in a machine shop. Evicted from their home twice, the boy absorbed a fear of the poorhouse which he never forgot. But he was supported always by the thought of his O'Neill ancestry. Ignoring his immediate forebears, who had been a race of mere farmers, he dwelt in thought among ancient Irish kings, and in his old age he particularly loved to regale his grandsons with the exploits of John the Proud, Lord of the Red Hand.

Eugene's father, James O'Neill, with his Black Irish eyes and hair inherited from some sixteenth-century Spanish Armada sailor, his frame of flowing grace and rich, liquid voice like heady wine, was a natural for the stage. From a walk-on beginning he rose rapidly to leads in Cleveland's stock company and soon was starring in romantic melodramas all across the country. In 1875 he was invited home to dinner by the wealthy parents of eighteen-year-old Ella Quinlan and fell deeply and permanently in love.

At twenty-nine James O'Neill was a hard-drinking, loquacious, sweet-tempered matinee idol. Unhappily, his magnetic charm had been the undoing of two lovesick women, one killing herself out of hopeless infatuation and the other giving birth to an unwanted child. Over the years this unwelcome son kept popping up to demand attention and embarrass him before his wife, and this shameful past was an irritant that complicated the couple's passionate union.

Ella naturally knew nothing of this episode at the time of their wedding. A slender, pretty girl, Irish like her husband but, unlike him, respectably middle-class, she had received an expensive education including such refinements as Latin and piano playing. At the convent she had dreamed of becoming a nun, but the Mother Superior, observing her tendency toward the dramatic, had wisely temporized, and on meeting the dashing actor with the caressing eyes and tender baritone she forgot all such thoughts. Thus two utterly incongruous personalities were caught and bound together by an unreasoning passion like a ring of iron, inside of which they fought and struggled and lacerated each other.

Fate, like a talented stage designer, provided the perfect setting for their wedding. The bride was radiant in white satin and orange blossoms, the groom stunning and romantic in his cutaway. But the day itself was full of terror, sky black with rushing clouds, air suffocatingly heavy and foreboding. June 14, 1877, had dawned late and unwillingly, as if dreading to dawn at all, and instead of brightening seemed to grow darker as the hours advanced. The New York *Times,* reporting the eerie phenomenon next day, called the scene "weird beyond description and silently menacing." Eugene O'Neill, a master at stage effects, could not have planned a better prologue for the O'Neill family drama.

Despite their rapturous love, intimations of trouble began appearing soon. James' fondness for stopping in at saloons on the way home came as a shock to the unsophisticated girl. And life on tour proved less delightful than anticipated. The only people she met were "stage people," and agents, actors, and stagehands were hardly suitable companions for Ella Quinlan of St. Mary's Academy of the Sisters of the Holy Cross. "Their life is not my life," she said sadly. Regarding them as inferior, she began to imagine that by having to associate with them she had herself lost face with her former friends, and she withdrew more and more to the dingy hotel rooms that were her only home.

A suit brought against James by the mother of his son was a further humiliation, and even though the suit was dismissed and Ella knew James to be unreservedly faithful, her wounded pride never quite recovered.

In 1878 the birth of little Jamie brought a new interest into her lonely life. And then another momentous event came, the first appearance, in 1882, of James O'Neill in a drama based on Dumas' novel *The Count of Monte Cristo.*

This romantic melodrama, which was climaxed by the Count's thrilling escape from prison crying triumphantly, "The world is mine!," was such a success as occurs once in a generation. James toured in it steadily for twenty-five years, giving six thousand performances and earning $50,000 a year.

In spite of this success, however, he never outgrew a certain odd stinginess, his ingrained dread of the poorhouse making him economize at irrational moments. At the same time he fell for every kind of wild business scheme—salt mines, gold mines, copper mines—which invariably faded into mist. The result was that he was always driven to taking out *The Count* for "just one more tour." At the end of his career he spoke bitterly of a wasted life and a talent sacrificed to commercial success. But in 1882 none of this was visible on the horizon. Then he was simply a generous, kindly man popular with public and co-workers alike.

When James Junior was five, little Edmund was born. But two babies were too much for Ella to care for in hotel rooms so she recruited her mother to move in and look after them while she went on touring the country with her husband.

This was the beginning of Ella's lifelong tragedy, indeed the tragedy of the whole family. During her absence on tour little James caught measles and, wandering about the hotel suite, entered the room where two-year-old Edmund lay asleep. The baby caught the disease and a few days later he died.

Ella was frantic with remorse. But being psychologically unable to carry her burden of guilt alone she was forced to shunt it off onto others. She persuaded herself that the fault was Jamie's, that he had always been jealous of his baby brother and had deliberately exposed him to the deadly contagion. So Jamie was packed off to boarding school and virtually exiled for nine years.

During the next lonely three years Ella's depression deepened. Simultaneously O'Neill, who tried unsuccessfully to star in other plays but was always forced to go back to *The Count*, saw himself becoming a one-part actor and began to lose heart. It was into this gloomy atmosphere that their third son, Eugene, was born, in October, 1888.

Eugene O'Neill's first memory was of his beautiful mother mourning her dead baby. As he grew older he learned that his brother had been responsible for the infant's death and further that he himself had been brought into the world chiefly to console her for this loss. Unfortunately, however, it seemed that he had failed in his mission, for instead of consolation his birth had brought her additional pain and somehow made her an invalid. Responsibility for this invalidism seemed to be shared by his father in some unexplained way. The picture altogether was dim and obscure, but the sum of it was that his father, his brother, and himself were all to blame for this beautiful lady's woe.

Eugene grew into a delicate, remote child without friends other than the stage hands and actors who played with him on tour. While he adored his mother, her attitude toward him alternated between affectionate concern and a strange dreamy detachment, and periodically she disappeared altogether, gone away, he was told, to be made well of some unnamed ailment. Always she was sad and appealing, and always he felt vaguely guilty. Then, at seven, he was sent to convent school. There, after learning the Creed, the Commandments, and the Sacraments, he took communion and felt the heavenly relief of knowing he had received the grace of God and been absolved of all his sins, whatever they were.

In his twelfth year the world collapsed. The mystery of his mother's ailment was uncovered when he came upon her giving herself a morphine injection, and in her wild defensive tirade she spewed abroad the blame for her addiction—on Eugene, whose birth had caused her pain and sickness, on the cheap hotel doctor who had given her the drug at that time, on the miserly husband who had called in an incompetent man, and on both boys in general for their roles in her tragedy.

Terrified by his mother's addiction and his own guilt, Eugene turned blindly to prayer, promising to live a saintly life in return for her cure. But no miracle occurred. So then, his offer rejected, he turned on the church that had promised him help and cursed it for its betrayal.

From this time on, Eugene O'Neill was locked in a life-and-death conflict with his Catholic faith, defying it yet terrified of it, fighting it off yet unable to let it go. In *Days Without End*, written when he was forty-five years old, he was still obsessed by the torment of his struggle and his yearning to retrieve his lost faith, a hope he never fulfilled.

Jamie did nothing to help him in his crisis. For Jamie was crumbling under his own insupportable burdens. Ten years older than Eugene, he had long known of his mother's addiction and his own childhood part in it and, like her, was too weak to carry it alone. By his teens he was already mired in a despairing cynicism, drinking heavily and bent on destroying himself—and, it seemed, his malleable young brother as well. Expelled from college, he took the boy on drunken New York weekends, introducing him to his personal collection of saloons and prostitutes and later chuckling to a friend, "Gene learned sin more easily than other people. I made it easy for him."

With this help Gene's attitude toward women was established early. He knew only two kinds, his virtuous mother and Jamie's friends. And while he loved his helpless, befuddled mother, he could not respect or trust her. "Bad" women, on the other hand, were one of the basic elements of life and he saw even the coarsest and most depraved of them as symbols of the earth mother, creating, enveloping, forgiving. In their company he felt relaxed and secure and for many years he distrusted any other kind.

Thus his adolescence was spent wintering with Jamie in New York while his parents were on tour and summering with them in the family cottage in New London, Connecticut. This seaport town had a year-round population of simple sea folk and a summer colony of rich New Yorkers, and though Monte Cristo Cottage was a comfortably furnished house, it was a snakepit of confused emotions. For Ella once again felt herself victimized, too good for the local people and, as an actor's wife, not good enough for the New Yorkers.

The boys, meanwhile, joined her in a three-pronged attack on their father's miserliness. His pleasure in working his own garden was interpreted as unwillingness to hire a gardener, and even the sinking of a well was taken as a cheap avoidance of water taxes. Thus mother and sons allied themselves against the father while, paradoxically, husband and wife privately continued as devoted lovers.

When college time came, Princeton, for no very pressing reason, was Gene's choice. He did little there but loaf and drink, his grave self-concern earning him the nickname of Ego, and after one year he and Princeton parted with mutual satisfaction. His father then shoved him into a routine office job. But this year was as unfruitful as the last and was distinguished solely by a meaningless, almost absent-minded marriage.

Kathleen Jenkins was the unusually beautiful daughter of a divorced New York woman of wealth. She and Gene were violently attracted by each other's good looks, but their parents were not so moved. The O'Neills objected to the match not only because of Gene's youth and lack of funds but Kathleen's Protestantism and background of divorce as well; Mrs. Jenkins had a correspondingly firm set of objections. To prevent the marriage, James dangled a fascinating gold-mining expedition in Honduras before Gene's eyes and he consented to go. But the strategy failed of its purpose, for just before his departure he and Kathleen slipped away to New Jersey and were secretly married.

His winter in a tropical jungle yielded him no gold—nothing, in fact, but a case of malaria and a mélange of vivid impressions. But the latter more than compensated for the former, for ten years later they gave him his first real success, *The Emperor Jones.*

During his absence Kathleen wrote that she was expecting a child, and in a panic Gene confessed the full facts to his father in a letter. This disgusted man stormed over to the Jenkins home with shouts about an annulment, and when the girl feebly objected to losing her husband, he burst out, "What do you want him for anyway, the drunken no-good bum!"

Arriving in New York about the time the baby was due, Gene nervously hid out in a saloon near Times Square. But Fate ran him down anyway. On May 6, 1910, the bartender, grinning wickedly, handed him a newspaper headlined, "The Birth of a Boy reveals

Marriage of 'Gene' O'Neill. . . . Son of Actor Was Wed Secretly Last July to Kathleen Jenkins."

Eugene O'Neill's actions toward his wife and child have no explanation save simple cowardice. He never went near Kathleen. Once when she was out he did manage to visit his son, and after breaking into tears he rushed out to sit all day on a park bench thinking sickly of suicide.

As in most crises, self-pity came to his rescue. He persuaded himself that he had been trapped into the marriage and, thus relieved of any obligations in the matter, agreed to join his father on tour. Not long afterwards Kathleen helped him out further by suing for divorce and assuming all responsibility for little Eugene Gladstone O'Neill, Jr. (Toward the end of his life he said ruefully that the only woman who had never given him any trouble was the one he had treated worst.)

Eugene's tours with The Governor were exercises in rebellion and resentment. Now, hating his father's flashy melodramas and overblown histrionics, he took out his disgust in drinking and embarrassing him publicly. Then to escape the resulting sense of shame he left the company and crawled back to New York.

But this escape did not take him far enough. Still haunted by his desertion of wife and child, he suddenly signed on a sailing vessel for South America. In Joseph Conrad's *The Nigger of the Narcissus* he had read, "The true peace of God begins at any spot a thousand miles from the nearest land," and there he thought to find this peace and to escape from the mutterings of conscience.

It is true that there no one asked questions or looked reproaches, and so among the ship's rough crew he found his first congenial friends—his "particular brothers," he called them, loyal and generous, crude but honest. Encumbered by no subtleties and wearing no protective masks, they made no demands that he could not fulfill. With them, as with the prostitutes, he felt safe and relaxed, neither judging nor being judged, and during the next fifteen or sixteen months, despite excruciating hardships and degradation, he enjoyed a simple, affectionate companionship he had never known before nor ever would again.

Part of the pleasure of reaching the very bottom, he often said, was the fact that, having no lower to go, one could rest there in peace. This pleasure he found in Buenos Aires; sleeping in parks, panhandling for food, he had no cares or any thought at all except for getting the next drink. All the time, nevertheless, a corner of his besotted brain stayed clear. The tales the sailors told and the chanties they sang, along with several of the men's personalities, remained sharp and vivid over the years and figured eventually in no fewer than nineteen of his plays, long and short.

Between voyages he saw neither Kathleen nor his family but lived at Jimmy-the-Priest's, a filthy saloon on the waterfront, spending his days at the bar and his nights on the roach-infested floor upstairs. His friends were stevedores, seamen, prostitutes, and thieves. One of his closest companions was a great apelike stoker named Driscoll seemingly bursting with unthinking self-assurance, and when O'Neill heard later that Driscoll had thrown himself overboard he was shocked and mystified. What strange element had had the power to so shake this stolid soul? Eventually his long ponderings resolved themselves into the play *The Hairy Ape*.

Death, never far from O'Neill's thoughts, was to him the final solution to all problems. During another tour with his father and mother his drunken escapades forced cancellation of their last eighteen weeks' bookings, and once more he deserted the company to hole up in a remorseful stupor at Jimmy-the-Priest's. Finally in despair he swallowed a handful of Veronal tablets and lay down to die.

This suicide attempt may have been no more than a melo-dramatic gesture, from which he was glad enough to be rescued by the timely entrance of two friends. But it did not rid him of his obsession, for of the forty violent deaths met by his characters, nine of them are self-inflicted.

The Governor, torn between parental love and desperation, was always making one more try to bring his dissolute sons back into the fold, and in the summer of 1912 he persuaded Gene to join a New London newspaper. Jamie, by now a settled alcoholic, also consented to exchange New York saloons for New London ones. Ella was home from the sanitarium; and thus the whole family was gathered in Monte Cristo Cottage.

But harmony was not in the cards. After some months Gene caught a severe cold and in early December was found to have developed tuberculosis, a disease then considered not only incurable but highly contagious. James, ever solicitous of Ella, decided Gene must leave the house. And in this instance his family's charge of miserliness does seem to fit, for his choice of a sanitarium was the state charity farm.

Gene's self-pity now exploded out of all control and twenty years of resentment focused on this one offense. He never forgot or forgave it, and it was the crux of one of his best-known plays.

When O'Neill began to write he looked no farther than his family circle to find a mountain of material. In no fewer than fifteen plays its members, in one combination or another, figure centrally: *The Great God Brown, All God's Chillun Got Wings, Ah, Wilderness!, Beyond the Horizon, The Straw, Mourning Becomes Electra, A Touch of the Poet, A Moon for the Misbegotton, Welded, The Iceman Cometh, The First Man, Desire Under the Elms, Dynamo, Days Without End.* But most personal of all is *Long Day's Journey into Night,* in which he tore upon the festering sore of that day's memory to let the poisoned blood flow out of his veins.

The writing of *Long Day's Journey,* his wife said later, was a daily torture. "He would come out of his study . . . his eyes red from weeping. Sometimes he looked ten years older than when he went in in the morning." It condenses into one hideous day the essence of that 1912 summer and fall. Under the name of Tyrone the O'Neill family is stripped naked, its faults, vices, and hates fully exposed for the first time. Ella's addiction is there, the disclosure of it having caused O'Neill the keenest anguish. There too is her feeling of being snubbed by New London society. The alcoholic Jamie is there, blaming his ruin on unrequited love for a beautiful actress (in reality the screen star Elsie Ferguson). James is there, assailed by his wife and sons as an Irish peasant and bogtrotter. And so is Eugene himself, there a young poet ill and neglected and on the point of being banished to a charity hospital. The play is full of agonized self-pity, but when it was produced several years after O'Neill's death many people called it his greatest because of its tragic intensity.

Following the events of that original "long day," O'Neill went to the state farm for treatment, but in a few days his father softened and sent him to Gaylord Farm, a progressive sanitarium. There he was happy and content and came away six months later permanently cured.

During his sojourn one of the patients, a pathetic Irish girl at the point of death, fell in love with him, and the episode later inspired him to write of her in *The Straw.* But except for the drama of it the episode meant little, for at twenty-four Gene was an old hand with women. "There was something apparently irresistible in his strange combination of cruelty (around the mouth), intelligence (in his eyes), and sympathy (in his voice)" a Princeton classmate recalled enviously. "One girl told me she could not get his face out of her thoughts. He was hard-boiled and whimsical. He was brutal and tender, so I was told. From shop girl to 'sassiety queen' they all seemed to develop certain tendencies in his presence."

Though his manner toward "nice" girls was carefully deferential, the dark brooding eyes and slightly sinister reputation worked on all kinds equally. And while never bothering to be faithful to any girl, he pursued an innocent affair with a young New London girl for two or three years, exchanging hundreds of letters and poems and in time immortalizing her in his nostalgic comedy *Ah, Wilderness!*

Gaylord Farm he regarded as his spiritual birthplace. Brought up sharp after seven years of violent, unthinking physical action, he was forced to remain sober and do nothing but think for days on end. Further, he was driven to reading. And suddenly the written word seized him. He read everything in the hospital's library, and one play by the Swedish playwright August Strindberg may be said to have changed his life.

The Dance of Death was a revelation, the love-hate relationship of its characters opening his eyes to the love-hate of his own parents. Drama, he saw, could hit the mind like a sledgehammer, and in his Nobel Prize acceptance speech he credited Strindberg with having inspired him to become a writer.

This revelation had struck in 1913. But as with Saint Paul on the road to Damascus, the light was so blinding that it was some time before he could see his way ahead. In the meantime, living on an eight-dollar-a-week handout from his father, he floundered awkwardly, writing scores of incredibly bad one-act plays whose only virtue was that they were unlike anything else ever written.

He spent a year at the famous English 47 drama workshop at Harvard, but the emphasis there was too much on the same drawing-room comedy dramas as his father's productions; he wanted to write about real life, ugly perhaps but true and therefore not really ugly.

So from there he dived to the gutters of Greenwich Village, where, haunted for nearly a year by his lost Catholicism, he sat swilling whisky and mumbling "The Hound of Heaven," Francis Thompson's frightening poem about a pursuing, inescapable God. His friends, who knew of his fascination with death, were fearful lest they see this rehearsal for oblivion slip into the real thing.

Home during this period was another Jimmy-the-Priest's, a saloon known as the Hell Hole, where during flush periods he rented a room for three dollars a month. In impecunious periods he slept with friends in the Garbage Flat, a garret so called for its beds made of sacking, its newspaper blankets, and packing-box chairs. Carpeting was a solid layer of cigarette butts and oyster shells, oysters and onions being the standard hangover cure. His bewildered father still wistfully sent him an occasional ten-dollar peace offering, but Gene never looked up anyone but Jamie, who was rehearsing for death in his own hell hole a few blocks to the north.

This whole sodden year O'Neill hardly wrote at all. Nevertheless he was working in his own ordained way, watching and listening. In the Hell Hole, as in Jimmy-the-Priest's, he had found his own people, "real" and therefore not ugly who, remaining permanently drunk, kept their pipe dreams intact until the Iceman came and put an end to all. One of these men, a professional bum who talked brilliantly and read Greek classics in the original while panhandling for liquor, became O'Neill's spiritual mentor. It was this Terry Carlin, with his long Irish face "like a pitying old priest," whose aphorism, "words only conceal thought, they do not express it," set O'Neill off on his use of masks and asides. It was Terry whose mistress was the original Anna Christie. And it was Terry who, resisting all modes of work for himself, inadvertently introduced O'Neill to a lifetime of hard work.

Besides the Hell Hole's deadbeats, a number of reporters, writers, and artists came there regularly to drink and listen to Terry's startling, nihilistic conversation. They spent their summers in Provincetown, a Cape Cod fishing village, and Terry, taken along as a mascot, was housed in the hulk of an old wreck. In 1916 Terry invited O'Neill to come along.

The previous year some of these artists, intent on encouraging unknown American playwrights, had started putting on short plays in the fishhouse of an old wharf. This barnlike structure they named the Wharf Theatre and themselves they dubbed the Provincetown Players.

Terry, having settled his guest and his battered portable in the old hulk, wandered through town greeting his friends, and on the street he encountered Susan Glaspell, one of the Players. "I'm hunting a play for our first bill," she told him. "Have you by any chance been writing one?"

"I don't write plays," he said. "All I do is think. But O'Neill has a trunk full of them."

"Tell him to bring one over tonight and read it," she said.

Of such stray accidents are careers born.

Too shy to read his own play, O'Neill hid in the next room while someone else read it aloud. But when the last word of *Bound East for Cardiff* faded into silence, there was a burst of rapturous applause and he was surrounded, patted, thumped, embraced, and kissed. In that moment many things happened: one floundering, aimless soul slipped out of chaos into his predestined niche; a number of ardent amateurs found the perfect instrument to play upon; and the American theater entered upon a new and exhilarating phase.

Till now the Broadway theater, wholly dependent on a few unadventurous producers, hardly knew the word *realism*. Its fare was largely imported drawing-room comedies having little or no relation to everyday life. Now the Provincetown amateurs, with O'Neill pouring out arresting, earthy one-acters about sailors, Negroes, and farm folk, coalesced into a highly professional company of actors and directors. Moving to New York and their own Playwrights Theatre in Greenwich Village, they attracted to themselves other playwrights inspired by the new freedom offered them. The names that became famous during this movement made drama history. Ninety-three new American plays were produced in the next ten years, and copying them, nearly two thousand independent Little Theaters sprang up across the country.

Broadway too benefited, for without this new thrust there would have followed no Theatre Guild combining artistry and commercialism as it produced many of O'Neill's most successful plays.

The reception of *Bound East for Cardiff* was a shot of adrenalin into O'Neill's veins. He and Terry acquired a real house, a shack out of whose back door they threw their empty tin cans and on whose front door they nailed a sign that read: GO TO HELL. But he was still morose and withdrawn, often sinking into moods of black despair. "There was no such darkness as Gene's," Mary Heaton Vorse wrote later. "He would sit silent and suffering and in darkness."

The Players, impressed and intimidated, tiptoed respectfully past the shack all but crossing themselves at the thought of the masterpieces being born inside and the attendant agony. The suffering was, of course, largely nothing but a hangover. He would drink himself into a week-long stupor and then pull up sharply, swim the liquor out of his system, and throw himself back to work. He never, he said, combined liquor and work.

During his dry spells he gave his friends four more sea plays, *In the Zone, The Long Voyage Home, The Moon of the Caribbees,* and *Ile,* all staged next winter in New York in the parlor of a brownstone house. He sat in on rehearsals, and very soon developed his lifelong feud with all actors, regarding them as parading peacocks unwilling or unable to submerge their own personalities in his characters.

Having been rejected for war service in 1917 as an arrested TB case, he settled down in Provincetown to a new long play. Its title was suggested by a little boy on the beach.

"What's beyond the ocean?" he asked.

"The horizon," O'Neill answered.

"And what's beyond the horizon?"

This was a stiffer question, and O'Neill spent a good part of his life trying to find the answer.

Gradually he formulated his philosophy of life. The most significant thing about man, he said, is his "hopeless hope," his effort to reach his unreachable dream. "The higher the dream is," he said, "the harder it is to realize. . . . Any man who has a big enough dream must be a failure and must accept this as one of the conditions of being alive." Realization being thus impossible, the important thing is the dream.

His new play, *Beyond the Horizon,* dwelt on this theme of the unattainable and was expressed in bitter autobiographical terms. Two brothers are in love with the same girl. One (O'Neill) dreams of the freedom of life at sea, but having declared his love for the girl, he is trapped into marrying her. He thus loses his freedom, having to settle for a stultifying farmer's life while his brother gains the dream he has lost.

This triangular love affair reflects his situation of the moment, for he and his close friend John Reed both loved a girl named Louise Bryant. Being already married, she could not marry either of them, though professing to love both. Living first with Reed, she moved over to Gene when Reed went to Russia; then, when Reed returned, she went back to him—altogether a situation confusing enough to satisfy the most dramatic nature. O'Neill made the most of the drama while it lasted. But soon he met another girl of more permanent consequence.

Agnes Boulton Burton was a tall, good-looking widow of twenty-four who wrote stories for pulp magazines. She had a small daughter, Barbara, whom she frequently left with her parents for long periods (a parental habit that was ironically repeated twice more in the course of the family history). Slumming one night at the Hell Hole with a friend, she was attracted by a thin dark man with a mustache and large haunting eyes. They talked and he walked her home, and as he left her he said startlingly, "I want to spend every night of my life with you from now on." Shortly thereafter he bought two tickets on the Fall River Line and took her back with him to Provincetown.

Their affair was stormy from the start. He loved her, he said, because she made him feel sure of himself, but believing life essentially tragic and all dreams doomed, he could not really accept their happiness. In his "Black Irishness" he periodically worked up a drunken quarrel that ended in gutter invective and battered faces.

In the spring of 1918 he sold *In the Zone* to a vaudeville producer. Till now they had lived chiefly on his father's seven dollars a week, but on this weekly royalty of thirty-five dollars they decided to get married. O'Neill found a Methodist minister to perform the ceremony, and afterward this unhappy Irishman with the lost faith wrote wistfully of that other man's sweet childlike sincerity: "I caught myself wishing I could believe in the same gentle God he seemed so sure of."

For a while marriage had a stablizing effect. While Agnes did housework and ground out her magazine stories, O'Neill, unconscious of everything about him, labored on *Beyond the Horizon*. Always a compulsive writer, he worked seven or eight hours a day, his desk neat and orderly, with twelve pencils freshly sharpened, reference material in careful files, and notes organized in handbooks. (His handwriting, always small, became so cramped as palsy affected his hands that his secretaries had to decipher it with a magnifying glass.)

He overwrote endlessly. During a play's development he had for it the intense protective love of a mother for her infant—it was the finest, the most original, the most important thing ever produced—and any attempt by actor or director to cut it was a personal insult. Once produced, however, and taken over by the actors, it became no longer his and he lost all interest, even in time turning on it in disgust.

When *Beyond the Horizon* was finished he sent it off in a state of exaltation, innocently anticipating an immediate production and immediate success. That, however, was two years distant, and while waiting he turned to the story of Carlin's mistress. At the same time, the Provincetowners were putting on his short plays and the critics had begun coming and taking note. The tiny theater's weekly gross did not permit the payment of royalties, but O'Neill was receiving something he needed more than money: experience and recognition.

At this period he met two men vital to his career. *The Smart Set,* modestly dubbed "A Magazine of Cleverness," had actually paid him $75 for publication rights to *The Long Voyage Home,* and out of this contact developed a fast friendship between O'Neill and George Jean Nathan, its editor and drama critic. The two men, one solemn, sloppily dressed, and lacking any trace of humor, the other elegant and urbanely witty, had a common contempt for the current condition of the theater, and together writer and critic did much to bring American drama to maturity and pave the way for such men as Arthur Miller and Tennessee Williams.

Richard Madden, the agent, was no less important in O'Neill's life. They met over lunch to discuss a business deal and afterward

Madden told his wife, "I saw this gentle, clear-eyed man and I fell in love with him." With never a written contract between them Madden nurtured him, fought for him, and when necessary lied for him sturdily until his death.

O'Neill had a gift for inspiring this kind of friendship. Stark Young, the critic, said, "As was usual in his case I felt vaguely an emotion of pity and defense. Though there was nothing particularly to defend him against, I wanted to defend him, to take his part." And Lawrence Langner, the Theatre Guild producer, said, "The kindness of his smile, the gentleness of his spirit, the philosophical detachment of his mind, his Olympian view of human destiny, were not only inspiring but so endeared him to you that you wanted to lay down your life in his service."

There were many who did all but lay down their lives, some gladly, some because they had to. He himself, having discovered his genius, gave his life to it like a priest to his religion and, wearing himself out in its service, demanded the same of others.

So single-minded was this dedication that he received news of Agnes' pregnancy with dismay. At the time of their marriage he had told her he wanted no children, for, he said, "I don't understand them. They make me uneasy." Considering this, he should not perhaps be judged too severely for his behavior when he got them. He did, moreover, plead with Agnes to have an abortion. But she did not or could not oblige and so on October 30, 1919, Shane Rudraighe was born, so named in honor of his ancestor King Shane the Proud. During the lying-in O'Neill was absent, drunk, but later he reported with satisfaction that the baby had "a good Black Irish look." Honoring his birth, the child's grandfather presented the couple with a real home, a converted Coast Guard station near Provincetown.

This surprising generosity typified the changing atmosphere in this father-and-son relationship. Eugene's metamorphosis into a family man and his growing success were arousing his father's pride, and when *Beyond the Horizon* finally opened he and Ella were present and beaming. The old actor was puzzled by the harsh realism of this pitiless tragedy—"What are you trying to do, send them home to commit suicide?" he wailed—but the complimentary reviews, the prospering box-office and, in time, the Pulitzer Prize were convincing enough, and he would drop in at the Players Club to receive congratulations and remark that though people had said Gene was a wild good-for-nothing he had always had faith in him.

Gene's attitude toward his father likewise changed. With a little success his resentment toward him softened, and as the old man's health declined and he became fragile and appealing, the son looked backward with regret. "We had had a running battle for a good many years," he said later. "He'd just about given me up. . . . He was too patient with me. What I wonder now is why he didn't kick me out." And when the old man's death seemed near he mourned the prospect of losing him "just at the time when he and I, after many years of misunderstanding, have begun to be real pals."

Another change just as remarkable was Ella's rehabilitation. At sixty-three she decided to go to a convent of cloistered nuns, where she spent her time talking to the nuns and praying. At the end of a few months she returned home completely and permanently cured. Further, after her husband's death she suddenly emerged as an astute businesswoman, taking competent hold of his chaotic estate and proceeding to restore it to order and solvency. Even her appearance altered, with the bedraggled look replaced by chic black gowns and consciously elegant coiffures.

The ultimate miracle followed. Jamie, galvanized by his mother's transformation, decided to remain cold sober and devote himself entirely to her service, with the result that they went about together happily for a couple of years, dining in expensive restaurants and attending Gene's openings in style. Finally, she became so lively and good-tempered that not only Jamie but Gene enjoyed her company.

Then she and Jamie went to California to sell some of James' real estate. There she died suddenly, and just as abruptly Jamie fell apart again. With her coffin in the baggage car, he drank his way across the country, trying with the aid of a prostitute in the Pullman to forget that other woman in the car ahead. In New York Eugene, sick with disgust, had to watch his hopeless disintegration and finally take him to a hospital where he died of delirium tremens in November, 1924.

Jamie's death left Gene sole heir to their parents' wealth. But it left him another legacy as well, the gruesome memory of an alcoholic's death throes—a story that would haunt him until he could write it out under the name of *A Moon for the Misbegotten.*

It was now more than two years since *Beyond the Horizon* had made Eugene O'Neill a name in the theater. During that time the Provincetowners had given him several more productions that, without making any money, had consolidated his position as a playwright. Then in 1920 had come *The Emperor Jones,* souvenir of his Honduran jungle days. Opening off Broadway to ecstatic notices, it had been moved to Broadway and gone on to productions in Europe, South America, and Japan. At this point, Gene, noting the box-office lines, plucked up courage to ask for a small royalty, and fifty dollars a week was found for him.

The following year George Jean Ntathan talked a prominent producer, Arthur Hopkins, into putting on *Anna Christie,* and at last O'Neill had a solid straightforward commercial success. True, some critics murmured faintly about the love story's "happy ending," which they felt unworthy of a great tragic dramatist, but O'Neill hotly denied that the lovers' reconciliation was really happy. The two would, he was sure, be very unhappy later.

His mother's death and Jamie's relapse coincided with rehearsals of *The Hairy Ape,* and on the night of the opening, instead of listening to the audience's wild applause, he was at Grand Central Station meeting his hysterical brother and arranging for the disposition of the coffin. Afterwards he walked the streets all night with a friend pouring out the mournful story of his lost father and mother and now of his only brother. "I'm the last of the O'Neills now," he cried. "The last of the pure Irish."

The prosperous run of *The Hairy Ape* furthered O'Neill's career but it gave the coup de grâce to the Provincetowners. Though personally loyal to many of them as friends, O'Neill found Broadway's greater professionalism more satisfying. And this was logical enough. The group had evolved in protest against Broadway's lack of a bold creative spirit; they themselves had spawned such a spirit, fostered and protected it in its growth, and now it was inevitable that they should fall away like an outgrown shell.

Nevertheless a fresh shell formed the next year with some of the same personnel. Robert Edmund Jones, a stage designer, Kenneth Macgowan, a former critic, and O'Neill himself joined together to put on plays of importance. *All God's Chillun Got Wings* was announced for production. This play dealt ostensibly with the mismating of a white woman and a black man, but actually it was a story he used several times, the cross-current marriage of his own "shanty Irish" father and his convent-bred mother. The miscegenation aspect of it obscured the real theme, for in 1923 intermarriage was so sensational that there were efforts to prevent the opening, threats of bombings, and such a flood of obscene letters to the leading lady that her mail had to be screened before being given to her. On opening night policemen were stationed at the door just in case, but the performance went through as scheduled—having incidentally benefited richly at the box-office from all the excitement.

By now money problems, though still pressing, wore a more glamorous face. Intoxicated by the royalties from *Anna Christie* and the prospects of his inheritance, O'Neill began running into debt on an impressive scale. No O'Neill in modern times had owned a country estate, so now this descendant of kings bought himself Brook Farm, a large house and thirty-two Connecticut acres complete with swimming pool, formal garden, four-car garage, stables, and a barn. Agnes groaned in dismay at the size of it all but he grandly engaged her a staff to go with it, a cook, a gardener, two housemaids, a laundress, a nurse for Shane, and, for himself, an Irish wolfhound, traditional pet of Irish kings. Now he *belonged,* as his father in New London had never belonged.

The beauty and peace of the lovely countryside was not matched inside the house. Eugene was alternating between frenzied work and frenzied drinking, and between violent love for Agnes and violent antipathy. Turmoil was his concept of marriage, and sometimes, coming to himself after a volcanic scene, he would be gratified to be told of the dramatic heights his passion and fury had attained.

The basic difficulty between himself and Agnes was the fact that she had been a working writer before her marriage and could not see herself now as merely an appendage to his genius. But this was an affront to his art. Serving it selflessly himself, he expected his wife to do no less.

Further, his solitude was disturbed by her lavish and frequent entertaining. Her drinking parties outraged him, so he escaped them by retiring to his room to drink alone, or by leaving altogether for a week in the Hell Hole with his old cronies, where she often had to come looking for him in a state of high indignation.

All this confusion and discord naturally bewildered the golden-haired little boy who wandered about the estate lonely and silent or hung onto the skirt of his French nurse, Gaga. Agnes, busy with writing or entertaining, had little time to talk to him, as, likewise, did Gene. Occasionally he had a playmate when Agnes' ten-year-old daughter Barbara spent a few weeks with them. But experience had taught the children that one did not make noise under the window of the dark frowning father except at one's own peril.

Following the success of *Anna Christie,* O'Neill's first wife Kathleen wrote him out of the blue. She had married a second time, but her husband was not rich and she wondered if Gene would care to meet his son and perhaps help with his education? Encouraged by Agnes, he agreed, and the twelve-year-old boy was brought to the O'Neill door and left to go in alone.

Eugene Junior was a handsome boy, extremely intelligent but

nervous and sensitive. When he was six his mother, soon after her remarriage, had sent him to boarding school but, homesick and miserable, he had run back home. Over and over he had run back home and always been promptly returned. So obviously he was not wanted there. Since early childhood he had heard much talk about his famous, handsome father but never having seen or heard from him, he had naturally assumed he was not wanted there either. So there was only one conclusion to be drawn, that there was something terribly the matter with him.

The masters at his school were worried about the boy. All tests had proved that his mind was well above average, but he seemed unable to study and his marks were steadily declining. So a sympathetic teacher took the trouble to probe gently, and it turned out that he believed himself to be an illegitimate child. The meeting with this strange father therefore was a paralyzing prospect.

When the two met, however, they were both trying to behave their best and the result was that they ended by liking each other. The father was surprised and gratified by the son's intelligence and grace of manner, and the son was reassured by his friendly reception. So now he was able to accept the schooling O'Neill provided and in time went on to make a brilliant record. But the underlying fear about their relationship had sown its insidious seed.

Success in the theater, welcome as it was, O'Neill found to have its drawbacks, for the demands on his time of production details, the endless conferences, the prima-donna tactics of actresses in rehearsal, all rubbed his nerves raw. Agnes and he were continually having jealous quarrels in which each accused the other of too great interest in outsiders. The burdens and expenses of fatherhood, especially since the appearance of Eugene Junior, were becoming ever more onerous. And so when Agnes told him that she was again pregnant everything within him screamed, "Escape! Get away!"

At first he tried the old alcohol route. But this was no good, for when he came to he found nothing had been settled.

So then he tried physical escape. A doctor obligingly said a change in climate would be good for his nerves, so, not yet quite ready to break all family ties, he took wife and children with him and moved to Bermuda. There he bought a large house on the waterfront, which was to be his haven from the problems of New York, Provincetown, and Connecticut.

But still he had not escaped. And gradually he faced the truth that he had really known ever since he watched the horrors of Jamie's delirium tremens. Alcohol itself was his problem. And there was only one way it could end. So on January first, 1925, he swore off liquor.

Not long before this time he had finished *The Great God Brown* and was now in the throes of *Strange Interlude*, both plays dealing with man's successive layers of conscious and subconscious. In *Brown* the characters were given masks to conceal their real selves, and in *Interlude* they revealed them only through asides. Both devices had evolved from the newly popular discipline of psychoanalysis, of which he had made a deep study. And so now, recognizing his need, he turned to it for help with his own problem.

"He told me," said Kenneth Macgowan, "that he was scared, that he couldn't continue the way he was. Agnes was no help to him in that respect; she drank along with him. During the analysis Hamilton the analyst had Gene lie on a black leather couch, in traditional Freudian style. When it was over Gene told me he had no trouble understanding that he hated and loved his father, and that he was suffering from an Oedipus complex."

In a family such as this, with its record of psychological miracles, even such a rarity as the cure of alcoholism by analysis is possible, and this miracle Eugene O'Neill achieved. Except for two slips of limited duration he remained sober the rest of his life.

Grateful though he was for his new well-being, this man, with his Black Irish temperament, could not be happy with it. Normality and sobriety did not feel natural, and he was lonely without the "companionable phantoms" of his drinking days. A friend once twitted him about the pleasure he got out of being tortured, and now he admitted to a "vague feeling of maladjustment to this 'cleaner, greener land' " within his soul. He needed turmoil to feel at ease.

This need was to be satisfied soon enough. His escape to Bermuda had not worked, and the whole family returned to Maine for the summer. His agent Richard Madden, rendering his client a service he had never intended, suggested a cottage near that of his partner, Elizabeth Marbury. There the O'Neills settled down, Agnes slim and loquacious and O'Neill handsomer and more distinguished than ever with his deep tan and graying hair. Accompanying them were fragile little Shane, the black-eyed baby Oona, the nurse Gaga, and, at various times, Eugene Junior and Agnes' Barbara.

O'Neill worked in the mornings propped up in bed on pillows, a work habit acquired at Gaylord Sanitarium, while the children were kept at a distance. In the afternoons the O'Neills exchanged visits with the other residents. One of Miss Marbury's guests was an actress celebrated less for her talent than for her dark, exotic beauty—Carlotta Monterey, born in California, educated in Europe, and married three times.

Miss Monterey was celebrated also for her opulent way of life, her daring clothes, and her ribald wit. O'Neill and she had met once or twice in New York, but on the afternoon the O'Neills dropped in at Miss Marbury's, her coolly indifferent greeting was an immediate challenge. At their first moment alone O'Neill turned his deep searching eyes on her and said, "You don't like me, do you?"

"Why, Mr. O'Neill," she replied, raising arrogant eyebrows, "I hardly know you." It was enough; very soon he was seeing that she did. There were seemingly accidental meetings and fortuitous errands, a lost scarf, a swim in the lake. Gradually her immaculate chic made Agnes look untidy and sloppy, and Agnes' breathless chatter seemed vapid after her easy wit. Carlotta on her part warmed to his somber charm and massive intellect. When her visit ended he asked for her New York address. And at the end of the summer he sent his family back to Bermuda, remaining himself in New York "to oversee the sale of Brook Farm."

At the first opportunity he telephoned Carlotta and almost daily visits began. "He talked and talked as though he'd known me all his life," she recalled later, "but he paid no more attention to *me* than if I had been a chair. He talked about how he'd had no home, no mother in the real sense, no father in the real sense, and how deprived his childhood had been.... I thought it was terrible that of all people to be so stricken, it should be this man, who had talent and had worked hard. And his face would become sadder and sadder.... Well, that's what got me into trouble with O'Neill; my maternal instinct came out.... One day ... he looked at me with those tragic eyes and said, 'I need you.' ... never 'I love you, I think you are wonderful'—just 'I need you.' "

His excuse for remaining in New York petered out after a month and he reluctantly returned to Bermuda. For months he continued to play out the role of husband, home-owner, and father, but the children were unhappy witnesses to many scenes over "that woman." During all the turmoil he finished *Marco Millions* and *Strange Interlude* for the Theatre Guild, and later in the fall he returned to New York alone.

One night in December he dined with Benjamin de Casseres and his wife. Suddenly Mrs. De Casseres, who had never met him before, said to O'Neill, "I'm interested in palmistry. May I look at your hand?" With a smile he held it out.

On touching it, she felt what she described afterward as "an inner illumination" and began to speak slowly, as if hypnotized: "You are not a poet, you are a psychologist." Then she rushed on, barely hearing what she said. "You explore. You uncover the roots of things. You are never going back to Bermuda. You will live in Europe and San Francisco. You have a long journey before you. You are leaving your wife. Another woman is in your life now .... There will be a great deal of publicity, and you will have a struggle for a divorce before you are able to marry her. Your plays will be successful. You will live for twenty-five years." O'Neill looked at her blankly and soon left, too stunned to speak. No one in the world knew he and Carlotta planned to marry, and neither he nor Mrs. De Casseres could ever account for this forecast which, except for the final statement, was completely accurate.

If his plans needed any consolidating, this prophecy supplied it. After the openings of *Marco Millions* (to mild success) and *Strange Interlude* (to hosannas, tremendous business, and another Pulitzer Prize) he and Carlotta began plotting their escape.

Agnes was to be told nothing at all. Young Gene, now a brilliant student at Yale, was told and sworn to secrecy. O'Neill's chief confidant, Macgowan, who had given the love affair his blessing, knew all. ("I encouraged Gene's relationship with Carlotta, because I thought she would keep him sober, which I didn't think Agnes could do.")

Little Shane received a letter designed to cover the lovers' tracks. O'Neill wrote that he had to go to California to see to the production of a play, *Lazarus Laughed,* and he feared it would be a long, long time before he saw either Oona or him again. But he loved them both and they were not to forget their daddy.

This elopement was an odd repetition of a familiar pattern. As Agnes had left her daughter Barbara with her mother to go with O'Neill, so now O'Neill was leaving his children with their mother to go with Carlotta and she was leaving her eleven-year-old daughter Cynthia with her mother to go with him.

The runaways sailed for London in February, 1928, heavily incognito. On arriving, O'Neill wrote Agnes reminding her of their long-standing pledge that if either fell in love with someone else, that one would be instantly released—with no alimony. He also recommended that she go back to work. "You are never going to amount to a damn so long as you depend on me for everything. . . . My happiness cannot be complete until I know that you have gone back to work."

Meanwhile he wrote to Macgowan ecstatically, "I'm simply transformed and transfigured inside. A dream I had given up . . .

has come true." As to their actual plans, these depended on Agnes' cooperation in the matter of a divorce. While waiting for her to act, they would go motoring through France.

Despite all their attempts at secrecy rumors began to spread in New York, and at the same time Agnes unexpectedly turned stubborn. The terms he offered, wrote her lawyer, were insufficient for the two children. O'Neill was indignant and said so. Letters flew back and forth, increasingly acrimonious. "She's trying to take me for all I've got," he complained bitterly; but fear of scandal precluded an open fight. "What a rotten mess to have wished on one! . . . It's the lousiest situation I was ever placed in."

Had O'Neill been lucky enough to have a sense of humor he might have seen the situation differently, but as it was, obsessed by a sense of personal martyrdom, he lost all control and drank himself insensible. This made Carlotta furious, which in turn increased his rage at Agnes. "Believe me, Kenneth," he wrote, "once I'm free of that baby I'm going to . . . make her pay for this." Unhappily, it was not Agnes who paid the most.

As soon as his current script, *Dynamo,* was delivered to the Theatre Guild he and Carlotta started on a round-the-world cruise. But they got no farther than Shanghai, for with nerves raw with pent-up fury he picked a frightful quarrel with her and flung off to an obscure saloon in the slums. By this time his presence in Shanghai had become known to the newspapers, though not his immediate whereabouts, and now the guessing game "Where is Eugene O'Neill?" was played out in the presses of the world. Carlotta kept up her own frantic private search.

After two weeks he was found in a sleazy hospital, very near a nervous breakdown from sheer fury. A psychiatrist had been called in to treat him for alcoholism, and finally the mental violence subsided and he was taken back to the hotel. Their one idea now being to avoid further notoriety, he was smuggled out of Shanghai as the Reverend William O'Brien (even now he could not leave behind his Irish identity). But it did him no good, for the New York *Times* quickly penetrated his disguise.

Carlotta's presence escaped detection in the muddle, but her maid got into the news as "O'Neill's secretary, Mrs. Tuwe Drew, a Swedish masseuse, who described herself as also a graduate physician."

This devastating experience killed their interest in anything but peace and solitude. Carlotta had always maintained "What my Irishman wants he shall have," and so they hurried back to France.

While looking for a home they heard that Agnes had agreed to a Reno divorce charging desertion and to a settlement which, in recognition of Carlotta's independent fortune, gave Agnes and her children approximately one third of O'Neill's income. As soon as the divorce was granted he and Carlotta were married in a double-ring ceremony. The place was Paris, the date July 22, 1929. Immediately thereafter they moved into a home of their own.

Carlotta always declared that she lived to make a perfect home in which her husband could write his plays, and the workroom she now presented to him was surely unique. The Château le Plessis at Saint-Antoine-du-Rocher in the Loire Valley had forty-five rooms and a 600-acre game preserve. It also had no electric lighting, no heat, and no bathroom, but such a circumstance was simply a challenge to this dynamic woman. Besides a bathroom she installed a swimming pool, a roof garden, and a gymnasium. Her "tough Irishman" at first feared he might be suspected of going soft or putting on airs, but under her influence he soon came to enjoy having his meals served by a butler, with the menus inscribed on little marble tablets in front of each diner's place.

Even when they were alone she dressed for dinner, delighting his eyes each night with a different gown, and on the theory that it was good for his psyche to have everything he had hitherto lacked she talked him into ordering a huge custom-made wardrobe including seventy-five pairs of shoes, and a racing car capable of 95 mph. On her own she gave him a specially made writing chair complete with headrest, shelves for reference books and knee-board, and a mink-lined overcoat.

When the bills began coming in he was somewhat appalled and nervously wrote his publisher that he had been offered $50,-000 for his manuscripts and wondered if he could get him a hundred thousand. The sale never went through, but the spending went on anyway without catching up with them for many years.

Château le Plessis was, of course, on the sightseeing itinerary of every New York acquaintance, and not one returned without some engaging anecdote or impression. One wrote reverently that "the bronzed, handsome, greying Mr. O'Neill" was "the ideal of what a great melancholy and brooding playwright should look like." Another reported with relish that cocktail time in the Château garden consisted of the host and hostess sitting in royal Chinese robes sipping an American soft drink called Moxie. All agreed that they had never seen a man and woman more passionately in love. Carlotta did everything she could to bring a smile to her husband's face, acting as wife, mother, housekeeper, secretary, typist, nurse, mistress, companion—almost tailor. At times, overcome with gratitude, he would break off work to scribble a paean of impassioned praise: "Mistress, I desire you, you are my passion and my life-drunkenness, and my ecstasy.... Wife, you are my love, and my happiness, and the word behind my word.... Mother, you are my lost way refound, my end and my beginning." (O'Neill recognized honestly his lack of the poetic gift. "Oh, for a language to write drama in! For a speech that is dramatic," he wailed to a friend. He longed to be a poet, and though he never succeeded he never gave up trying.)

On her part, Carlotta told a friend, "I am so desperately desirous of giving him back some little bit of all the great beauty and happiness he gives to me."

One other role there was that Carlotta played, sometimes indeed overplayed—that of buffer. O'Neill, lacking strength of will to refuse callers himself, gave her the job, so she always answered the telephone, screening out strangers and pushers and, to their eternal indignation, early Greenwich Village friends such as Terry

Carlin who antedated her regime. But even she could not shut out the Hell Hole cronies; he might not see them, but a call for help never went unanswered. To the end of his life those down-and-out days were his favorite topic of conversation.

In 1930 young Gene came to visit. A handsome, articulate young man with a resounding voice, he was building the record at Yale that two years hence was to win him highest honors and three prizes in classics. His surface poise, however, covered a deep insecurity. His mother and step-father had suffered financial hardships, and his young step-brother, of whom he was very fond, had recently committed suicide. That side of his family had his affection and sympathy, but at the same time there was a plaintive, worried adoration for his father, who had rejected him as a child and now accorded him cordiality and respect.

O'Neill was in fact so impressed by his son's scholarship ("He's too erudite for me, I can't even talk to him") that his interest in young Gene's special study of the Greek classics contributed to his own next great work.

While on his way to Shanghai in 1928 O'Neill had written in his notebook: "Greek plot idea—give modern Electra figure in play tragic ending worthy of character." Eighteen months later he wrote Shane that his current work was the biggest and hardest he had ever tackled, and that after a year he was only then one third through the second draft. It was still another year before he sent the final draft to the Theatre Guild.

Mourning Becomes Electra is actually three plays in one, and when finally produced it ran from five P.M. until nearly midnight with a break for dinner. The Aeschylus story of lust, incest, and murder had been transposed to 1850 New England, but this retelling of the Greek "trilogy of the damned" was, on a deeper level, one more treatment of the haunted O'Neill family locked in a love-hate relationship. In this instance Eugene is represented by a daughter, Lavinia, who after being involved in the various adulteries, murders, and suicides of her family, and being herself guilty of incest with her brother, locks herself in her own prison-house to die. "I'm the last of the Mannons," she cries. "I've got to punish myself."

When Jamie died, O'Neill had cried, "I'm the last of the O'-Neills," and the whole story of his prototype Lavinia is an uncanny projection of himself, not only of his life up to that time but onward into the future.

After the October, 1931, opening the play, hailed as a masterpiece, was compared to the Empire State Building towering over Manhattan. It sold out for months, and if O'Neill and Carlotta had chosen to remain in New York they could have been toasted at some dinner party every night of the week.

Instead they chose Georgia. Le Plessis had palled even before their three-year lease on it was up and they ended by building another mansion on fashionable Sea Island, where Gene could swim and sit in the endless sun. Here, on their Blessed Isle, they luxuriated in every comfort, even down to washstands high enough to eliminate stooping when brushing the teeth. It and they attracted so much interest that eventually an eight-foot wall had to be added to keep out inquisitive tourists.

At this time O'Neill was, in a sense, at the peak of his career. He had produced in the last twelve years the remarkable total of nineteen full-length plays, of which nine were genuine critical and financial successes. Ahead of him lay eight more, but Broadway saw only three of them during his lifetime, and only one of these, the strangely atypical *Ah, Wilderness!*, was a real success.

Like *Desire Under the Elms,* which had come to him fully outlined in a dream, this slight domestic comedy broke into his labors on the unhappy *Days Without End,* demanding to be written forthwith. A dream in every sense of the word, it was a never-never-land picture of the O'Neills as a happy, humorous, and well-adjusted family, and when produced it was something of an embarrassment to him, suggesting as it did that he had had a happy childhood. Taking note of this misinterpretation on the part of the press, he asked Brooks Atkinson of the *Times* to interview him so that he could make clear that he had really had a very miserable one.

After this vacation from tragedy O'Neill returned to his native element. In the blistering, blinding heat of south Georgia he began working out a staggering new work plan, a cycle of plays following the Harford family down through the generations. At first he projected four, then five, and finally eleven plays, starting back in the Revolution. Always fascinated by the past, from now on he lived in it, brooding on the Harford curse that dogged one generation after another. His concept of a divine power, a Fate merciless and inescapable, was his substitute for the "gentle God" he had glimpsed wistfully on his wedding day. It was what he lived with all through life, and it proved an unhealthy fellow traveler.

After several years the heat of their Blessed Isle, which forced him to write sitting on a bath towel, with bookkeeper's black sleeves on his arms and blotters under his hand, made the strain of his enormous project almost unbearable. He managed to rough out a first draft of *A Touch of the Poet,* the cycle's first play, and began *More Stately Mansions,* sometimes working all night and emerging in the morning more ghost than man. But finally, after an Island summer in Hades, they left for the Northwest, where O'Neill planned to do research for the Harford saga.

Once again they built a house, this time one near San Francisco with a magnificent view over mountains and valleys. But by now his health was giving serious trouble—neuritis in his arm, which prevented his writing for months at a time (dictating blocked his imagination), and a palsy in his hands that was advancing with frightening speed. Nevertheless he struggled on with the Harford cycle.

But there came a time in the late thirties when, living behind electrically controlled gates in an isolation fiercely maintained by Carlotta, and watching the terrifying rise of Hitler abroad, his inner despair seemed to spill out and encompass the world. So, washing his hands as it were of everything external, he returned to his private domain and to those days "at the very bottom where there was no further down to go" and nothing remained but a dream.

The Iceman Cometh, a play about the unattainable dreams by which men exist and the Iceman at the end of all, has been exhaustively analyzed from psychiatric, religious, and metaphysical points of view. O'Neill regarded it as the best thing he had ever written; there were moments in it, he told a friend, "that suddenly strip the secret soul of man stark naked . . . with an understanding compassion which sees him as a victim of the ironies of life and of himself."

With the advent of World War II all their servants went into defense work. Carlotta had never learned to drive a car and Eugene's palsy precluded his driving, with the result that their contact with the outside world depended on farmers and a nearby hardware man. In the ensuing silence and solitude O'Neill sank ever deeper into his own unhappy past, and so, again abandoning his "damned cycle," he faced head on the ghosts he had been fencing with ever since the Monte Cristo Cottage days.

Long Day's Journey into Night took O'Neill two years to write, and during that time Carlotta often feared to see him lose his mind. "It was terrible to watch his suffering," she said, and she herself, typing the manuscript, often wept for him. But he had to write it; after all this time he now believed he could approach his family honestly, with "deep pity and understanding and forgiveness." (The manuscript, he decided, was not to be made public until twenty-five years after his death, and when finished, it was sealed and stored in his publisher's vault. In 1956, however, Carlotta released it for production.)

O'Neill's use of the words *pity, understanding,* and *forgiveness* reveals this strange man at his strangest. A genius he certainly was, and as Mrs. De Casseres said, a psychologist and explorer. But the psychologist who is blind to his own motives is a psychologist manqué. Pity there may have been in his painful revelation of his family's weaknesses, but his picture of himself as their poetic, persecuted victim has less forgiveness than resentment and self-pity.

He was blind, indeed, in whole areas of his life. Obsessed by the damage inflicted on him by his parents, he was yet utterly unconscious of the damage he was inflicting on his own children. Shane had suffered neglect since babyhood—unwanted before birth, left afterward to the care of Gaga, at nine deserted by his father. Gaga's death and the boy's exile to boarding school had followed, and there he had been deeply humiliated by the constant questions about his famous father and his lack of anything to tell. His letters to O'Neill were generally handed over to Carlotta, who told him later that she had "loathed" answering them. At eighteen he asked permission to visit his father to talk about his future, but he was refused, it was not convenient just then. Soon thereafter he was dropped from school. By this time he was drinking heavily.

So began for Shane a disordered existence of drunkenness, drug addiction, and squalor. There was a haphazard marriage and a baby dead from neglect, sessions in jail and psychiatric wards, and several attempts at suicide. For over twenty years he was periodically in the scandal sheets, embarrassing his father. But long ere this both the O'Neills had washed their hands of him altogether.

O'Neill's lingering hatred of Agnes virtually estranged him from his daughter as well. But Oona was different stuff than Shane; as tough and resilient as he was flabby, she early knew her own charm and power. With black hair, an amusing nose, and a wide, impish grin, at sixteen she was thoroughly and self-confidently herself. Her amused compliance with gossip columnists and photographers and her laughing remark "We O'Neills are just shanty Irish" outraged both her father and Carlotta, who referred to her coldly as "that girl." Voted New York's Number One Debutante of the Year in 1942, she subsequently went to Hollywood for a screen test, where her mother introduced her to an old friend, Charlie Chaplin. Chaplin offered to coach her for the test, and shortly afterward, as soon as she reached her eighteenth birthday, they were married. At the time Chaplin was fifty-four. Lacking a real father, she had married a substitute one, and the arrangement seemed to suit them both very well.

O'Neill never spoke to her again, though she tried several times to see him. "Oona broke Gene's heart," Carlotta said. He never could understand how his children could so betray him, and both Oona and Shane were cut out of his will.

Eugene Junior was still friends with his father and Carlotta, though he saw them seldom while they were on the West Coast. But after the war, with O'Neill's palsy accelerating and Carlotta exhausted from bedmaking, nursing, cooking, and typing, they gave up their California house and came East for a production of *The Iceman*. Then young Eugene saw them frequently.

By now a recognized authority on Greek drama, he had become an assistant professor at Yale, and his proud father enjoyed his learned conversation. But he had also developed a drinker's paunch and a reputation as a communist, neither of which Carlotta enjoyed. She came to dislike him intensely, and he saw that his father was going to have to choose between them.

These strained relationships were, unhappily, not the only emotional hazards in the family. For the unbelievable had happened. The blazing Eugene-Carlotta passion, for so long a mutual adoration, had degenerated into the vixenish love-hate of his parents. His old friends had always believed that Carlotta was taking his demands for isolation too literally, and certainly now, on his return to New York, he acted like a man released from prison. Looking up old friends, he opened his arms to new ones also. His health bloomed, he went to races, ball games, prizefights, and night clubs. Requests for interviews and speeches were graciously indulged. And he flirted with young actresses, mildly enough but all too publicly.

Carlotta was not amused. Whereas their wedding anniversaries had habitually brought forth messages of worship and gratitude, their fifteenth anniversary yielded only a note of apology and appeal: "Forgive all the mistakes and injuries . . . our marriage has been the most successful and happy of any we know—until late years. Here's for a new beginning!"

But Carlotta, still believing that too much of this New York exertion might reduce him to invalidism and dependency, was not moved, and his plaintive request not to "sneer" at his love, his heartbreak, his need, went unheeded. Each expected all the concessions from the other, and at length there was an impasse. Early in 1948 she left their house.

"My frau has flown the coop," he phoned to a friend. But to her he wrote, "You are all I have in life. I am sick and I will surely die without you. You do not want to murder me, I know." Carlotta still ignored his appeal, and nine days later, as if trying to carry out his threat, he fell and broke his shoulder.

Moved to a hospital, he was showered with attentions by friends who did their best to bring him and Carlotta together. Young Gene also begged him to come and live with him in the country. He considered his son's offer, but in April Carlotta decided to return, and then he told Gene, "I have to go back to her, I can't live without her." This, the young man knew, was the end for him, his ultimate dismissal.

Already for some time young O'Neill had been coming to pieces. Twice married and divorced, he had also been through a number of short-lived alliances. Then followed a series of disheartening blows: loss of his post at Yale and unsuccessful tries at acting and lecturing. The woman he had lived with for several years refused to marry him ("I couldn't, there was insanity in his eyes.") and finally came his father's total rejection. In September, 1950, he killed himself.

The final years of Eugene O'Neill read like one of his own grisly dramas. For a lifetime he had dwelt in his private world of hopeless hope and inescapable despair wherein tragedy was the fate of every man. His prototype in *Mourning Becomes Electra* accepts, indeed embraces, the fate that "becomes" her, and as she goes into her house she says almost gloatingly, "I'll never go out to see anyone. I'll have the shutters nailed closed so no sunlight can ever get in. I'll live alone with the dead, and keep their secrets, and let them hound me, until the curse is paid out and the last Mannon is let die!"

He could not, surely, have foreseen his own future. But his son Gene once said, "The concept of Fate in the Greek sense had a tremendous influence both on his work and on him . . . 'It will get you in the end,' he once said." And certainly his concept of Fate got O'Neill. After Carlotta's return they forsook New York and deliberately searched out an isolated house on a cliff overlooking the Atlantic. There they shut themselves in away from the world.

It is possible that this subconscious living out of his own prophecy might have run true to the end, except that in one respect he departed from his own text. Rather than shutting himself up alone, he went with Carlotta. And so the pattern was broken.

But it adhered to another well-established one, for their relationship fell into the classic love-hate mold. One day he would say, "You are my love, forever my love, Sweetheart." The next he would glare at her, spitting out curses. After young Gene's suicide they sat so long in the silent house glaring at each other that both became temporarily unbalanced. They were taken off to separate hospitals and brought irrational lawsuits against each other, he demanding legal guardianship over Carlotta and she in turn suing for separate maintenance. But at last reason and their mutual dependence drew them together again and they went to live in a hotel in Boston.

It had been now twenty years since *Ah, Wilderness!*, O'Neill's last financial success. *The Iceman Cometh* had done moderately well in 1946 and his published plays still brought in some royalties, but his name lacked the weight of former days. In 1952 they were actually in debt.

It was then that the old play about Jamie, *A Moon for the Misbegotten*, which had never been produced, was brought out in book form. It served to ameliorate somewhat their financial worries, and a copy of it also served to carry the last message he ever wrote to Carlotta or anyone else: "To darling Carlotta, my wife, who for twenty-three years has endured with love and understanding my rotten nerves, my lack of stability, my cussedness in general . . . I am old and would be sick of life, were it not that you, Sweetheart, are here, as deep and understanding in your love as ever—and I as deep in my love for you as when we stood in Paris, Premier Arrondissement, on July 22, 1929, and both said faintly, 'Oui'!"

Early in 1953, sick of life and anticipating his death, he began worrying about his unfinished cycle, dreading the tampering of alien hands. He and Carlotta had already destroyed some manuscripts, and now he ordered her to bring him the rest. Sitting before the fire, he started tearing the pages, a few at a time because of the tremor of his hands. She tore them too, making piles of the scraps and feeding them to the blaze. "It was awful," she said. "It was like tearing up children."

Eugene O'Neill had lived, as much as any writer can, for his work. Now that that was done with he had no further interest in living. But still his old unanswered question worried him. "When I die, get me quietly and simply buried," he said. "And don't bring a priest. If there is a God and I meet Him, we'll talk things over personally, man to man."

And still his sense of drama did not desert him. As he felt himself going he half raised himself in bed and clenched his fists. "Born in a hotel room," he muttered, "and God damn it—died in a hotel room!" Death come on November 27, 1953.

Thomas Wolfe
(1900=1938)

Thomas Wolfe
(1900-1938)

"THOMAS WOLFE," said a critic in reviewing one of his novels, "has a magnificent malady: it may be called gigantism of the soul."

Others have seen Wolfe's malady as a monstrous overcharge of electricity, a force throwing him about like a live wire, blindingly brilliant but perilous to approach too nearly. Even the man himself suffered from this overcharge, and all too soon he was burned out from a sheer excess of energy.

From the very first Tom never had a chance at tranquillity. The last of eight children, he was dropped into a swirling cauldron of animosities by two eccentric parents savagely mismatched. The resulting irritations kept him raw-skinned and bleeding, but if Freud is to be believed this environment may have been the perfect breeding ground for such a genius as this one.

Wolfe's mother, Julia Westall, was a genuine "character." One of nineteen children born in North Carolina just before the Civil War, she was such a wretched skin-and-bones baby that her embarrassed mother kept her hidden from the neighbors' prying eyes. Nevertheless, she survived the privations of war and defied calamity and death for eighty-six years. Once, with an infected leg hideously swollen and blue, she was told that it must be removed to save her life. Pursing her lips in a tight line, she snapped, "The leg stays with me." And stay it did and served her obediently and well.

As a girl small, thin, and steely, she supported herself teaching country school, in her spare time selling books door to door in Asheville, North Carolina. With her first $125 she bought her first piece of real estate and at twenty-one built her first house. "She's the stingiest girl in town," the neighbors muttered, "measures every stick of wood to the square inch." From that time on she lusted after property like a man lusting after drink.

Her marriage was singularly devoid of sentiment. While plying her bookselling trade she stopped in at the store of one W.O. Wolfe, who cut and sold marble tombstones. After buying one of her books he expressed interest in another on her list. Several days later she brought it. While he was completing the purchase he surprised her by asking her to be his wife. It seemed that, twice married and widowed, he yearned to settle down again and had been watching her approvingly as she passed his shop.

"All men liked me," she told a friend with calm satisfaction, "but I had made up my mind to be an old maid and I told him so." When he persisted she joked, "Well, I tell you—I'll open the book and on the right side, the middle of the page, whatever it says we will abide by it. . . . And what do you suppose it opened to? 'Till death do us part.' "

The romantic Mr. Wolfe, believing himself in receipt of a sign from heaven, insisted on the marriage, and for Christmas he sent her a marble doorstop with their initials carved on it together. He added a few handkerchiefs . . . just in case, he said, she ever regretted the step she was going to take.

The handkerchiefs were an appropriate enough gift, though this tough little warrior was no weeping willow. Her prime interest in life was real estate, while the tall gaunt husband, as warm, sensual, and open as she was flinty and hard-headed, preferred poetry and song. His roaring voice intoning the mightier passages of Shakespeare, his dramatic hyperbole of speech, his gusto for living, fitted not at all with her dry matter-of-factness.

And when she found that she, an implacable temperancer, had married a drunkard, she drew back in outrage and fear. It was not too long, however, before she recovered her poise, and when he came home shouting and waving his arms he would shortly end up crushed and weeping under her relentless glare.

Husband and wife stuck together mainly out of habit. He called her the most hard-hearted woman he had ever known, and she retorted smartly that that came from having married a marble man. There was a certain hot attraction nevertheless, and the children came and came in a long string. Thomas, the eighth, was born in 1900.

In 1906 the ambitious Julia, impatient with the life of a stone-cutter's wife, decided to better herself. Buying an old mansion around the corner from their Woodfin Street house, she opened "Mrs. Wolfe's Old Kentucky Home" with rooms for nineteen boarders. Her husband remained at the Woodfin Street house and their daughter Mabel kept house for him there. Effie, the oldest child, was married and gone from home, the older son Frank was already a drifter sunk in drinking and drugs, and one little boy had died in childhood. But the younger sons, Fred, Ben, and Tom, were swept off to the Old Kentucky Home on Spruce Street.

This split in little Tom's home life seems to have left a split in his soul. Used to the noisy maelstrom of brothers and sisters ("Julia's wolves," her relatives called them), where the father's laughter and songs and rages kept the air quivering with life, he was dragged off and buried in "that great chill tomb" on Spruce Street.

During the day Mrs. Wolfe was busy with housekeeping and real estate deals, and in her spare hours rocked and gossiped on the wide porch where her filing-cabinet memory poured forth endless reminiscences. Unnoticed, the boys would wander back to the warm and friendly ambience of Woodfin Street, and Fred and Ben often spent weeks there. But every evening the mother gave her apron string a yank and dragged home the beautiful little boy with the long curls. She suckled him till he was four, and when she slept he was beside her in the bed. Not until his ninth year could he induce her to cut his curls . . . and even then it was only when he got "things" in them.

Having two homes the future novelist virtually had none, and later was to blame his lifetime of turmoil and confusion on this strangled situation. Tied to his mother against his will and yet heavily dependent on her; hating her dark gloomy house with the TB patients rocking and spitting on the front porch; chilled by its loneliness; deprived, as he saw it, of the supporting strength of a father, his life became a search, a series of clutching hopes and disappointments. "The deepest search in life," he once wrote, is "man's search to find a father, not merely the father of his flesh . . . but the image of a strength and wisdom external to his need and superior to his hunger, to which the belief and power of his own life could be united."

Four times in his life he would find, or think he had found, this superperson, this tower of supporting strength, and four times, as his demands went beyond all reason, the idol would disappoint him. These disappointments he saw as crass betrayals, the grossest kind of hoax. How *dared* they fail him when he needed them to cling to?

Besides these four, two other persons were to let him down. Ben, the brother eight years his senior, who had cared for him when his mother was busy elsewhere—Ben, whom he idolized all through his early years—Ben died of pneumonia when Tom was eighteen, leaving him dismayed and desolate and resentful.

And his mother—time and again he would find her letting him down. She who had kept him so close and made him so dependent —very soon she was failing to "understand" him. By the age of eleven his complicated needs were beyond her satisfying, and he had taken on a substitute mother. Yet in love and exasperation and sheer hate, that dependency on his mother, that bond, held fast, and though he railed and spat at her this was the one real constancy of his life.

The deputy mother was a lovely woman perceptive enough to recognize the odd, untidy boy's poetic potential, to hail and nurture it. Margaret Roberts was the wife of the principal of one of Asheville's public schools and while helping her husband correct English papers she came across an almost illegible essay startlingly superior to the rest. The Robertses were planning to open a private school the following year and they asked that young Thomas Wolfe be enrolled (an advancement encouraged by the loving Ben but resented by Mabel and Fred, who were older and therefore presumably more deserving). His four high school years were thus spent under Mrs. Roberts' watchful and proud eye.

From the age of five, books rather than games or sports had been Tom's passion, and by his teens he was said to have read every book of fiction in the Asheville Public Library, good and bad. There had been much trash among the lot, but Mrs. Roberts opened up "the shining Eldorado of good literature" to him and he spent more and more time at her home.

This "mother of his spirit" watched over his health as well as his studies. To square out his ridiculous beanpole frame already approaching six feet she pushed him out of doors into school athletics. But contests bored him; instead he would wander for hours about town observing, absorbing through eyes and nose and ears the atmosphere of the place and its people.

Not wholly due to Mrs. Roberts' encouragement and praise was Thomas' confidence in his own superiority. Already he was turning inward with that intense self-awareness that was to characterize both his life and his work. Like his mother he had a filing-cabinet memory and like her he shared his thoughts volubly, pouring them out in an excited, stuttering flood. One moment he sailed through the air on exalted wings, the next thudded to the earth in moods of black despair. Mrs. Roberts understood them all and when he graduated, not yet sixteen but covered with honors in literature and oratory, her pride was as great as his own. It was an accepted fact between them that he was to become a great writer.

Chapel Hill, North Carolina, was W. O. Wolfe's choice of college for Tom, while Tom yearned for the University of Virginia with the halo of Edgar Allen Poe upon it. But, already ill with the malady that would one day carry him off, Mr. Wolfe saw in Tom the son that could glorify the family name, first as lawyer, then as

politician, finally as governor. For this assignment the boy would
need many contacts within the state, so Tom, fretting like a restive
colt, was forced to submit to the hand that held the whip and the
purse strings.

His four years at Chapel Hill were much happier than in
retrospect he cared to admit. Throughout life he was the giant hero
of all his books, and seeing everything oversized, he later pictured
himself enduring gigantic woes and humiliations. The loneliness of
his freshman year actually was common to all students, but in *Look
Homeward, Angel* he added to his normal state of isolation a load
of special hardships from the past—the early-dawn paper route he
had been "forced" to run, the magazine vending on the street, the
handing out of Old Kentucky Home cards at the depot. Even
worse because more immediate were the visits his mother was
making now on campus, embarrassing him by talking up the Home
among his classmates. "She's r-ruining me!" he wailed to Mabel. A
further cross was his height. In 1917 to be six foot six was to be
a monster and he suffered deeply, imagining himself the butt of
secret laughter.

The miseries of Eugene Gant in *Look Homeward, Angel* were
overdrawn consciously, for he believed that the story of any student could be true *in spirit* only if he were represented as lonely
and unappreciated, since all students, no matter how well accepted, *felt* like neglected outsiders. In reality his last three years
were both successful and happy, and he contributed heavily to the
college newspaper, *The Tar Heel.* He was elected to a literary
fraternity and even in time to a social one.

With success came self-confidence and with confidence came
ease of manner. His stuttering, outrageous nonsense and horseplay
won him the friendly reputation of a "character" on campus, and
in his last year he was a genuine Big Man, editor-in-chief of *The
Tar Heel,* class poet, and member of the Senior Council. He was
voted Best Writer, Wittiest, and Most Original, and the yearbook
dubbed him "a genius"; and at graduation, while W. O. and
Mrs. Wolfe sat beaming, the university president whispered

of the great future that lay ahead for their son.

This success was doubly remarkable for occurring in spite of Tom's glaring social deficiencies. One soon found that a conversation with him consisted either of listening to a monologue or answering a stream of probing questions on some particular subject. He was incapable of team sports; he was too ungainly to dance; and his disregard of such trifles as clean shirts, haircuts, and tended fingernails led to serious speculations about the date when he was known to have last stepped into a tub. (The rumor that he was suspended from his fraternity for "unbearable sloppiness" has been hotly denied, but descriptions of him in the act of dressing have been rendered in hushed and awestruck tones.)

Tom's reputation for brilliance was founded partly on achievement and partly on promise. During his first two years he had written haphazardly. But in 1918 Professor Frederick Koch arrived on campus bearing with him a reformer's zeal and a passion for folk drama. Declaring stoutly "we write from our hearts," he dismissed decadent "society plays" and set his students to combing the newspapers for stories about fishermen and farmers. Tom, all on fire, wrote *The Return of Buck Gavin, A Tragedy of the Mountain People,* and acted in it himself. Later he turned out a number of earnestly folkish dramas which were published in the college magazine. From then on, for all too many years, playwriting was his passion and his undoing.

Professor Koch had been a pupil at Harvard of the eminent George Pierce Baker of English 47 Workshop fame, and he urged the course on Tom. But Tom needed no urging, his heart was already afire with the "enchanted promise of the golden cities." Ben had long been pressing him to break away, to go north and escape their small town's limitations, and Ben's death had left him utterly alone, with the "great wild pattern of the family" shattered. He must go.

But W. O. Wolfe, weary and ill, shook his head. Tom had had his education; now it was time he earned his living. Writing was foolishness anyhow, the law was what he should aim for. But still

Tom pleaded and argued and so the old man said shortly, "Get the money from your mother then—if you can."

Tom turned his guns on Mrs. Wolfe; writing was his destiny, didn't she understand that? Couldn't she realize there were things one had to do? If she would only advance him a year's tuition he would make her a bargain—she could deduct it from his share of his father's estate when he died. At last she gave in: all right, one year. Mrs. Roberts was delighted; this was what she had always hoped for.

On Koch's recommendation Professor Baker welcomed Tom into his "sacred circle" of twelve students and encouraged him to continue mining his Carolina folklore vein. A tragedy about backwoods people battling their hopeless environment was Tom's first project, and for long he lived in a state of "pure exaltation." Not only was the tide of creativity rising within him but he had found a superperson even more inspiring than Mrs. Roberts.

For a full year George Pierce Baker was "the infinitely wise and strong and gentle spirit who knew all, . . . could solve all problems." Tom wallowed in his adoration, living and breathing the Workshop, and Baker, who relished enthusiasm and individuality, took him to his heart.

The student body was less enchanted. Wolfe's appearance was scruffier than ever, and it seemed that his principle was to wear a garment until it rotted off him and then buy a new one. With no sense of time, he was always drifting into Workshop rehearsals late and talking about himself too much and too long. Harvard could not summon up Chapel Hill's easy-going tolerance, and he reacted to his classmates' disapprobation by ridiculing their "affected" talk of aesthetics. (Later he went through a hyperaesthetic phase himself, frothing on and on about Art and Beauty. And finally, gaining a sense of proportion, he returned to the ridicule—this time actually turning some of it on himself.)

Now however there was no sense of proportion about anything. Driven by a hunger to know everything in the universe, his reading went beyond all reason, so that eventually he claimed to have read twenty thousand books. The Widener Library's million and a half volumes loomed up like a monster to be vanquished, and the thought of the uncountable numbers yet unread drove him nearly mad. He pictured himself tearing the entrails from a book as from a fowl, clocking the pages meanwhile to see how many he could conquer in an hour. But even as he read he would suddenly remember the teeming streets outside and dash out to catch up on that part of life, rushing through the crowds and peering into each passing face.

He made lengthy catalogs of the places he had seen, the people he had known, the women he had slept with, the meals he had eaten. Then while gloating over this opulence he would break off to despair over the greater number not seen, not known, not slept with, not eaten. Long lists of projects scrawled on greasy bits of paper were found among his papers after his death, testifying to his hunger to "devour the earth."

This fever to swallow everything all at once may have been heightened by the frightening discovery one day of blood on his handkerchief after a fit of coughing. He had always been haunted by the TB patients on his mother's front porch and a wave of terror almost engulfed him. Was he going to die soon?

But as no further evidence appeared the fear was forgotten, except for occasional hints to his mother as bids for sympathy. At those times she responded with lectures about nourishing food and no cigars or cigarettes. Liquor she had not yet learned to include in her fears for him.

Wolfe spent two years at Harvard without returning home and Baker invited him back for a third. He had wrung the necessary funds from his mother by continuous appeals variously cajoling, reproachful, adoring, cynical, humble, proud, and despairing. He described the Workshop productions of his plays and sent her a copy of *The Mountain* with the filial note, "All the critics in the world may *say* it's good, but a man's mother will *know*." Eventually she came through with the full three years' fee.

Then in June, 1922, W. O. Wolfe died suddenly, and Tom

went home. Though never irrationally bound up with his father as with his mother, Tom had adored the man's exuberance, his "earth-devouring stride" and great ringing cry of "Merciful God!" This death shocked and bewildered him, anticipated though it had been, and the loss intensified the search for a father of the spirit.

The summer in Asheville was relieved by long hours with Mrs. Roberts, who exclaimed when he read her his plays, "Boy, nothing can stop you!" This was the meat that fed him. But Asheville itself, seen through new and critical eyes, disgusted him. Walking the streets, dropping in at bars and workshops, reading the political news and listening to the town's elders, he saw it as a place in whose slime flourished "the knave, the toady and the hog-rich." Returning to Harvard, he wrote Mrs. Roberts that he had gathered material for a new play.

This *Niggertown* occupied his entire third year. Landing squarely on miscegenation and race riots, with side excursions into politics and business, it called for forty-four actors and ten scenes and ran more than four hours. But Baker, excited by its vitality, scheduled it for Workshop production, only pleading for cuts and a change of title.

Tom obliged with the new title, *Welcome to Our City,* but the cutting consisted of taking out one set of lines and putting in another. Baker went humorously mad. "I've got a student," he wrote a friend, "who's a crazy, wild, six foot five Southern boy. He's written one of the most brilliant plays ever submitted in English 47, and we're trying to put it on in spite of him. He's shy, he stammers, and he upsets the cast. When anything goes wrong he bellows at them." Wryly he implored someone, anyone, to take him out and drop him in the Charles River, adding hopefully, "And tell me if he gurgles much."

"Mama, get down and pray for me," Tom had written before the play's first performance, and apparently Mrs. Wolfe did her best. Though it was considered somewhat too candid by some viewers, Baker stood staunchly behind it. He promised, indeed, that if Tom would *really* cut it he would recommend it to the prestigious Theatre Guild.

Uplifted, Tom wrote his mother, "I am inevitable. The only thing that can stop me now is insanity, disease, or death." In his next letter he went further. "This thing inside me is growing beyond control. I don't know yet what I am capable of doing but, by God, I have genius."

After revising his play but even now failing to shorten it much, he floated down to Asheville to wait for the Theatre Guild's letter of acceptance. But the old family arguments were as irritating as ever: Mable and Fred were resentful of his "living on them," and he was soon ready for a padded cell. To relieve the tensions he got into a drinking bout that ended him in jail, and Mrs. Wolfe, already a martyr to her husband and Frank, received this new development with despair. In shame he retreated to New York.

After three months the Guild rejected the play. But stubbornly he persisted in passing it around, and in time it fell into a pair of hands that were to mold his entire future life. Meanwhile he leaned heavily on Baker.

Ever dependent on his mother, he persuaded Baker to write to her extolling his talents and his worthiness of generous support, which Baker did more than once. But when he rebelled at Baker's criticism of his play and the professor replied briskly that not squealing at criticism was the mark of a first-rate artist, he began to think he saw clay feet below the idol's robe. And in time he took a very disenchanted view. "In *Of Time and the River* he satirized the Workshop bitterly, saying of Baker that "the man was half sawdust. . .lacking in warmth, in greatness and humanity. . . unable to see the genuine quality in a man." Baker had had his day.

By now the family's openly expressed opinion that it was time he earned his own living had sunk in. His record at Chapel Hill and Harvard easily obtained him a post teaching English at New York University, and he chose its Washington Square branch for its proximity to Broadway's theaters.

But there was a second reason for his choice. "I teach! I teach! Jews! Jews!" he wrote a friend, admitting to a strong prejudice held over from his childhood which made him wish to study this strange breed at close quarters.

Now for the first time on his own, Wolfe suddenly developed a capacity for work that was the marvel of all who knew him. Though detesting his job, which included laboriously correcting 104 papers a week, he still gave it his most conscientious attention, leaving himself scant time for his own writing. For six years, off and on, he slaved in this education-mart. But the first two were the hardest, for then all the creative forces surging up within him had no outlet, and he found release only in cursing, brooding, roaming the streets, and drinking.

Since *Welcome to Our City* had been wandering up and down Broadway without settling down anywhere, he decided to make a break for Europe on the strength of his savings, some funds from his mother, whom he had won firmly to his cause, and the university's promise of a post when he returned.

Mrs. Roberts was as ardently behind him as his mother. "Tom, you are a star, and you must make your words shine like stars," she wrote, exhorting him to *live*, to drain the cup of experience to the dregs. "But," she added hastily, *"to* the dregs. No more!" Too many geniuses, she warned, had swilled the cup dregs and all, ruining their lives and tainting their talents. She had seen Tom too often turning in his frustration to "magic, proud liquor," and she watched him, praying but still hopeful.

He sailed in October, 1924. In his suitcase was a half-finished play and in his mind the determination to pack the months ahead as full as a Strasbourg goose. In London he roamed the queer, crooked old streets looking, talking to people, and stuffing the essence of them into his notebooks. But in Paris, lacking any knowledge of French, he could only roam alone and watch the passing faces.

His loneliness there was relieved by the appearance of a Harvard acquaintance with two girl friends. In the ensuing celebrations the relationships of the four became dramatically scrambled, and for a month they did Paris in accepted American tourist style. When January came he wrote his mother frantically begging for means to stay longer, and while awaiting her generosity he sought sustenance elsewhere.

For some years Wolfe had been light-heartedly casual in his relationships with women, his Gargantuan appetite for sensation leading him to gulp sex on the same scale as he gulped food. (A sample breakfast: a dozen eggs, two quarts of milk, an entire loaf of bread.) He had been "in love" any number of times, without any pretense of seriousness; that was his normal condition.

Also normal to him was his dependency on older women, thus far his mother and Mrs. Roberts. Now he found it natural to be taken care of by two other older women. The first was an American widow who lent him her apartment when he was stranded, the second an erratic countess who fascinated him by drinking horses' blood for her anemia.

He escaped from both of these unscathed. But then, sailing home in August, he met a beautiful, extravagantly talented Jewess eighteen years his senior. They made love on deck the night before they landed and said good-bye next day, supposing it was forever. Instead, it was the start of one of the most famous love affairs of the era.

Aline Bernstein was the daughter of a wild, unpredictable Jewish actor, Joseph Frankau, and his New England wife, her mixed background giving her a soft feminity and an appreciation for beauty combined with almost masculine forthrightness and common sense. Following childhood in a colorful, disordered, and casually amoral home, she was orphaned and then married in her teens, more for security than for love, to a successful young broker, Theodore Bernstein. After the birth of a boy and a girl she studied painting, then applied design, and in 1915, when the famous Neighborhood Playhouse was founded, she became its stage designer. Very quickly her vaulting creativeness backed up by hard work made her pre-eminent in her field. And her laughter, her warmth, her capacity for enjoyment won her almost universal affection.

She had come to some sort of understanding with her husband. He loved her devotedly, they were the most congenial of companions, but he was essentially humdrum, preferring bridge to the art world in which she lived, and without destroying the outward form of their home she had had several love affairs by the time she met Wolfe.

On shipboard that night in August, 1925, she was knocked almost off her feet by Wolfe's explosion of emotion right after their introduction. In a book written years afterward she described the scene: "This young giant seized her by the arms, shaking her, shouting at her, 'Where did you get your face, raised in that dung-heap the theater among evil and rotten people?. . .Answer me, where did you get your eyes of love, your mouth of love, your flower face, did your mother cheat and lie with an angel? Answer me!' "

Overwhelmed by his passion, her head swam, but finally she pulled herself out of his arms and found breath to shout back, " 'You madman, you like the theater yourself, you want to be a part of it; you wrote a play, I've read it.' " Rushing on, she told him that at that moment his play was reposing in her suitcase. She had thought it remarkable and had taken it to England to try to get it produced. She still hoped to get it put on at the Neighborhood.

He was not to be put off. " 'I don't want your theater. . .don't get me mixed up with such people, that is not what I want. I can make my own way without them. I want you, my beauty, I want to know your skin and your lovely rich clothing, do you change your underwear every day? And the sheets on your bed. How much do your nightgowns cost? Clean washed skin, honey skin washed clean every day and wrapped in soft silk, but what do you know, you can know nothing of a life or a mind like mine.' "

Exhausted, she had dragged herself away from him that night, and they had parted on the dock next day. He had gone south to see his mother, but quickly, on returning, he had written her a stiff, formal note. Eagerly she answered, telling him to meet her at the Playhouse, where she took him backstage, introduced him to the actors, showed him her drawings and costumes. They were uncomfortable and tremulous, watching each other sideways, unsure and yet already sure. Afterward she said that her falling in love had been like a Japanese maiden's ritual leap into a volcano—she knew it would kill her but she could not stop herself.

This love affair was like a bridge, its two ends rooted in widely disparate countries but coming together and making one strong and indivisible whole. On his side it began as a light, exultant thing, his frustrated ego buoyed up by the frank admiration of this elegant and distinguished woman. For her, it was her fascination with his monumental genius housed in a lonely boy, helpless and baffled by simple problems like eating regularly or organizing the day's work. In her woman's way she was as highly electrified as he, and their two currents met and fired, welding them together so powerfully that any separation meant destruction of one or the other.

Imperceptibly Wolfe's light-hearted amour turned into an all-consuming passion. But more than finding a lover, he had found a new superperson, another image of strength and wisdom to cling to. In Aline's warmth and security he could wrap himself away from the cold, on her admiration set himself up higher. And as his loyalty shifted toward this woman it turned away from that other down in Asheville. His mother's newly perceived "materialism" began to grate on his sensibilities, and in reciting to Aline's sympathetic ears the other's lack of appreciation, the jealousies and animosities he had endured at home, he dramatized them into such proportions he was soon a seething mass of resentments.

Now persuaded that he had been brutally victimized by his mother, he complained not only to Aline but to Mrs. Roberts that he had been "forced into work for which I had no affection. . . . Money has been held over me like a bludgeon. Recently what little help I have secured from home. . .has been withdrawn."

To his mother herself he wrote, "There are few heroic lives; about the only one I know a great deal about is my own. . . .Year after year, in the face of hostility, criticism, misunderstanding and stupidity, I have been steadfast in my devotion to the high, passionate, and beautiful things of this world."

His tales of youthful struggles and trials had to Aline an epic quality of grandeur. "Write them down, write all this down," she cried, and only too eagerly he poured it all out onto paper, scene after random scene as they came to him.

After a few months of discreet concealment they took a skylight loft in Greenwich Village together where he could live and she could come to work on her designs. It had no bathroom (he soaked himself periodically at his friends' apartments or at the Harvard Club) and no cooking facilities other than hot plates. But here, an artist of *haute cuisine,* she prepared him exquisite meals and for a few hours each day they found a heaven of laughter and love and trust.

Meanwhile she pursued her domestic life unbroken. At her evening parties he appeared, brushed and polished, as "one of Aline's protégés" and was introduced to the cream of the theatrical and publishing sets. These encounters were not always beneficial, however, for in this conspicuously successful company he was either overpolite or rude and defensive, according to how much gin he had braced himself with beforehand. And his plays, no matter how often she showed them around, did not, would not, land.

At last Aline began gently suggesting that perhaps his particular genius was not suited to the tightly constricted form of the drama. His canvases were too wide, his vision too comprehensive; take the story of his youth, now—he had almost written a novel as he talked it to her, she *saw* these people, they breathed and walked. If he wanted to write a novel she would stake him to a year abroad where he could write in a congenial atmosphere. And she would go along, there was some business she could see to in London.

So they had a summer in England. And there was a certain day —she described it afterward as the happiest day óf her life. Two Theatre Guild friends called for them in a rented Rolls-Royce and invited them for a long ride. When they drove up they looked at her face in amazement; she looked, they said, as though she had swallowed a fifty-watt lamp and it was shining right out of her.

It was a high blue English morning. Wolfe behaved charmingly and they all laughed and talked. She thought he had enjoyed himself as much as she had. But after they left she found him looking sad. " 'You love those people more than you love me. You want to leave me and go back to your work, to your fine successful friends! Dearest!' And he held her close. 'Don't leave me, ever, stay with me, dearest, and love me forever.' She told him that never, so long as there was life in her body, would she stop loving him. And it was the truth."

Had she known it, this touching, endearing jealousy of her two friends was in reality a warning glimpse of the "half-monster" within him. In the fall she sailed for home, leaving him to work on his novel, and very soon he began entertaining nightmares of jealousy. Unable to forget that she had had lovers before him, he was haunted by the slimy remark of an acquaintance, "She *likes* young men—I'm sorry, but that's the way it is."

His uncontrolled imagination drove him to fantastic accusations. She cared nothing for him. Leaving him alone with his enforced chastity, she had rushed home on a "bawdy mission" to be with another man.

Often he reverted to his ancient prejudice, taunting her with snarls of "Grey-haired Jew!" In milder moments she was "my Jew." And in his diary he mulled over the question of "what to do about the Jew." Between times he apologized for his "abominable ravings," writing her that "love made me mad and brought me down to the level of the beasts." In extenuation he explained that the throes of writing set up within him such a conflict of forces that he seemed to be struggling with the whole wide world, lashing out not only at people he distrusted but those he loved best.

Often his letters left her crushed and bewildered; but when he arrived home in January, 1927, she met him as loving as ever, and they fell into each other's arms ecstatically. She would have paid his rent until he got settled—not, she explained, out of her husband's money but out of her own—but this time he maintained his independence. New York University was glad to take him back on a shortened schedule, and he taught there intermittently while working on the novel he had started in England.

This book had had its inception on a sunny day in the country, and later, remembering its every moment, she wrote of it with love. They had been lounging on a grassy hillside. Holding a large blankbook opened on his lap, he had looked at her with a solemn, prophetic gaze. He was, he told her, destined to be a great writer. He would write and write about her, and long after she was dead she would be famous because she was entombed in his work. A woman less spellbound might have resented the egotism. But Aline Bernstein had grown up among creative people, and realistically she recognized that genius must be judged not by how it behaves but by what it produces.

That day on the hillside was the first of nearly two years of days spent on his book. Month after month he pushed himself to exhaustion, writing his own life story. Seized, possessed by his vision, he Thomas Wolfe was as it were a microcosm containing all experience, all truth, and in dealing with his life he dealt with the universe. Every remembered detail of it, every quarrel and bitterness as well as the lovely moments of youth, had to go in to make the pattern complete.

This compulsion to "pour it out, boil it out, flood it out" left him no peace. Badgered by a million memories that came most clearly in the midnight silence, he wrote until dawn; then after a few hours of fretful sleep he rose and wrote again, flogging himself on with fifteen or twenty cups of foul coffee. Often he forgot to eat at all until Aline came bounding up the stairs, eyes shining and arms full of groceries, to prepare his one enormous meal of the day.

In March, 1928, this sprawling manuscript three times as long as the average novel was finished, and Aline began trying among her friends to get it published. In his ignorance he had expected it to be snapped up at once, but its length and incohesiveness frightened off editors who were otherwise impressed. At last in disgust he turned it over to an agent and made off alone for Europe sick at heart.

Tragically, this trip was half to escape Aline. The long strain of writing and then the disappointing result had brought him near a breakdown. He had been carrying on his classes only by benefit of his "magic, proud liquor" and, unable to vent his frustration on his students, had turned it on Aline. Both mistress and mother, she had made the mistake of holding him too close, and their duels of words, which had been for laughs at first, now drew blood. There were curses and cries and then floods of tears. Knowing her own faithfulness, she burned with indignation when he phoned her house at three in the morning to check on her whereabouts. And knowing the generosity of her love, she plied him with vast, magniloquent reproaches which he could not help but resent.

The moment he escaped to Europe, however, he forgot that she interfered with his work and that he wanted freedom from her to live and grow and change. He wrote her that gazing at the skeleton of a Bronze Age chieftain's wife had made him think of his love for her, a love so enduring that it would "hover above our bones when the great towers of America are forgotten." And when, after a brawl in a Munich beer hall, he lay in a hospital with scalp wounds and a broken nose, his thoughts crept back to her like a sick child's. But he was coming back to her now, and they would forge some kind of life together again.

But her place in the sun had slipped by. Now, as the rays moved past her, another figure was emerging to take the light—a new image of strength and wisdom for him to cling to.

No one suspected what was lying ahead, least of all Wolfe. All he knew was that a Mr. Maxwell Perkins, editor of Scribner's publishing house, had written him in Europe that he had read his manuscript and would be glad if he would telephone when he returned. Wolfe landed in New York on New Year's Eve and on January 2, 1929, he phoned. Mr. Perkins invited him to come right over.

The man awaiting Wolfe in the managing editor's office was a slim erect patrician with handsome features and keen blue eyes. If each human being can be said to wear an aura, Maxwell Perkins' aura was integrity. To any profession he would have brought honesty and decency; to this one he brought as well patience, judgment, and a special empathy with the writing mind. His private radar system alerted him to a new author's capabilities; through it he sensed the man's inner necessities and the reasons for his sometimes incomprehensible behavior. And operating on the premise that a publisher's first duty was to respect and foster talent no matter in what rocky soil it might be growing, he had become the most famous and respected editor in America.

Grounded through many generations in his country's history, Perkins had long dreamed of finding a book that would speak for America as Tolstoi's *War and Peace* had spoken for Russia. He had already induced his old and conservative firm to break new ground with Scott Fitzgerald and Ernest Hemingway, and now great was his joy over the intensely American Thomas Wolfe.

At the time of their meeting Perkins was forty-four, tall and grave, his only peculiarity a gray fedora hat which he seemed never to take off. (Colleagues thought that, being a trifle deaf, and shunning a hearing aid, he used the brim as a kind of sounding board.) Glancing up as this giant entered, he noticed that the giant's hands were trembling, and he invited him in gently, waiting for the other's heart to slow down.

Finally he began speaking about a certain scene in the manuscript; it would make a perfect story for *Scribner's* magazine. Wolfe's heart rose and sank simultaneously; it would be wonderful to sell a story to a magazine, but tragic if that was all the editor was interested in. However, Perkins went on to speak admiringly of the entire manuscript, referring to a thick batch of notes in his hand. When Wolfe realized that this great editor had actually analyzed every page of his manuscript he was so touched he nearly wept. And by the end of the interview, when he saw that, subject to cutting and revision, it was virtually accepted, he rushed out onto Fifth Avenue with his head reeling.

Dazedly he started up the avenue. Hours later he came to 110th Street, having walked from 48th without knowing how he had got there. And for a week the trance persisted, till on January 9 he wrote in his diary; "On this day I got letter from Scribner's confirming their acceptance of my book." Under the entry he wrote two names, "Aline Bernstein" and "Thomas Wolfe."

For Aline was still a part of his life. To one of the Scribner's editors he described her as "the great and beautiful friend who has stood by me through all the torture, struggle, and madness of my nature for over three years." But the break had been made; from day to day he oscillated, now kind, now cruel, but often and oftener savagely irritated, and she was reduced, this proud handsome woman, to cringing apologies and excuses. Dutifully he dedicated the book to her, but the internal pressure to be free became ever more insistent.

For six months Wolfe cut, revised, reorganized, meanwhile working part-time at the university. Perkins early saw that alone he would never reduce the book to publishable size and gently suggested helping him after hours. So for two months the men slaved nightly with blue pencils, deleting finally 100,000 words. Wolfe's heart bled over every syllable, but Perkins was his new hero and this was the hero's wish. As a result, in October, 1929, *Look Homeward, Angel* was safely published.

The first review was a dash of cold water. Sardonically titled "Ah, Life, Life!" it conceded Wolfe's strength and promise and emotion, but the overall tone was ridicule: "Musings over destiny, fate, love, ah me! ah me!" But he had only twenty-four hours of agony, for next day the front-ranking Sunday New York *Times* gave it a solid rave, a genuine "selling review"; next week came another in the *Herald Tribune,* and the rest of the country followed suit, comparing him with Melville, Whitman,

Dostoevski, Joyce. The book was off at a gallop.

Wolfe likewise was off running. His high-keyed emotionalism roused a high-keyed response in many readers, notably the young,who found there an expression for their own unbridled turmoil. He was besieged on all sides; invitations came from women, amorous and otherwise; offers came for lectures, and requests came for autographs. For seven months he did nothing but deal with the blissful distractions of his fame.

The month before publication Wolfe had gone home to Asheville. Knowing what was in the book, he had planned in some trepidation to warn his family, but he never got up the courage. Just before he left he seized his sister's arm nervously. "Mabel," he whispered, "when I come again I may have to come incognito or wearing false whiskers," and she was vaguely disquieted. He must have been writing about sex or the Negro problem or something.

The commotion in Asheville when the book finally did appear is still remembered there. "Eugene Gant" and his relatives and friends were in it, all too plainly recognizable, some of their names not even changed. Worse, in drawing their portraits he had abstracted their salient characteristics and emphasized them like a newspaper cartoon, some far from flattering. His use of local scandals, whispered before but never publicized, hit some very tender spots, and his mail contained curses, obscenities, and threats.

His granite mother dealt with all condolences over her portrait by curtly refusing to see any resemblance between herself and "Eliza Gant." The rest of the family likewise denied any injury. And indeed, the glare of publicity had a not unpleasant afterglow as the details faded out and only the distinction of being famous remained.

Not so the rest of Asheville. Those other people received no such reflected glory, and so icy was the town's hate that for seven years Wolfe dared not show his face in town.

Perhaps most hurt was Mrs. Roberts, "the mother of his spirit." A copy tenderly inscribed had been sent to her, but when she read it she found her husband so unkindly distorted that she wrote a bitter protest ending "You have crucified your family and devastated mine." It was many years before this breach was healed.

Wolfe had feared some such reaction, and he and Perkins had discussed its possibility. Later Perkins wrote in his defense, "The writings of every great novelist are in some considerable degree autobiographical...*David Copperfield, Pendennis, War and Peace,* etc., are very close indeed to autobiography, but everything in them is different from what it really was, has been transmuted in passing through the imagination of the writer. It is this way with Thomas Wolfe. None of the people are literally as he presents them, nor are any of the happenings. They are the basis out of which he creates a world."

As an editor Perkins sincerely believed it was the novelist's prerogative to use what he knew, and that the danger of offending individuals paled beside the writer's greater responsibility to stay with his vision. Later his sincerity was to be put to a cruel test, and then it shone as hard and clear as a diamond.

With the *Angel* safely put into orbit Perkins began gently nudging Wolfe toward another book. Tom had started one but lost interest and now was floundering wastefully, citing his teaching chores as an obstacle to work. Perkins thereupon removed the obstacle by funding him until royalties started flowing. A Guggenheim Fellowship for work and study abroad was also arranged, and so now there was nothing to interfere with another long spell in Europe. Nothing except Aline.

She received the news of the project tragically, and there were dreadful scenes. He swore he still loved her but that he must have freedom to write, and she swore that if he loved her he would stay in New York and let her support him. He told his troubles to Perkins at tremendous length; Perkins had never met Mrs. Bernstein, but from Wolfe's accounts he could see little future for the affair and said so. So then Wolfe told Aline that Perkins had advised him to leave her.

So murderous were their fights and so pitiable her sufferings that some of her friends intervened, even saying that for her sake the whole thing should be ended. This he seized on eagerly, from then on persuaded that he was leaving her at the behest of her friends. He sailed in May, 1930, for ten months of wandering, trying to forget the woman suffering at home but never quite able to.

The new novel went haltingly; he was having "second book trouble," for now he was a personage to be watched, a comer whom even Sinclair Lewis had mentioned in his Nobel Prize speech. Self-consciously he felt the eyes of the critics study'ing him—did he have another book in him? More important, would it surpass the first? The weight of the world seemed to be lying on his shoulders. And the worst of it was that he *had* no book in him, no concrete plan, no one thing he had to say. So for a while he simply loafed about Paris, wasting his time in drinking unhappily and brooding.

Gradually the "softness" of Paris began to irritate him. Then, from irritation, he went to dislike and hate. Hating Paris, he began to think of America and became so homesick that he had to sit down and write about it, all the things he remembered—corn stalks in rows, an iron railing along Atlantic City's boardwalk, the sound of an American train crossing a bridge. Gradually, from a dead stop, the wheels of his mind had begun turning and soon he found himself racing through acres of memories, putting down anything and everything that occurred to him, without form or continuity filling huge ledgers that piled up in his bedroom. He had, he said, discovered America, and from the moment of that discovery the line and purpose of his life was shaped.

There were, of course, mundane distractions. At Perkins' suggestion he looked up Scott Fitzgerald, who was stuck in the middle of a novel and, with a mentally ill wife, badly needed cheering up. They saw Paris night life together and Wolfe was amazed to find that Fitzgerald could outdrink him. He also spent a bibulous week with Sinclair Lewis, whose tragic disintegration he later recorded in *You Can't Go Home Again.* And in November he learned that the Great Depression had caught up with Ashe-

ville and that his mother, with her ambitious real estate investments, was wiped out. Immediately he wired Perkins to send $500
to Asheville out of his earnings. One could squabble with his family
when things were rosy but when trouble came you all stuck together.

After ten months he sailed home. With him came a mountain
of ledgers containing random scenes, one-paragraph impressions,
long meditations—somewhere between 200,000 and 400,000
words—and with iron determination he dodged the distractions of
New York literary life and holed up in a Brooklyn basement.

The Brooklyn hideout was of course chiefly a refuge from
Aline. On sailing the year before he had written her two affectionate notes and, guilt-laden over his heavy indebtedness, had written a will dividing everything between herself and his mother.
But, determined on a final split, he ignored her pleading letters for
the rest of the year. Looking for reasons to be angry with her, he
persuaded himself that she had set Fitzgerald and others in Paris
to spying on him. And so when she cabled wildly reproaching him
for his silence and threatening to kill herself he was angry and
frightened but he made no reply. When he returned he swore his
friends to secrecy.

The papers, however, smoked him out. When she read them
she tried over and over to see him, and then in a final wave of
despair swallowed a massive dose of sleeping pills. For three days
she appeared to be dying; then, dragged violently back from that
death, she succumbed to pneumonia and again courted oblivion.
But at last the doctors prevailed on her to let them help her and
she returned to the world.

In her book she described what followed. She saw herself
walking through Central Park and sitting down in a wisteria arbor.
Suddenly the whole sky was filled with a light like dawn and in the
calm and silence she found that she who had been broken in
pieces was miraculously whole. Furthermore, she knew herself
with a new certainty—knew herself free and independent. "Her
life was her own, to do with as she wanted. . . .She was her very

own, herself. She had learned that through the desolation that had come to her. . . .For a supreme moment in the rustic arbor, her ego had left her body and mingled with the great unknown."

This was some advance. But more than flashes of such peace was not her portion yet, though it did come in time. Tom guiltily visited her in the hospital once or twice, but anger and resentment had petered out into simple boredom and he avoided her for years.

As Aline faded from his life Perkins loomed ever larger and closer, friend, companion, adviser, father, the superior being to whom he could attach himself. Conversely, Perkins, who had five daughters but no son, accepted the father role gladly, giving himself not only as editor, shield, conscience and guide but, finally, as victim.

Daily he served, guarding and guiding every department of Wolfe's muddled life. As he was leaving his office Wolfe would turn up with some story or problem and go on talking for hours, perhaps all evening, till calm had settled again. And as the "nine-headed monster" of a manuscript grew, Wolfe needed him more than ever. Like one hypnotized he went on writing without form or direction, long catalogs of things and places and people remembered, all getting nowhere, telling no coherent story. By now there was material for ten shapeless books but no clearly defined single book.

This compulsive boiling out, pouring out, went on for four incredible years before Perkins in desperation took a hand. Wolfe, stung by the taunts about his autobiographical fixation, had been writing all around the edge of his story without settling on a central character, and Perkins, reading scraps of it here and there, realized he must pull it together.

One day he said, "Look here, Tom, face it—everything you have written is really about Eugene Gant. Why not use it just that way—take up Eugene's story where *Look Homeward, Angel* left it off. Then everything will fall into place."

As simply as turning a key he had unlocked Tom's mind, and with a fresh burst of energy Wolfe took the inchoate mass and began giving it shape. Now the writing was not a compulsive, aimless exercise but a purposeful sweep forward, and he worked in a state of delirium crossed with periods of Olympian calm.

Finances were now very tight. *Scribner's* magazine had bought several excerpts from the novel but the lucrative short story field defied his excessive wordiness, and he was living chiefly on the advance on the new manuscript. But still the end seemed no nearer than ever, for he had written almost a million words and was adding fifty thousand a month in a sort of hypnotic trance. His physical condition besides worried Perkins; unable to sleep before dawn and tortured by nightmares then, he relied on alcohol to keep him going, and at last Perkins began to fear for his very sanity.

At last, in December, 1933, Perkins decided on an unprecedented move. Calling Wolfe to his home, he said in a voice he strove to make casual, "Listen: your book is finished. I have read disconnected bits and I know it is finished. I want you to go home and put the pages in order and then bring it to me to read straight through."

Wolfe howled in outrage; the book needed six months more work. Then suddenly he relaxed. Like a drowning man feeling solid earth under his feet he threw up his arms in wild joy. He would do as he was told. The torture was over, and Perkins was his savior. Only later did the resentment set in.

Began now a solid year of nightly meetings. The manuscript, taking up from *Look Homeward, Angel,* covered Eugene Gant's life from his departure for Harvard up to and including his affair with Esther Jack. As a first step in preparing it for publication Perkins divided it in two, the first half ending with the meeting of Eugene and Esther, and the second covering the love story itself.

Cutting even this first half would be a mammoth job—one chapter alone, a night's train ride across Virginia, ran over 100,000 words, and a single conversation equaled two hundred printed pages. And even so it lacked some connective scenes that he still had to write. Night after night, from dinner till midnight, they argued. Perkins would get out five thousand words and next day Wolfe would appear with seven thousand more. He admitted that Perkins was right in all things, nevertheless the manuscript, his child, had been "taken away from him" and he began to brood.

As the announced publication date drew near his resentment turned into mulishness. Perkins grew desperate, and at last he finished the cutting and sent the manuscript to the printer while Wolfe was out of town.

The upshot was an explosion, still the angry wail about six months more work. And when the galley proofs came back for correction he was still mulish. Inevitably the proofs contained many errors, for his writing was an illegible scrawl and he had not bothered to correct the typist's errors, so once again Perkins and another editor struggled to correct them.

But when the pages came through in their next-to-final state Wolfe found a host of imperfections. Charging through with a reckless pencil, he slashed and added and rewrote. But now alterations were a costly operation, and the bill was a staggering $1,180.60. According to standard practice it was charged to him, and his indignation sizzled in the back of his mind for a year.

Finally in January, 1935, the presses were locked and run and the finished book began to appear. "The battle seems nearly over," Perkins wrote a colleague in weary triumph, "and I am still alive."

During this year-long battle Wolfe had vacillated between rage and adoring gratitude. But when the book was finally done, gratitude predominated, and he wrote a blow-by-blow account of its composition with special emphasis on Perkins' part. But Perkins, sensing the unwisdom of this revelation, persuaded him to reduce his fulsome "dedication" to eight lines. Later, however, Wolfe expanded it into a speech and then into a slim book, *The Story of a Novel.* Unfortunately, written as it was in a glow of love and gratitude, it was to have exactly the opposite effect from what either could have desired.

Of Time and the River was due out in March, 1935. Wolfe, remembering the scandal induced by *Look Homeward, Angel,* decided this time on a strategic retreat. So, leaving a huge case containing the second half of his manuscript in Perkins' home, he sailed in a flurry of suitcases, bags of fruit, loose shoes, notebooks, and old laundry.

He awaited the publication in Paris in an alcoholic depression. Then when his book received a shower of applause and flowered into a best seller he began to worry lest best-sellerdom connoted mediocrity.

It would seem that among this man's array of Gargantuan moods depression was a basic one, for despite all the good news about it he kept brooding over the lost six months' work and on the slurs of a few New York critics. Among these were the charges that he had no sense of humor, that his characters were all seven feet tall with megaphone voices, that his style was, at its best, wondrous and Elizabethan, and at its worst hyperthyroid and afflicted with elephantiasis.

Suffering, he wrote Perkins complaining of America's treatment of its creative artists: "In Christ's sake, Max, what is wrong with us in America? . . .Why do our best writers, poets, men of talent turn into drunkards, dipsomaniacs, charlatans, cocktail-cliquers, creators of pop-eye horrors, pederasts, macabre distortions, etc.?" There was in America, he went on, a sterile and perverse lust for death that wished to destroy the very people who had something of value to give. One day it would set up these young men, proud of spirit and athirst for glory, praise them to the skies, and the next turn on them with cynical scorn, distrusting their talent and destroying their power.

His complaint was hardly justified in his own case, for at that very moment he was on the brink of his greatest acclaim. His return to America was a return to glory. Perkins met him at the dock saying that never had he seen such a quantity of fan mail nor such a weight of newspaper clippings. Sales were skyrocketing and there would be abundant riches for all.

Their celebration started at lunch and went on for a tour of Wolfe's favorite hangouts. At one point they passed the attic where he had written *Look Homeward, Angel,* and in a prankish mood the two, hulking giant and dignified New Englander, climbed the fire escape and crawled in for a look at the young eagle's nest.

The evening ended on a Brooklyn hotel roof overlooking New York Harbor. The city, harsh, defiant, unconquerable, had been conquered and reduced to submission, and looking down on it, Wolfe's spirit hit the stars. "It was a moment," he wrote, "when the whole wine of life seemed to have been distilled and poured into his veins. . .when he possessed the whole of life, its power, beauty, pity, tenderness, and love, and all its overwhelming poetry —when all of it was his." Standing by the dauntless friend who had made it possible, he was swept by a wave of love, a moment unforgettable to which he would return when all else was slipping away.

Now for the first time there was plenty of money. Having learned the knack of condensation, he was even being bought by magazines. And revolting against dark side streets without a view, he moved into a river-view apartment on the East Side, whose furniture included a living-room cot for his mother. That Christmas he gave a tremendous party and in an expansive gesture he reached up and scrawled on the ceiling, "Merry Christmas to all my friends and love from Tom," a jolly message that beamed down on him for the two years of his tenure.

Women pursued him in droves, sadly enough Aline still among them. Even after five years she had not accepted her fate and the year before had had an actual breakdown and spent time in a sanitarium. Now, reading of his triumphant return, she sought him out at his favorite restaurant and confronted him as he sat drinking with Perkins. Anxious to avoid a public scene, they hurried her around the corner to Scribner's offices. Wolfe, who had never repaid her loans, now took Perkins into another room to make an arrangement to do so, and when they returned she was just putting a vial of pills to her mouth.

Whether this was a forlorn gesture or the real thing no one

knows. She had actually swallowed no pills and came to no harm. But all she gained was a momentary reconciliation based on grudging pity, and in a few months, gradually accepting the finality of Wolfe's boredom, she was able to turn back to her work and find surcease there.

The next year saw him traveling all over Europe, and during a trip to Germany he saw Nazism raw and was horrified at its treatment of the Jews. In a story, "I Have a Thing to Tell You," he scolded the German people roundly and belatedly included himself among the guilty. He did not send Aline a copy but reading it in the magazine may have slightly salved some of her wounds.

During this year he achieved, besides short stories and some lectures, plans for a series of six books covering the last 150 years, but before undertaking this monstrous task he faced a decision about the rest of the manuscript in Perkins' basement. Now he found he had lost interest in it, and the editor was not anxious to arouse it for it was the part containing the affair with Aline. Knowing that such a manuscript existed she had threatened to do "anything in her power" to block its publication and he was glad to escape that public brawl.

Wolfe's decision lifted Perkins off one hook handily. But it impaled him on another hook even sharper. For said Wolfe, "I think I'll write a book about what happens to a fellow who writes a book."

Perkins had always subconsciously known this was coming. With a sigh of resignation he remained true to his editorial standards and told Wolfe to go ahead. To a friend later he wrote, "God knows what the result will be, but I suspect it will be the end of me. A worse struggle than *Of Time and the River* unless he changes publishers first."

Unless he changed publishers first! For years this would have been the wildest jest, a totally unthinkable thought. But a change of mood was evident in Wolfe. After his great success with *Of Time and the River* his letters had carried a different tone, a shade less subservient, a shade more commanding. And there were other signs—a misunderstanding about royalties, though when Perkins explained his position Wolfe subsided penitently; a squabble with Wolfe's former agent over a commission during which he accused the editor of siding with the sick woman against himself; and the old one about the printer's bill for corrections in *Of Time and the River.*

But none of these differences would have arisen without one common basis—Wolfe's growing rebellion. Like the five-year-old who clings to his father's hand for safety and then, with the danger past, shakes off the hand, he was finding it imperative to assert his independence.

The feeling was brought to a head by a review of *The Story of a Novel.* Bernard de Voto had been no admirer even before this; in reviewing *Look Homeward, Angel* he had referred unflatteringly to "meaningless jabber, claptrap, belches, grunts and Tarzanlike screams." Now he zeroed in on the point that had worried Perkins, the clear evidence that "one indispensable part of the artist has existed not in Mr. Wolfe but in Maxwell Perkins. Such organizational faculty and such critical intelligence as have been applied to the book have come not from inside the artist, not from the artist's feeling for form and esthetic integrity, but from the office of Charles Scribner's Sons."

At first Wolfe took the blow well. He admitted that on first reading the article had made him angry but then he had recognized that when a thing hurt that was a sign there was truth in it. Also that "if a thing has something good in it, it is indestructible and will be saved. . .and if a thing has no good in it it cannot be saved."

But this philosophical level could not be maintained and he slipped back into resentment, obsessed with the necessity of going it alone to prove that he could. Since Perkins' office had been his second home, used as post office, bank, and sometime bedroom, his first move now was to open a bank account of his own and order his mail sent to his apartment.

This disengagement was hastened by his new manuscript, the

story of the fellow who wrote a book. When his new agent Elizabeth Nowell read its opening chapters her hair rose and in alarm
she showed it to Perkins. During the thousands of hours he had
spent with Wolfe, Perkins had made the mistake of talking freely
about his firm and its personnel, and now his hair rose too. But he
told her, "I have always said an editor's first duty was to his author,
and that his only criterion should be the artistry of the manuscript.
So I shall not try to suppress Tom's book. Scribner's will publish it.
And then I shall resign."

But there were no resignations yet, no open break, only more
sparring over minor grievances. From a small-town reactionary
Wolfe had turned into a talkative radical; Perkins feared that the
injection of politics into his work would turn him into a mere
pamphleteer and so gently discouraged it. But Wolfe saw this as
an effort to block his creativity.

At another time, when two libel suits were brought against
him, he felt Perkins had failed to protect him sufficiently. He had
looked to his editor as one capable of all miracles and when he was
forced to pay minor damages he felt personally betrayed.

During the course of this estrangement he wrote Perkins several letters severing the relationship, one of them twenty-three
typed pages long, only to write others later retracting them. But
at the same time the personal affection held. Wolfe all but lived at
the Perkins' home and though Max grew weary of Tom's com-
plaints against his firm he never wearied of the man, hoping that
he would "come around in time."

In the spring of 1937 Wolfe was notified that his mother was
being forced into bankruptcy by old creditors, and while detesting
the Old Kentucky Home on his own account he resolved that she
should not lose it. So after seven years he went home to face
Asheville's wrath.

But to his surprise he received a cordial welcome. No one
hated him now, the only unfriendly citizens being those he had
left out of his book. He had happy reconciliations with his relatives
and Mrs. Roberts and impulsively decided to take a summer cabin

in the woods nearby where he could "set a spell and think things over."

Think he did; but the summer did not work out well. Like a tourist attraction he was stared at and spied upon. Moreover his family at close range had the same disturbing effect as before. High-strung and garrulous, they chivvied him and distracted him from his work. His mother and Mabel fought jealously over him; Frank, home ill after a life of drinking, disgusted him. He still loved and admired his brittle, dauntless mother but to Fred he wrote of his disappointment. The family reunion was so different from what he had hoped. "I've just found out," he declared, "a man must stand alone."

Having completed a section of his manuscript while sequestered in the woods, he felt the need of an outside opinion. Still trusting Perkins as no one else, he was just steeling himself to forget pride and ask for it when a new attack from De Voto appeared. This was the decisive straw. After fortifying himself with several stiff drinks he picked up the phone and began calling New York publishers. Five times a slightly blurred voice said over long distance, "My name is Wolfe. Would you be interested in publishing me?" Five times he received vague, noncommittal answers from men who suspected a practical joke.

But one of them was intrigued enough to call up Scribner's and report the conversation. Thus Perkins learned that the man whose career had been for eight years the foremost interest of his life had finally broken with him. Patience has its limits and that day he voiced aloud his indignation and grief.

When it got around that Tom Wolfe had actually "done it" other publishers began wooing him, eagerly outbidding each other with flattering offers. On the last day of 1937 he signed with Harpers a contract that was to last the rest of his life. As he scrawled his signature he solemnly quoted Martin Luther's words on the occasion of his great decision: "I can do no other."

Whether he was replying to his own conscience is not known; at all events he wrote to a friend afterwards describing the "strangely empty and hollow feeling...the sense of absolute loneliness." Nevertheless it was true that in obeying the impulsion of his own nature, the need to cast off and be free, he could indeed do no other.

That break with Scribner's was, in a sense, in line with the disappointing attempt to return to his family. Both epitomized an important development. "You can't go home again," he wrote... not to childhood, not to romantic love, not to a young man's dreams of glory and fame, not to the father, wherever he might be found, in whom would rest strength and wisdom and safety.

In the past he had written as if looking in a mirror. But he was weary of that narrow preoccupation with himself. "I think," he said, "my interests have turned more and more from the person who is writing the book to the book the person is writing." And as he freed his vision for a wider view he saw that one seeking a father to lean on was seeking what a father stood for, self-government and self-reliance, and that these qualities could not be borrowed from another. It was indeed a large discovery and it came just in time.

For Thomas Wolfe had not much time left. At the turn of the year he had just one more chance to see his discarded idol. A manuscript dealer was attempting to blackmail him and he needed his editor as a witness. Perkins gladly consented to testify, and his appearance in court touched Wolfe to tears. For the first time in his life he was wearing a hearing aid, especially bought and fitted for the occasion lest he muff the lawyers' questions.

After the successful conclusion of the case they went out to lunch and then made a round that lasted through dinner. Excited and happy, Wolfe talked on in the way Perkins had listened to for nine years, pouring out everything that had happened. But now, Perkins noticed, there was less egotism in his tales and a new objectivity and humor about life. Most noticeable of all, there was even the ability to make fun of himself. It is pleasant to think that Perkins had a glimpse of him thus. For it was the last time he was to see him at all.

All through the spring of 1938 Wolfe wrote furiously. He was happy about what he was writing, for the Eugene Gant of former books had become George Webber, and this man had a new and wider point of view. Working longer hours than ever in a fury of impatience, he was growing heavy and sick looking; he had dark circles and shaking hands, and as always at this stage of composition he was unable to sleep until exhaustion overtook him.

In late spring he was invited to speak at Purdue University, and having reached a good stopping point in his manuscript, he laughed and said, "I'm no speaker, but I can d-do a hell of a lot of s-stuttering for th-three hundred dollars." So he went west, leaving the whole huge mass with his new editor, Edward Aswell. It was raw and disorderly, and he anticipated another year's work on it, but he wanted Aswell to have some idea of what lay ahead. (Had Aswell actually seen what lay ahead it is likely he would have fainted, for he had material there for three books and was going to have to bring it to publishable condition without any help from Wolfe.) *The Web and the Rock* was Wolfe's title; but when Aswell needed others for the second and third volumes he chose *You Can't Go Home Again* and *The Hills Beyond.*

It was May when Wolfe left New York. After his successful stuttering speech at Purdue he started off on a whirlwind tour to the Coast. There he picked up two men and with them drove 4,662 miles through the national parks, going sixteen hours a day for thirteen days and then drinking most of the night. Stopping in Seattle, he found an ecstatic wire from Aswell, *Your greatest novel so far,* and in his elation decided to go on to British Columbia by steamer.

It was on shipboard that he caught a cold that took him, against his proud will, to a hospital. All his life, remembering the TB patients on his mother's porch, he had had a dread of tuberculosis, and now he was told he had it. Other doctors called it pneumonia. Either way, he was terrified. "I don't want to die out here," he wailed to the acquaintance who took him to the hospital. "Don't let me be kept out here to die!"

Fever and delirium came and went, came and went, but his vitality sank steadily. When Perkins heard of his illness he wrote him a light, cheerful letter about his wife's garden and his new grandson's "fierce-looking ears," and during one of Tom's better moments he replied in a shaky hand, "I'm sneaking this against orders, but 'I've got a hunch.' " He had, he said, been to a strange country and seen the dark man very close, but he knew now that he was just a grain of dust and felt as if "a great window has been opened on life I did not know about before." Whatever happened, he wanted Perkins to know that he would always feel about him as he had on that glorious day they celebrated *Of Time and the River* together.

Grasping at life, he reached out to other sources of life he had known and thrust aside. He telephoned Aline, but his voice sounded drunken, and having heard many wild statements about his health before, she did not believe him this time. When she learned the facts her pain and remorse were indescribable, and she tried to go to him, but Perkins in his greater wisdom dissuaded her.

When the Seattle doctors lost confidence in their ability to save him they sent him, with the newly arrived Mabel and Mrs. Wolfe, to Johns Hopkins in Baltimore. There surgeons operated and discovered tuberculosis of the brain. He died three days later, on September 15, 1938.

He was buried in a huge, specially made coffin in the Asheville cemetery among his father's marble gravestones. The family and many friends stood around the grave, but Perkins stood off by himself among some trees. Friend extraordinary, he still had one more service to perform: according to Wolfe's will, he was administrator of all his literary affairs, and so it was that this erratic genius came again under his care, even though his last novels were published by someone else.

F. Scott Fitzgerald
(1896=1940)

F. Scott Fitzgerald
(1896-1940)

DURING HIS lifetime Scott Fitzgerald occasioned more than his share of raised eyebrows, and after his death the world remembered him chiefly as the playboy prophet of an empty-headed age. But those who knew him better remembered him for very different reasons. His sensitive concern for others was the motivating force of his life, and to make people happy was, he said, "more fun than anything."

"He was as spiritually generous a soul as ever lived," said the woman who above all others was in a position to know. And his eagerness to do honor to other writers, even to exalting them above himself, went at times beyond their own comprehension.

This is not to say that he did not recognize his own worth as well. He knew long before Gertrude Stein said it of him that he had "created the contemporary world" and in inventing the phrase The Jazz Age had given it an enduring name. And even in his moments of deepest despair he claimed the right to "some small immortality," though he wistfully discounted the probability of attaining it. (Actually it was only after his death that the steady radiance of the man's spirit became visible through the kaleidoscopic flicker of his bizarre behavior.)

Francis Scott Key Fitzgerald was the scion of Maryland gentlefolk, one of whose forebears was the author of "The Star Spangled Banner," and a certain graciousness of spirit was the thing he always remembered best about his father. A gently unaggressive wholesale grocery salesman, Edward Fitzgerald lived by a code of

"good instincts, honor, courtesy and courage," and this mild-man-
nered man with the trim Vandyke beard and the white piping on
his vest was for many years his son's ideal of a man.

Mollie Fitzgerald, on the other hand, was a sore embarrassment to her son. True, it was her McQuillan money that gave him
his expensive education, but the McQuillans were only 1850 immigrant Irish and Mollie was personally eccentric in clothing and
behavior. So when young Scott came to writing stories his glamorous heroes' mothers were always as unlike his own as possible.

Scott Fitzgerald and his mother got off, as it were, to a poor
start together. Just before his birth, which took place in St. Paul,
Minnesota on September 24, 1896, Mollie's two older children
died in an epidemic, with the consequence that a normal upbringing was an impossibility for the new baby. In her terror of losing
the little blond treasure she handled him like a Venetian glass
figurine. His first concept of himself, therefore, was as a fairy-tale
princeling who owned ponies and yachts and royal palaces. In
adolescence he dreamed himself the football hero saving the big
game in the last thirty seconds of play, and when at thirteen he
started driving the homely family car he slouched arrogantly at the
wheel, like a millionaire's son whipping about in a red Stutz Bear-
cat.

But by fifteen he had seen through his dreams to the drab
reality. He knew by now that the uncouth mother and unsuccessful
father would be no help in making the dreams come true. And so
he recognized that if he wanted to live the princely life he must
manufacture it for himself.

Fortunately for his ambitions he was so pleasing to the eye—
slim and delicately featured, with hair of pale gold and eyes of
blue-green jade—that the most aristocratic doors opened to him
easily. But that did not end his problems. While the McQuillan
money had eased him into St. Paul's most fashionable dancing
school, which in turn eased him into St. Paul's most fashionable
society, his parents were not invited to the same grand houses.
Among people of "family" he had no such reassuring background

and deep in his heart he never completely belonged. Though moving among the elite with easy grace he still felt tremulous inside, dreading to make some false step that would expose him as an imposter. Later he told a friend ruefully, "I spent my youth alternately crawling in front of the kitchen maids and insulting the great."

So he was always trying. Memorizing book titles, he discussed the books learnedly as if he had really read them. Too slight for sports and secretly hating exercise, he went out for them doggedly for their prestige value. And in the arena where he did feel confident he swaggered openly. "Eleven valentines from girls last year and fifteen this year," he boasted the spring a few hairs began to grace his chin.

This bumptiousness was a stage he had to go through. But with his innate sensitivity he passed through it more quickly and easily than most and arrived in short order at an oddly mature and courageous self-knowledge.

Sent east to a small select Catholic school in New Jersey, he was soon forced into self-examination by the coolly unimpressed upper classmen who merely laughed at his pretensions. Before his first year was out he had drawn up a chart of his own qualifications. The virtues he listed as follows: he was handsome, he had great athletic possibilities as yet undeveloped, and was an extremely good dancer. He had personality, charm, magnetism, poise, and the ability to dominate others; also a "subtle fascination over women." Mentally he was talented, ingenious, and quick to learn.

About his faults he was realistic, outright merciless. Morally he rated himself below normal. Secretly unscrupulous and anxious to influence people, even for evil, he was fresh, cold, and cruel; he lacked a sense of honor and was selfish in the extreme. Further, he had a streak of weakness and, in the last analysis, no real courage, perseverance or self-respect.

He did not list among his virtues, because he did not recognize their existence, his honesty or the perceptiveness that was to make him F. Scott Fitzgerald the writer. Nor did he recognize as a fault his taste for alcohol. The father he idolized was known in St. Paul as "a man who drank," and at fourteen the son was already sharing a bottle of drugstore sherry with another boy and getting as drunk as possible. He made the maximum drama of these episodes, pretending to sag at the knees after a single glass of beer, and afterward added a few comic or sensational touches each time he told the story. During his writing years these drinking exploits furnished him with rich literary fodder; at first they were light and funny, but in time they passed into the grim and tragic.

To a boy with insatiable social ambition and a bent for literature and drama, his natural choice of college was one allowing full scope for his various talents. Princeton had football, the number one road to success. It had, further, the Triangle Club, whose annual musical comedy written and produced by the members was its second most prestigious activity. Scott had been writing and acting dazzlingly in school shows for several years, and Triangle should be a safe bet for success even if he muffed the first squad in football.

Other slightly inferior avenues to prestige were available— *The Tiger, The Daily Princetonian,* and *The Nassau Lit.* But if one hoped to make one of the social clubs which in Princeton took the place of fraternities and to graduate a member of the Senior Council, one set his sights at the top. So immediately after learning he had passed his entrance examinations in September, 1913, Fitzgerald wired his mother, *Send football pads and shoes.*

But being slight and only five foot seven, he had to forgo his football dreams after a single day on the field. So then came the Triangle Club and *The Tiger.* He bombarded both with poems, jokes, sketches, and libretto lyrics and by the end of his freshman year had placed numerous pieces in both the show and the magazine. True, his marks had suffered but these were of minor importance.

His sophomore year he suffered the usual harrowing visits from members of the social clubs inspecting prospects. Hiding his anxiety under a facade of wit and easy-going urbanity, he had the satisfaction of receiving four bids, from which he chose Cottage. Then he relaxed, knowing the rest would be easy.

Anything, he was convinced, was possible to a man if he worked hard enough and, happily self-confident, he made large demands on life, remarking, "I'm only interested in the best." With his slim golden looks ("like a jonquil," said one girl), his gravely listening attention, and his smile "like a flash of confidence in you," he always ended up with the number one charmer at any party. It was thus in the cards that when Ginevra King visited Minneapolis that Christmas vacation he and she should be drawn together.

In the jet set of 1915 Ginevra was a junior comet sweeping across the skies of the East and the Middle West. A dramatic brunette beauty, at sixteen she had already perfected her technique of conquest and, concerned more for quantity than quality, ticked off her proposals each week like a hunter counting his bag.

With Scott it was different. Meeting her only two days before the holidays ended, he fell completely in love, and when they parted forty-eight hours later, he to Princeton and she to Westover School, he had given his heart without measure.

For a while his love was returned, and their ecstatic correspondence was a network of poetry weaving back and forth. That spring of 1915 was altogether so glorious that when he walked he scarcely seemed to touch the ground, for besides the marvel of Ginevra's love there was his membership in Cottage, the secretaryship of Triangle, and a place on *The Tiger* editorial board, all pointing logically to campus leadership. And, lighting up the months, there were also snatched meetings with Ginevra—quick visits, rigorously chaperoned, between Princeton and Westover, a few theater dates in New York, and meanwhile those passionate but strangely innocent letters. In June, on a glimmering night of dancing on the Ritz Roof, they discovered in amazement that all this love had been packed into an incredible fifteen hours together. Surely no one since Romeo and Juliet had ever had such a romance.

For Scott this was the beginning of two years of loving, hoping, planning. All girls were meaningless puppets seen through the obscuring haze of Ginevra's beauty. And when he started writing, all his early heroines were Ginevra in one form or another. Every letter from her was stored away carefully, and years later he had all 227 typed up and bound, to be kept with him until he died.

This intensely focused emotion was the keynote of Fitzgerald, for his calendar had no room for casual love. Promiscuity and obscenity alike offended him, and sex was a total commitment of the spirit, all bound in with tenderness and reverence. One critic has observed of his work: "No one, I think, has remarked how innocent of mere 'sex,' how charged with sentiment is Fitzgerald's description of love in the jazz age," and indeed it is strange that *This Side of Paradise* and *The Beautiful and Damned* should be remembered as sex novels.

Inevitably, Ginevra tired of him; their aims were too different, and the wholesale attention she demanded ruled out the one-to-one exclusivity he wished for. They were too different in other ways as well. Ginevra King was exorbitantly rich, and her "old" Chicago money, which gave her such superb self-confidence, only made his family's means seem embarrassingly meager. A remark overheard while he was visiting her in Chicago, "A poor boy should never think of marrying a rich girl," dropped onto his sensitive skin like acid, eating it to the bone, and he nearly shriveled away in shame.

When she lost interest in him he blamed his poverty, and from then on a wistful over-the-fence reverence for wealth tainted his outlook. The rich had always had a sheen that set them apart ("The very rich are different from you and me," began one of his most famous stories), and now their apartness gave them a terrible power to hurt.

But during those first spring months in 1915 all was sublimely right. He loved and was loved. Accepted by his peers, he belonged at last. The path of eternal pleasure lay ahead and all he had to do was walk it. However, then the very excess of pleasure betrayed him.

In the bustle of *thés dansants* and proms, of rehearsals and script conferences, of editorial sessions and Cottage committee meetings, ordinary studies were all but forgotten. Exam time hit him unawares and, suddenly frightened, he crammed and failed. Re-examined, he failed again, this time paralyzed with fear. And suddenly, scarcely crediting his ears, he heard the word *probation* —no more extracurricular activities, no Triangle, no *Tiger,* no *Nassau Lit.* Thus in a moment stripped of excitement and honors, no longer now ever to be a big man on campus, he saw his entire life ruined. "And all," he moaned, "because I couldn't do chemistry!"

The humiliation left him less secure than ever, and he plumbed the depths—not now a real Princeton man, never, never now *one of them.*

Though the pain of the blow was never forgotten, he did in time wring a blessing out of it. For, one road to distinction blocked, he turned to an alternative. Already he had felt vague stirrings toward serious writing, and even while giving social distinction first priority, he a few times surreptitiously sought out a group of intellectuals known scornfully as "birds." Despite the danger of appearing a bird himself, he joined in bookish discussions with future judges, editors, critics, explorers, and writers, among whom was Edmund Wilson, an aloof *literateur* to whom professors spoke with respect and ordinary undergraduates hardly dared speak at all.

Having decided to plump for a literary career, he approached his new vocation with an ardor that amused and yet intrigued the future critic. "I want to be one of the greatest writers who ever lived," he exclaimed impetuously to Wilson, who smiled with lofty patience. Nevertheless in this youthful enthusiasm Wilson saw promise of growth, and for years he watched over the Fitzgerald career like a paternal sheepdog, snapping at the cheapnesses, guiding the wayward brilliance, and nudging his charge to an ever higher standard of excellence.

"Come now," he would write briskly, "clear your mind of cant! Brace up your artistic conscience, which was always the weakest part of your talent! . . . . Concentrate in one short story a world of tragedy, comedy, irony and beauty! ! !" Fitzgerald listened humbly, and later declared his eternal gratitude to the man he called his intellectual conscience.

The crash of his college career had, in a curious way, not only led him to a better one but had enriched his equipment for it. Suffering, ecstasy, all emotions, the more personal the better, were the material he worked with. "Taking things hard," he immersed himself in *feeling*. The intensity of his friendships was his greatest charm, the probing eyes, the breathless listening smile and eager nod of agreement. All electric energy, he was constantly recharging himself with fresh experiences and emotions, and at the end he regarded it as his greatest tragedy that through caring about everything so deeply he had exhausted the capacity to care at all.

A Catholic youth who had gravely discussed possible priesthood with Ginevra, he was very conscious of himself as a sinner, and like everything else he took his failings hard. With merciless objectivity he recorded his derelictions in one book after another, from *The Beautiful and Damned* down to *The Crack-up*. This double identity of observer and observed caused him to suffer agonies during his wife's childbirth pains and yet at the same moment to take careful note of her every word and move.

Having been forced to repeat his junior year at Princeton, he was caught before graduation by the United States' entry into World War I. All his friends were volunteering for officers' training, so in November, 1917, he followed suit listlessly, arriving in Fort Leavenworth, Kansas, where his chief reaction was boredom.

He loathed sleeping fifteen in a room; he resented marching under a heavy load, and ingeniously gave his knapsack the necessary dimensions by filling it with an empty stovepipe. He concealed within the covers of *Small Problems for Infantry* the manuscript he was working on, and despite the efforts of his baffled superiors (including one Captain Dwight D. Eisenhower) he left Fort Leavenworth known wryly but affectionately as the world's worst second lieutenant.

Fortunately for the Allied cause, he never got to France. Instead he found himself, still bored, at Camp Sheridan, near Montgomery, Alabama. There, in July, 1918, he was relieved of boredom for the rest of his life.

No one meeting Zelda Sayre had ever been bored. Irritated perhaps; shocked, even outraged; but even the most censorious were intrigued by her fey recklessness. Still under eighteen, she was beautiful, red-gold, slim like a reed, and when Fitzgerald saw her at a country club dance everything inside him seemed to melt. He rushed over to be introduced, and there on the dance floor he set his feet on a path from which there was no returning. (Had he known what lay ahead he might have run in the opposite direction. On the other hand, with his eagerness for experience, he would probably still have traveled the whole sad road.)

The spoiled daughter of an Alabama Supreme Court judge, Zelda came from an old Southern family, unmoneyed but solidly aristocratic. Endowed with a wildly unpredictable energy, from childhood on she had obeyed every caprice, diving from greater heights than any of her friends, riding boys' motorcycles faster, smoking earlier, necking more openly. At the same time she had a kind of serene sweetness, an unshakable poise, that dignified even the most hoydenish behavior. Old ladies loved her; when she turned a series of cartwheels down Montgomery's main street it was indulgently smiled off as "Zelda's latest."

Some people called her complicated, but this was denied. Herself she described with frightening, prophetic accuracy as two simple people opposed to each other—one yearning to be fenced in, the other determined to break out.

To Scott, Zelda's beauty and quick repartee were only the beginning of her fascination. Life, for anyone caught up in the orbit of this spinning fireball, would, he told himself, be eternally fresh and exciting. He and she were two halves of a destined whole, and they had to come together. And as they skimmed about the dance floor cheek to cheek in the fashion of the day the same whispered comment followed them everywhere, "They're just *made* for each other." Zelda agreed vaguely to an engagement but made no binding promises.

In February, 1919, the army began demobilization. Second Lieutenant Francis S. K. Fitzgerald being "unusually dispensable," he was among the first to be let go. So then it was heigh-ho for New York and a quick success that would resolve Zelda's hesitation.

This, he soon found, was not going to be so easy. Much as she loved him, she was chary of committing herself to an unproven writer. Moreover, like Ginevra, her attitude toward exclusive possession was different from Scott's. He, on being shown a sleazy furnished room, was shocked by the landlady's wormy suggestion that it would be okay if he had girls in. For Pete's sake, what would *he* be doing with girls? He *had* a girl, hadn't he?

Zelda, on the other hand, had always made a point of kissing other men in front of him, and now her letters were full of dates and shows and Junior League dances. When he wrote wistfully that now he knew why they used to lock up princesses in towers, she replied that she could never *stand* being tied down, she loved him just terribly, more than anything in the world and she guessed they were sort of engaged, but she wanted to live in the great shining stream of life and the thought of marrying a poor man and carting home bags of groceries from the A. & P. was making her *nervous*. He knew how it was; sweet man that he was, surely he understood?

He understood perfectly. How could he blame her for wanting money, when next to herself that was what he wanted most?

His first word on reaching New York had been an exultant wire: *I declare everything glorious this world is a game everything is possible.* But after several months the best he had managed was a ninety-dollar-a-month job writing car-card slogans, and during all that desolate spring, divested of his smart officer's uniform and reduced to worn civvies, including shoes reinforced inside with cardboard, he sat up late writing stories he hoped would make him a quick fortune.

Instead, in the first five months he collected 122 rejection slips, which he defiantly pinned in a frieze around his dingy room. Meanwhile Zelda had been sending him data on her doings designed to drive him wild. More than once her "nervousness" had forced him to make quick trips to Montgomery to reassure her of his eventual success. But by June she was still unconvinced, and on his next visit she formally broke their engagement. If, of course, he was ever a real success, that would be a different matter. (When she saw him off at the station he climbed into a Pullman sleeping car with a grand air, but once under way he sneaked shamefacedly through into a day coach and sat up the rest of the way thinking miserable thoughts.)

Back in New York he went on a three-week drunk of forgetfulness and then, somehow purged, took a long look at his future. He had lost his girl. He had lost her solely through lack of money, just as with Ginevra. So it was true—a poor boy had no chance in the world of the rich.

Years later, in his confessional *Crack-up,* he recalled the bitterness, the animosity, he had felt toward the leisure class, "the smouldering hatred of a peasant ... distrusting the rich yet working for money with which to share . . . their lives."

Twenty-two, however, is hard to keep down forever. His short stories might have failed, but there was still that novel he had been writing in the army about Ginevra and himself and their crowd. Rereading it with mounting approval, he wrote Edmund Wilson his conviction that some morning he would wake to find that the debutante set had made him famous overnight, "I really believe that no one else could have written so searchingly the story of the youth of our generation." He would go back to St. Paul and finish it, and if he was right, that one debutante might change her mind.

Working around the clock, eating sandwiches and milk his worried mother set down outside his third-floor room, he labored through the heat of St. Paul's summer. In September he sent the manuscript, not by unreliable mails but in the personal care of a friend, to Scribner's in New York.

Less than two weeks later he received a special delivery letter. *This Side of Paradise*, wrote editor Maxwell Perkins, "is so different that it is hard to prophesy how it will sell, but we are all for taking a chance and supporting it with vigor." That day Scott needed no alcohol to intoxicate him; he ran along Summit Avenue stopping cars to tell stranger and friend alike of his good fortune.

The bounce back from despair carried him to the stars. And it did seem that Scribner's had primed the prosperity pump, for within three months he had sold several stories, including one to the hallowed *Saturday Evening Post*, and Metro had made him a flattering movie offer.

The result was that Zelda now promised to marry him as soon as the novel came out. And the result of *that* was a celebration in a New York hotel when he got roaring drunk, hired three bellboys to dress him for a party, and flooded the lower floors by leaving a faucet turned on.

Even with all these breaks he did not yet realize the extent of his good luck, for in Maxwell Perkins and his new agent Harold Ober he had stumbled on two men who were to guide him over the years with loyalty, sagacity, and taste. For a long time the arrangement looked very easy: all he had to do was simply to sit down and write what he remembered. If it turned into a book, Perkins had simply to correct his spelling and send it along to the printer. If it was a story, Ober simply notified the *Post* that it was available and that the price had gone up again. When, later, things got difficult, the two men tightened their belts and carried on.

In March, 1920, *This Side of Paradise* was published. Like most first novels it was autobiographical, the story of a young man's college experience and his coming of age. Princeton, naturally, is there with its *thés dansants* and proms and mandolins in the moonlight. Ginevra and he are there, drinking and petting. Above all, that new phenomenon the flapper is there, with her bobbed hair and rolled stockings and girdle parked in the dressing room.

Other books about flaming youth came out soon, but none in which every scrap of dialogue and every mental attitude were so precisely right. Fitzgerald had begun to write the social history of his time, and the country gasped at the emergence of a major prophet.

The youthful exuberance of the book caught the critics with their guards down, and he was mentioned in the same breath with such prodigies as Byron, Kipling, and the early Dreiser. Dangerous words like *artist* and *genius* were bandied about carelessly, and for a while he believed them all, living in a state of "manic insanity."

With publication Scott had wired Zelda to come up and keep her promise. The Protestant Mrs. Sayre had written him a few seasoned words of warning: "Your church is all right with me. A good Catholic is as good as any other man and that is good enough. [But] it will take more than the Pope to make Zelda good; you will have to call on God Almighty direct.... She is not amiable and she is given to *yelping*. But when she yelps just give her your sweetest smile and go quietly about your business." Undaunted and ecstatic, he carried off his bride to St. Patrick's Cathedral and they were married in the rectory on April 3, 1920.

The scene chosen for their honeymoon could not have been more appropriate. The Biltmore Hotel adjoined Grand Central Station and together they stood at the very heart of the city—a city which, like the rest of the country, was just recovering from the war and preparing for "the gaudiest spree in history."

If Scott Fitzgerald had been born either a few years earlier or a few years later, his history might have been quite different. As it was, he fitted into his moment like a key into a lock and, like a key, he opened the door to the new world. Nineteen-twenty America was just discovering that the war which had been expected to make the world safe for democracy had made it merely a mess. Cynicism became the fashionable attitude: if heroic effort had failed so dismally, the hell with effort and let's everyone concentrate on a good time. "It seemed only a few years," wrote Fitzgerald, "before the older people would step aside and let the world be run by those who saw things as they were." Right now, the "sincere" thing was to follow the impulse of the moment. "Let's have fun" became the watchword.

In a matter of months the Fitzgeralds, by their beauty and vivacity, their wild independence and virtuosity at living, became the symbols of the jazz age. Scott had promised Zelda that anything was possible and fate seemed to be upholding him, for six months after having been forced to bum Cokes from his friends in St. Paul, here he was besieged by magazines, book publishers, and movie companies. He who had walked the pavements with cardboard in his shoes was suddenly skimming the Ritz Roof in his new patent leathers. Best of all, he and Zelda were more in love than ever.

Two spirits soaring on the same high wind, they went riding down Fifth Avenue on the tops of taxis, diving into the fountain in Union Square, dancing on people's dinner tables, running hand in hand down Fifty-seventh Street after a Carnegie Hall concert. Sometimes alcohol was not even involved, it was sheer exuberance over being so happy—happier, they knew, than they could ever be again. And the saving grace in all their excesses was a kind of "golden innocence" and air of breeding. Always stopping short of vulgarity, their conversation depended for wit on neither the bedroom nor the bathroom.

Photographed and written about endlessly, these Sunday supplement celebrities fascinated the public not only by their exploits but by their touching, unashamed love, "clinging to each other like barnacles to rocks." Scott himself wrote of their "almost uncanny pull at each other's heart." Though before marriage he had been the more totally ensnared, afterward Zelda gave herself just as unreservedly. One afternoon he came back to their hotel to find her curled up asleep hugging against her cheek one of his old shoes.

At the same time they were jealous, not only of each other but of the attention each received from the public. Scott was reveling in his new glory, while Zelda, who had hitherto been the center of any gathering, fiercely resisted being known simply as his wife. She knew herself to be as inventive as he, with a verbal felicity nearly as great. Childish ego clashed with childish ego and, loving like children, they fought in the same way.

The diary of a Princeton friend, Alexander McKaig, was strangely revealing and prescient:

"April 20, 1920. Called on Scott Fitz and his bride. Latter temperamental small town Southern Belle . . . I do not think marriage can succeed. Both drinking heavily. Think they will be divorced in 3 years. Scott write something big—then die in a garret at 32. . . .

"June 13. Terrible party. Fitz and Zelda fighting like mad—say themselves marriage can't succeed. . . .

"Sept. 15. In the evening Zelda—drunk—having decided to leave Fitz and having been nearly killed walking down RR track, blew in. Fitz came shortly after. . . . Trouble is, Fitz absorbed in Zelda's personality—she is the stronger of the two. She has supplied him with all his copy for women. . . .

"Sept. 27. Fitz . . . new novel sounds awful—no seriousness of approach. Zelda interrupts him all the time—diverts in both senses. Discussed his success complex . . . Fitz bemoaning fact never can make more than hundred thousand a year . . . to do that have to become a Tarkington. . . .

"Oct. 12. Went to Fitzgeralds . . . Usual problem there. What shall Zelda do? I think she might do a little housework, apartment looks like a pigsty. If she's there Fitz can't work—she bothers him —if she's not there he can't work—worried of what she might do. . . .

"Oct. 16. Fitz has been on wagon 8 days—talks as if it were a century. Zelda increasingly restless—says frankly she simply wants to be amused . . . Great problem—what is she to do? Fitz has his writing of course—God knows where the two of them are going to end up. . . .

"Oct. 20. Fitz is hard up now but Zelda is nagging him

for a $750 fur coat & she can nag. Poor devil.

"Oct. 21. Fitz . . . much taken with idea of having a baby . . . Scott hard up for money in spite of fact he had made $20,000 in past 12 months.

"Dec. 11. Fitz and I argued with Zelda about notoriety they are getting through being so publicly and spectacularly drunk . . . I told them they were headed for catastrophe if they kept up at present rate.

"April 17, 1921 . . . Fitz confessed this evening at dinner that Zelda's ideas entirely responsible for 'Jelly Bean' and 'Ice Palace.' Her ideas largely in this new novel. Had a long talk with her this evening . . . She is without doubt the most brilliant and most beautiful young woman I've ever known.

"May 5. Fitzgeralds gone gloriously to Europe on the *Aquitania.* I miss them dreadfully."

During this year the Fitzgeralds had moved, always at the request of the management, from hotel to hotel, to Connecticut, back to New York, and then on to Europe, always in a clutter of liquor, smoke, open suitcases, and visitors. But with Zelda pregnant they decided to come back and settle temporarily in St. Paul.

In spite of all the symbols of success Scott's conscience, that *alter ego* he called his spoiled priest, was standing aside watching disapprovingly. Once, during a poetry course at Princeton, Alfred Noyes had told Fitzgerald he believed him capable of books of permanent value, and Scott had ecstatically dedicated himself to his muse. But that was before Zelda, and since then he decided to take the cash and let the credit go.

After a few months in the spotlight, however, he became vaguely unhappy. Reading *This Side of Paradise,* Edmund Wilson had dribbled acid all over its pages. "Your hero . . . as an intellectual . . . is a fake of the first water," his literary conscience had written him, "and I read his views on art, politics, religion and society with more riotous mirth than I should care to have you know. . . . Tighten up your artistic conscience and pay a little more attention to form."

Wilson's words seared, but as long as living expenses kept

increasing and magazines kept paying him ever larger sums, Fitzgerald turned his ear away from the nagging voices. At the same time the turbulence of his life was beginning to frighten him. Asked once by a struggling writer why he, with all his success, should call himself a "bewildered and despairing human soul," he shook his head and replied, "Wait till you're a success."

Out of this bewilderment and disillusion came *The Beautiful and Damned.* Though McKaig, reading a first draft, had found it "awful, with no seriousness of purpose," it was in reality an intensely serious response to Fitzgerald's own conscience. The story of Anthony Patch and his beautiful young wife, both "wrecked on the shoals of dissipation," is not so much a view of Zelda and himself as they were then as his shocked vision of what they might become. Its bleak outlook, she with her looks gone and he sunk in alcoholism, set some readers against the book. But it had a short vogue as a peek into the private lives of those fascinating, wild Fitzgeralds.

The Beautiful and Damned had been published in March, 1922. The previous October little Scottie had made her appearance in St. Paul while they were considering starring in a movie of *This Side of Paradise.* Max Perkins had shudderingly opposed that notion, and instead Scott had started writing "an awfully funny play that is going to make me rich forever."

Money was now, as always, his obsession. He had fallen into the habit of borrowing against his future earnings from his patient agent and publisher, pleading the impossibility of living on less than $36,000 a year. It wasn't, he explained, the *money* he wanted, it was the life money brought you, the travel, the entrée into cultured circles. There one acquired the quiet confidence and unlabored grace that were the height of charm. Some of this charm might be synthetic but, like bootleg gin, it had enormous power, and to earn it he sickened himself grinding out endless stories of flappers and sheiks. But one day he would strike it really rich and then he could stop and write the great American novel.

After their St. Paul year they came east to see to the production of his play *The Vegetable,* a satirical fantasy about politics.

There were numerous interviews with theater managers and numerous rewrites, but nothing happened for another year. Meantime, *Tales of the Jazz Age* served to keep the Fitzgerald name before the public—this, and their secondhand red Rolls-Royce and the Long Island house where they gave their chaotic parties.

To these parties came all of 1923's Café Society. To them also came a few genuine Old New York blue-bloods and a few of those strange men with no background and tremendous, unaccountable wealth. One of these, a man with a diamond-studded revolver who gave enormous parties at his great estate nearby, started Fitzgerald thinking of a character named Gatsby. He would write his story as soon as *The Vegetable* had made him rich.

The Vegetable, however, was this innocent's beginning of wisdom. Underlying his transitory doubts and despairs had lain a solid conviction that success was inevitable, that if you really tried you could twist life into any shape you chose. But on the night of November 20, 1923, at the Apollo Theatre in Atlantic City, with the mayor of New York and other notables attending, he learned better. The bored audience walked out in such droves that he went back to see the star after the second act and asked him, "Are you really going to stay and do the last act?" When the star said yes, he gave a laugh and went next door to a bar. Years later he told a friend that that humilating failure had wrecked forever his "magical illusion" of invincibility.

The failure, moreover, left him without a cent remaining of the $36,000 earned that year and, indeed, $5,000 in debt. Panicking, he went on the wagon, shut himself in a bare room over the garage, and in five months, working twelve hours a day, produced eleven stories and earned $17,000. Proud of his virtuosity but disgusted with the result (trash, trash, he called it) he began to worry seriously: was he deteriorating? Had he been drawing on his personal experiences so long he was running dry? Was he even actually incapable of fine work any more?

Searching for some remedy to his troubles, he succumbed to the bogus prescription, Leave where you are, go somewhere else;

in Europe everything will be different. So with Scottie and an English nannie they left New York and settled in France, where he tried desperately to write *Gatsby* clean, economical, true.

The prescription half fulfilled its promise: things were indeed different. But they were not better. Perhaps Zelda was bored while Scott immersed himself in his novel; perhaps she was jealous of his work and his fame; perhaps she needed a renewed sense of power. At any rate, while he dwelt in the world of Jay Gatsby and the woman he loved, he failed to see his own woman falling in love with someone close at hand, a French aviator, tall, athletic, handsome, and passionate. But after a few weeks he blinked and looked around. Then there were violent scenes and he roared the aviator off the premises like an infuriated watchdog.

Deeply as his pride and sense of possession were wounded, the real hurt went much deeper. "On the theme of marital fidelity," a friend once said, "Fitzgerald's eloquence has moved me to tears. . . . Where so many others are conscious only of sex, he is conscious of the soul." There, in his soul, he had loved Zelda and now it was there he suffered. In a couple of months he was able to persuade himself that the trouble was clearing away, and, six months later, that while he and Zelda sometimes had terrible drinking rows, they were still enormously in love, the only truly happily married people he knew. But their utter oneness had been violated. It was the first crack in the faultless enamel and eventually rust began to gather.

The drinking, which he had always regarded as good-natured sport, was now becoming a burden bowing him down; no longer was it funny to wake up bewildered in a foreign city or, black-eyed, in a police station. His sense of personal security, never strong, began wavering as he saw himself losing grip on the legacy bequeathed him by his father, good instincts, honor, courtesy, and courage.

He could not yet admit to outright alcoholism, for his pride was very precious, but, as after *The Vegetable*'s failure so now after the failure with Zelda, he was shocked into sobriety. Forcing himself onto the wagon and forgetting all else in his work, he finished *The Great Gatsby* in a triumphant blaze, knowing it to be good.

This, then, he had not lost, for into the book he had poured the purest artistry at his command. Much of himself he had put into it too—his foolish worship of the rich and, most painful, the two engagements broken on account of his poverty. The whole theme of the novel was, he said, "the loss of those illusions that give such color to the world, so that you don't care whether things are true or false as long as they partake of the magical glory."

He and Zelda were still abroad when *Gatsby* was published in April, 1925. *Excellent reviews,* cabled Perkins. *Sales situation doubtful*—five words that told the story. Excellent indeed were the reviews, which agreed that he had emerged from adolescent promise into maturity; gratifying were the letters from Edith Wharton and Willa Cather and Gertrude Stein. T. S. Eliot even called *Gatsby* the most important novel since Henry James' time. But the sales situation remained doubtful, for 22,000 copies sold would hardly repay his debt to his publisher.

Dismayed and shocked, he raged at the public; no one any more wanted to read anything but those new proletarian novelists, Caldwell, Farrell, Dos Passos. He wouldn't write that stuff even if he could, so he would hurry up with a lot of money-making stories and then do one more novel, something really new in form and theme. Or, he said grimly, like one contemplating slumming, if the stories didn't go, he would go to Hollywood and write for the movies.

Instead, he started to dream vaguely of doing a new novel while a year of "a thousand parties and no work" began. This was the year of Sara and Gerald Murphy, a couple who had changed the Riviera from a fashionable winter resort to a fashionable summer one simply by settling there. Sara was trim, quiet, and humorous, a perfect hostesss, while Gerald, slender, elegant, and witty, had the special power of bringing out the charm and wit of those around him. They were, observed John Dos Passos once, the golden couple that the Fitzgeralds dreamed of becoming. "They were rich. They were good looking. They dressed brilliantly. They were canny about the arts. They had a knack of entertaining. They had lovely children. They had reached the highest rung on mankind's ladder."

They also had taste, and though they were sincerely devoted to the Fitzgeralds, their love did not extend to all their capers. Nor did they hesitate to rebuke and even punish. One night at a dinner party Scott threw a very ripe fig at the naked back of a French countess. The party, including the target lady, maintained a stiff silence. Later he started tossing crystal goblets out into the garden. At this point Murphy, losing patience, forbade him the house for three weeks.

Scott accepted the exile, contenting himself by throwing the contents of a garbage can over the wall. But so genuinely apologetic was he always after these exhibitions that his friends forgave him as one forgives a wayward, winning child.

Zelda had her own moments of contributing lavishly to the legend she was creating. Less noisy than Scott, she maintained a lofty, almost angry dignity even in her most undisciplined periods. Late one night at the Casino she stepped forth onto the dance floor holding her skirts high over her bare midriff and pirouetted solemnly about the hall, head high and face impassive. Back at the table, she seemed in a trance, unconscious of the stares around her. But her friends were puzzled, for she was different from Scott; more and more she was doing these meaningless things, but with her it was often when she was cold sober.

All this time Fitzgerald had been intermittently struggling with his novel, which, he wrote Perkins, was to be about Zelda and himself and the hysteria of their recent doings in Paris. But the story had not jelled, and as he fell under the spell of the Murphys the hero, instead of remaining pure Fitzgerald, took on the coloration, the charisma of Gerald while retaining the personality and the weaknesses of himself. (Zelda likewise was part Sara, but as time and events moved on that story altered as well.)

Fitzgerald's attitude toward Murphy was almost hero worship.

But that was nothing new in him, for he had an infinite capacity for worship, particularly of other writers. His esteem sometimes expressed itself in carnival fashion, as when, invited to lunch with James Joyce, he anounced that out of the depth of his respect he intended to throw himself from the window. (Joyce blinked through his thick glasses and later murmured, "That young man must be mad.")

Once in New York, when Joseph Conrad was visiting his publisher, Scott and Ring Lardner drove out to Long Island and, to express their reverence, performed a ritual dance on the publisher's lawn. (No one responded but the caretaker, and he threw them out.) Dining with John Galsworthy, Scott cried, "You and Conrad and Anatole France are the three living writers I admire most in the world."

He was always discovering new writers and, like a birddog, bringing them proudly to lay at Perkins' feet. Ring Lardner he adored (he called this funny, tragic man his "private drunkard") and having got him settled with Perkins, sat up all night preparing Lardner's manuscript for the printer while his own work lay neglected.

But the writer for whom he cherished the most slavish devotion was Ernest Hemingway. Having read his first stories in obscure French magazines, Fitzgerald tracked him to one of his Left Bank haunts and introduced himself. Though famous while Hemingway was unknown, his admiration for the younger man was unfeigned; he sent him to Perkins, and when *The Sun Also Rises* came out he nagged critics into writing laudatory reviews, comparing that novel favorably with his own *Gatsby*. "There's magic in it," he said. And later, of Hemingway's book of short stories, he said, "Ernest's is so much better than mine."

His admiration extended to the man's burly, engaging personality, and during these first years there was a relaxed, kidding friendship between them. But the two men's escalators were going in opposite directions and as Hemingway moved up Fitzgerald watched him wistfully across an ever-widening gap.

Hemingway, no mean drinker himself, found Fitzgerald's drinking hard to take, and after several unwelcome visits he ordered their mutual friends not to give Scott his new address. Later, as his scorn increased, he referred in a story to "poor Scott Fitzgerald's worship of the rich and the wreck it had made of him." Scott cried aloud in pain, yet he never lost his admiration and kept asking Perkins for news of him to the last.

Hemingway's dogged attention to the business of writing was Fitzgerald's despairing envy, for his own novel had come to a halt on the Riviera, and he had failed to produce so much as a single story in a year. Finally he and Zelda returned disconsolately to the United States and Scott made good his sulky threat to go to Hollywood. The sum of that experience was a great deal of liquor drunk, a scenario written but never produced, $3,500 received out of an anticipated $12,000, and a further crack in the couple's love.

By now their "organized cat and dog fights" were as notorious as formerly their love had been. Scott, once asked his greatest ambition, had said, "To stay married and in love with Zelda, and to write the greatest novel in the world." But Zelda's affair had violated the sanctity of their relationship, and in Hollywood Scott, at thirty-one regarding himself as middle-aged, acted like a middle-aged man and became enamored of a pretty seventeen-year-old star. The flirtation, essentially just a wistful touching of fingers across the years, was more than half motivated by revenge for his own hurt. But it remained in his memory like a rosy dream, and the girlish figure of Lois Moran recurred often in his fiction, notably as Rosemary Hoyt in *Tender Is the Night.*

By 1928 the couple had retreated to a country house outside Wilmington, Delaware, where Scott was by God really and truly going to get that damn novel finished. Scottie, who had been leading a very colorful life for a little girl, could now play quietly under the old oaks. And Zelda, who was becoming increasingly restless, could give her various talents a workout. For some years she had painted not badly, with Scott's approval. She had achieved some success with her stories and articles. But to the public she was still Scott Fitzgerald's wife, and jealousy had been making her fretful, liable to sudden caprices and fits of gloom.

During their quarrels over Lois Moran, Scott, losing his temper, had snapped that at least the girl *did* something, she was not only talented but she *worked*. The gibe struck home, and Zelda set her jaw fiercely.

In her young girlhood she had taken dancing lessons. So now, at twenty-seven, she decided to become a professional ballet dancer, too late by twenty years for such a decision. The ferocity of her absorption was like the dancing madness of the Middle Ages. She took lessons every day in Philadelphia and practiced endlessly at home. Then nothing would do but she must study with a Russian teacher in Paris.

There it was still more classes, more private lessons, more hours of practice and merciless dieting. She dreamed of a position with the Russian Ballet, which made Scott roar cruelly (there was something about her "leaping and sweating" that irritated him beyond control), and when she received an offer from the Folies Bergère, Scott roared louder than ever. Bitter quarrels were followed by long bitter silences, and each watched the other's face sidelong, bewildered and helpless. Then in April, 1930, Zelda's mind gave way altogether.

As far back as 1925 Hemingway had said to Scott, "You realize, don't you, that she's crazy?" And even before that Rebecca West told a friend, "From the first moment I saw her I knew she was mad . . . a handsome face, but when one got the after-image it always showed a desolate country without frontiers." Now she was taken to a Swiss sanitarium in a state of acute terror, where she kept repeating, "It's frightful, it's horrible, what's going to become of me? I must work and I no longer can. I must die and yet I have work to do."

After long observation the doctor's report read: "It was evident that the relations between the patient and the husband had been shaky for some time and that for this reason the patient had tried to create a life of her own through the ballet (since family life and obligations were not sufficient to satisfy her ambition and her artistic leanings)."

Her case was diagnosed as schizophrenia (that split personality she had unconsciously recognized at eighteen) wherein she vacillated between wild irrationality and lucidity as bright as the sun. When she tried to run away she was brought back and soothed; when she tried to kill herself she was confined till the fit passed. Since for many months the very mention of a visit from Scott brought on an attack of agonizing eczema, he could communicate with her only by sending flowers, and he spent the next year wandering about Europe like a lost spirit. Years later, still wandering, he told a friend, "Our love was one in a century. Life ended for me when Zelda and I crashed. If she could get well I would be happy again and my soul would be released. Otherwise, never."

The doctors had reported that his drinking ran like a tormenting thread through her hallucinations. But stop drinking he could not. At times he tried to hold himself down to a pint of wine at dinner, but he was totally incapable of controlling his intake. However, he did what he could do—paid for her hospital treatment when she was sick and when she was better cared for her at home, where for long periods they had some of their happiest times.

He even encouraged her, as therapy, to start writing again. But the resulting novel, *Save Me the Waltz,* whose manuscript she sent to Perkins without showing it to him first, proved to be a rock upon which they nearly foundered. Scott had always used his own and Zelda's experiences in his writing; her ideas, her personality, even her letters and diaries, had been the material out of which he spun his stories, and his new novel, after many permutations, had resolved itself into a graphic treatment of their life together, including her breakdown. But now, when he saw her manuscript, he was stunned to find that it told virtually the same story. And his manuscript was only half finished.

His shock and indignation—"*I* am the professional writer, not you. That is all my material"—startled and frightened her. He insisted on vast changes before it could be published, and though she protested feebly she made them. Still, the book ended up as her version of her illness. His version of it would come later.

In 1932 he brought her back to America, where he rented a large old house convenient to a Baltimore clinic. There they lived a life so secluded that in two years they dined out exactly four times.

To Scottie he was an affectionate and imaginative father, writing plays for her to put on with her friends, making up historical games around a set of Roman and Greek lead soldiers, and performing card tricks with hands that were, these days, always shaking.

At last he had got seriously back to work on his book. In his working notes he described the hero as "a man who is a natural idealist, a spoiled priest, . . . in his rise to the top of the social world losing his idealism, his talent and turning to drink and dissipation. Background one in which the leisure class is at their truly most brilliant and glamourous such as Murphys."

Zelda's illness he drew honestly enough. But having been unable to learn from her mother of any childhood experiences to account for her breakdown, he invented a startling and melodramatic one. (Perhaps he could not quite accept the life they had lived together as good enough reason.)

Tender Is the Night was published in 1934, nine years after its inception. By now everything in life seemed to hang on its success—solvency, popularity, self-respect, perhaps even survival. It was, he said, his confession of faith, in which he told the things he had learned at such cost—that work was the real dignity, that money and beauty were broken reeds, that honor, courtesy, courage were the real staffs of life.

Having suffered the most for it, he believed it to be his best book. And if the public as a whole could have agreed with such men as John Peale Bishop, who wrote, "You have shown us . . . that you are a true, a beautiful and tragic novelist . . . with inimitable invention, gaiety, tenderness and understanding," he might have got the lift he so desperately needed. Some critics did indeed agree with Bishop. But Hemingway, whose word counted so much, scolded him for self-pity; and there were other impatient gibes. Why, one critic fumed, in the depths of a world depression, was he preoccupied only with a crowd of idle neurotics? The book had the poorest sale of any of his novels and the implied verdict on him brought him to his knees.

The financial blow was no less devastating than the psychological. With the Depression and the current craze for proletarian writing, prices for his stories had declined sharply. When Zelda was at home and nearly sane he tried manfully not to drink, but in his worried state he always failed. Then he would lose patience at her fumbling efforts at housekeeping and explode, which would only beget another damaging scene. Thus the two of them went on, she in and out of hospitals for years, and he struggling desperately to pay the bills.

He never stopped hoping for her recovery, though he tried to accept the hopelessness of it. He even tried to accept substitutes for her. Gradually as time pushed them apart they watched the separation widen sadly, she no less regretful than he. After one of his regular visits the half-person she had become wrote him: "Dearest and always dearest Scott: I am sorry that there should have been nothing to greet you but an empty shell.... The thought of the effort you have made over me, the suffering this *nothing* has cost would be unendurable to any save a completely vacuous mechanism. Had I any feelings they would all be bent in gratitude to you and in sorrow that of all my life there should not even be the smallest relic of the love and beauty that we started with .... I want you to be happy—if there were any justice you would be happy—maybe you will be.... I love you anyway—even if there isn't any me or any love or even any life—I love you."

Finally the doctors released Zelda in the care of her mother, who was now alone, and she lived there quietly, shielded from excitement. From time to time she had to return to the sanitarium for treatment, and for the last years of Scott's life she was simply a dim figure whom he wrote to dutifully—that, and a financial burden he could neither slough off nor properly carry.

Shattered by his disappointment over *Tender Is the Night* he wrote no new stories, but he did manage to gather a group of old ones for a collection, *Taps at Reveille,* which was at least a show of activity. Then, ill and penniless, he fled to a two-dollar-a-night hotel in Hendersonville, North Carolina, to think his life over. Suffering from cirrhosis of the liver and, he believed, tuberculosis, he found himself there on a certain Monday morning with two tins of potted meat, three oranges, a box of Uneedas, and two cans of beer. With him he had one pair of pajama pants and one shirt. It was then that he wrote *The Crack-up.*

These three articles were a postmortem on his own psychological breakdown. Honest, candid, shockingly naked, they analyzed "the blow that comes from within [when] you realize with finality that in some regard you will never be as good a man again." He whose entire wealth had always been the sum of his experiences —the encounters and adventures and relationships, and the richness of his own emotional response to them—now found himself drained and poverty-stricken. Scratching about in the pockets of his soul he had found nothing there.

At that, terror had seized him—and then, even worse than terror, leaden apathy. This was the final deadening defeat, that he no longer had the capacity even to care.

The articles caused a sensation, and book publishers and magazine editors were again on his trail seeking more juicy confessions. Once more Hemingway took him to task for whining in public: Fitzgerald, he said, had gone from youth to senility without manhood in between. But it was left for another man to give him the coup de grâce.

With his fortieth birthday approaching, a New York paper sent a reporter to North Carolina, who by wheedling succeeded in getting up to his room. The interview, Fitzgerald thought, had been pleasant and innocuous enough. But a few days later he read the front-page article:

"The poet-prophet of the post-war neurotics observed his fortieth birthday yesterday . . . trying to come back from the other side of Paradise, the hell of despondency in which he has writhed for the last couple of years." The writer described Fitzgerald's jittery jumping on and off his bed, his trembling hands, his twitching face "with its pitiful expression of a cruelly beaten child," the frequent trips to the drawer where a bottle lay hidden. It ended with Fitzgerald's comments on his contemporaries: " 'Some became brokers and threw themselves out of windows, others became bankers and shot themselves. Still others became newspaper reporters. And a few became successful authors.' His face twitched. 'Successful authors!' he cried. 'Oh, my God, successful authors!' "

Seeking escape in oblivion, he swallowed a phial of morphine. But the massive overdose made him vomit and he did not die. So, having survived the worst, the mechanical reaction of his nerves carried him in the only direction that remained to him—up. He started to fight.

Thirty thousand dollars in debt to agent, publisher, and friends, responsible for Scottie's schooling and Zelda's hospitalization, he looked inevitably toward Hollywood. There had been several short unsatisfactory visits already, and the *Crack-up* articles had made producers visibly leery of him. But Ober finally set him up at MGM for six months at $1,000 a week with options. Four hundred of the thousand was to take care of Scottie and Zelda and himself, and the rest was to pay back his debts. Eventually he ended up in the clear. His morale, after three terrible years, miraculously revived.

These years had been terrible for Scottie too. Most of her holidays had been spent with the Obers and other friends; Helen Hayes mothered her on one trip west and his cousin took her on visits to the South. And by mail Scott hovered over her like a prudish mother hen, insistent that she learn from her elders' mistakes.

His rules were many and detailed: no long radio listening or telephoning on school nights; no dates with sixteen-year-old boys with cars; no lip rouge. He tried to choose her courses and her friends. ("These are such valuable years, let me watch over the development a little longer.") He gave her tips on college etiquette and, deadly in earnest, wrote her about life. "All I believe in in life is the rewards for virtue (according to your talents) and the punishments for not fulfilling your duties." He smothered her in lists: "Things to worry about: courage, cleanliness, efficiency, horsemanship. Things not to worry about: popular opinion, the past, the future, growing up, people getting ahead of you, triumph, disappointments, pleasure, satisfactions. THINGS TO THINK ABOUT: What you are aiming at."

His letters were voluminous enough to fill a book—anxious, loving, angry at her spending, mournful over their quarrels, proud of her literary ability, furious over her silly escapades, sometimes showing off before her, sometimes cravenly humble, threatening, if she took a single drink before age twenty, to go on an end-it-all binge . . . but always ending up with dearest love, her Daddy.

Arriving in Hollywood in June, 1937, Fitzgerald shortly went to a party at Robert Benchley's home to celebrate the engagement of an English marquis and a pretty British columnist. He was immediately reminded of Zelda by the girl's blond beauty and asked to meet her. Though still wan and shaking he had not lost his power to charm and in a very short time they were friends.

Sheilah Graham's story was almost unbelievable. Born Lily Sheil to impoverished Cockneys in a London tenement, she spent her early years in an orphanage, afterwards coming home to nurse her dying mother. Brief turns as a maid and a salesgirl were followed by marriage at seventeen to a much older man who let her pursue unhindered a career as a chorus girl. With incredible willpower she educated herself out of her slum background, finally achieving manners and speech cultivated enough to pass her into the society of the wealthy and the titled.

How she made these people believe her tales of an upper-class family and education in a Paris finishing school is hard to imagine, and perhaps they never really did, but at all events she maneuvered herself into the London newspaper world and then on to New York. Finally she gained her goal, authorship of a Hollywood gossip column. Even a title had come within her grasp. But soon after her meeting with Fitzgerald the engagement with the marquis was broken and she and Scott became what was known in Hollywood as *a thing*.

But what Hollywood knew as a thing was something else to Fitzgerald. "I can't stand this casual business with a woman," he said. "With me, it isn't an affair . . . it must be the real thing, absorbing me spiritually and emotionally." And so it was now. With the love-making went the talking together—probing ever deeper, getting to know the very depths, giving more and more of one's self, demanding more and more of the other's.

Over the weeks she grew anxious and then frightened as she found him turning up her most guarded secrets. There was no escape from his questions, and she thought miserably that with the truth would come the end of his love. Instead, he was touched by her courage. Her elaborate impersonation of an aristocrat brought her close to himself; how, indeed, could he condemn her as an impostor when most of his life he had been one himself?

On her journey to the top she had encountered chiefly predatory males, and his tender understanding amazed and touched her, calling forth intense loyalty. And this was well for him, for at the time of their meeting he had been on the wagon, and when he fell off the shock was devastating. Nevertheless she stuck, and it is safe to say that her sticking made his last years if not good, at least bearable.

Since there was little the world did not know about the Fitzgerald history, his decision not to divorce Zelda was generally respected; so therefore was Sheilah's stand-in position. Very soon they took on the aspect of a settled married couple—hardly a humdrum existence, for his drinking kept it in disorder, but one made up of mutual need and understanding. She steadied him when his foot slipped, and he helped her continual efforts at self-improvement, making up monumental reading and study lists for her "college of one."

Meanwhile his position at the studios was precarious. He well knew that a Hollywood screen-writer's standing was based on the number of screen credits he earned rather than on the actual writing jobs he had held. There were, he knew, three steps to security—first, a screen credit; second, a hit picture; third, an Oscar. And for a while Fitzgerald was hopeful. His option was picked up and it seemed that his first assignment, though a collaboration with another writer, would earn him a credit based on a count of the lines he had contributed to the script.

But the producer was himself a writer, and the picture ended up with hardly a line of Fitzgerald's left in. The blow to his pride was one of the worst of his life. In fury and anguish he protested the implied slur. "For nineteen years I've written best selling entertainment," he wrote Mankiewicz, "and my dialogue is supposedly right up at the top. But . . . you've suddenly decided that you can take a few hours off and do much better. . . . Oh Joe, can't producers ever be wrong? I'm a good writer—honest."

Thereafter he dabbed ineffectually at one picture after another, *The Women, Madame Curie, Gone With the Wind,* and others whose names have sunk into the dust. No screen credit came through; short jobs were followed by long idlenesses; the MGM contract was not renewed a second time, and then there were illnesses and insomnia, with chloral hydrate and Nembutal for sleeping and digitalis for the heart. He was in and out of hospitals, with and without nurses, and there was a moment when a doctor threatened him with alcoholic paralysis.

Not for the first time, he touched some kind of psychological bottom. Reading that the Pasadena Playhouse was staging an adaptation of his story "The Diamond as Big as the Ritz," he decided to make an appearance at the premiere in Hollywood style. Renting a chauffeur-driven limousine, he took Sheilah to dinner at the Trocadero and drove to the theater in grandeur. To his bewilderment the lobby was dark and deserted, but he was directed to a studio upstairs, where he found the players, a group of drama students, and the audience, a dozen girls in slacks on wooden benches. Bravely he and Sheilah stayed and applauded. But the story got out—a hilarious bit of gossip—and that was when it took real courage to walk the Hollywood streets.

His failures at MGM and his periodic illnesses not surprisingly had driven him back into debt. Also they had driven him back to short stories. The $4,000 days were over, but he was glad to accept $250 for his Pat Hobby stories about a broken-down screenwriter. And he was planning a new novel. On the strength of his prospects he tried again to borrow from his agent.

Despite his fondness for Fitzgerald (or, more accurately, because of it) Ober refused to return to the old routine—implied discipline that made Fitzgerald cringe in pain. But in spite of the blow to his pride (or again, perhaps, because of it) the seething energy of the born writer kept driving him on.

The novel had always been his favorite form of expression. But he had lacked a theme and a hero. "Show me a hero and I'll write you a tragedy," he said more than once. And in Hollywood at last he found one. Irving Thalberg, the youthful production head of MGM, had run his gigantic studio with a touch never too light or too heavy, always sensitive, always responding to his conception of the finished product. Slight and delicately made, this man used his gifts with Napoleonic success. And when he died at the age of thirty-seven he left a void not to be filled by any one man again.

In Thalberg, a great power operating a great concern, Fitzgerald saw a man like Lincoln whose ending was a like tragedy for his world. He wrote a few chapters which Perkins called "a beautiful start—stirring and new." *Collier's* magazine promised $30,000 if it ended as well as it started. And he wrote Scottie in October, 1939, "I have begun to write something that is maybe great . . . I am alive again."

The year of life that followed was not one of unalloyed good; he still quarreled with Sheilah over his drinking, though the final months were free of that burden. He was still scraping for money, though he had high prospects ahead. He still received wistful disoriented letters from Zelda which tore at his heart (happily he would not know of her 1947 death in a fire). But in the main it was a good time. "I am trying desperately to finish my novel by the middle of December," he wrote Zelda. "It makes me happy. . . . Two thousand words today and all good."

But he did not finish it in December. Instead, in December the heart he had asked so much of gave out and on the twenty-first day he died, with *The Last Tycoon* only half done.

No one knows with certainty whether the unwritten part would have matched that left lying on his desk. But that part, a picture not only of Thalberg but of Sheilah and himself, contains even in its raw state some of his finest writing, sharp, clean, and powerful. When it was published in 1941 Stephen Vincent Benét wrote, "You can take off your hats, now, gentlemen, and I think perhaps you had better. This is not a legend, it is a reputation—and, seen in perspective, it may well be one of the most secure reputations of our time."

Ernest Hemingway

(1899=1961)

Ernest Hemingway
(1899=1961)

"N EXT TO WRITING," Ernest Hemingway said more than once, "the greatest pleasure in life is hunting and fishing," and he must have posed for a thousand photographs holding up a dead fish or sitting on a dead lion. To a close friend he added, not entirely in jest, "and I spend a hell of a lot of time killing animals and fish so I won't kill myself."

All his life Hemingway talked of suicide, analyzing the best methods down to such fine points as how to trigger a rifle with the big toe. Yet few men, surely, have radiated such exuberant life or appeared to get more fun out of it. Wildly contradictory, he was everything from a professional prizefighter to—really—president of a PTA. Generous yet mean, modest yet boastful, gentle yet brutal, brave yet racked by fear, he defied the attempts of critics to pigeonhole him. Yet one thing all concede: that this life, given so enthusiastically to destruction, still brought new vitality, indeed a whole new way of writing, to American fiction.

From birth Ernest Hemingway was beckoned opposite ways. His father was an ardent hunter and fisher and general outdoorsman who as a medical student had spent summers studying the Sioux Indians in South Dakota and working as cook on a surveying expedition to the Great Smoky Mountains. While in camp he startled the other men by producing a handsome pie made of wild blackberries and honey stolen from a beehive at great personal peril, the pastry of which had been rolled out with a beer bottle.

(This was, in fact, the only use he ever had for a beer bottle, being all his life a stern teetotaler.)

As a young M.D. building a practice Clarence Edmunds Hemingway had grown the full beard that was supposed to suggest maturity and competence to nervous patients, and indeed it did somewhat temper the dimpled good looks and the merry twinkle in the eye. The adventurer in him had yearned to go as a medical missionary to Guam or Greenland, but by the time of decision he had become engaged to the girl who lived across the street, and that was the end of that.

Grace Hall had just returned to Oak Park, Illinois, after studying for grand opera in New York, where she had appeared with the Philharmonic Orchestra and even been invited to sing for Queen Victoria in London. Her thrilling contralto quickly conquered the young doctor, and love nullified the previous plans of both. But forever after, in moments of marital stress, Grace's sacrificed career had a way of coming into the conversation.

The wedding was an impressive one—her gown had ninety yards of organdy in it—but the Halls were well able to afford such pomp. And besides, Grace Hall, though she had forgone opera for marriage, was still earning hundreds of dollars a week teaching and concertizing in the Chicago area.

In this, as in much else, the usual husband and wife roles were reversed: while the wife was presiding in the music room the young husband was averaging a mere fifty dollars a month at his practice, meanwhile taking care of the house, ordering, shopping, even cooking the meals. (On occasion, visiting a patient, he would borrow his telephone to tell Grace it was time to take the cake out of the oven.) His ideas of diet were far ahead of the surrounding community's—and, be it added, of his wife's as well. He fed their babies orange juice, meat, and fresh vegetables before they were even weaned, and Grace complained that he was going entirely too far when he brought the oldest baby to be nursed with onion on its breath.

This oldest baby, Marcelline, was born in 1898. Ernest came

the next year, followed by three more girls, Ursula, Madelaine, and Carol. Grace Hemingway had always thought twins very romantic and planned to have a couple at once. The first two babies, however, had failed her by coming separately and in different sexes, but being a woman of inflexible will she made twins out of them anyway. Marcelline and Ernest were clothed alike in fluffy, lace-trimmed little dresses and floppy hats; both of them had dolls and china tea sets to play with, and Marcelline was held back a year so that they could start school together.

Grace was also determined to have an orchestra in the family, and as each child came along it was taken to symphony concerts and operas and given an instrument to learn. When Ernest's turn came he was assigned the cello and he practiced it grumpily for years (though as time went on he secretly bowed with his right hand while holding a book in the left).

Thus the boy's early years were lived in a world almost totally dominated by females. He was, moreover, smaller than his "twin." As soon as possible he graduated out of girl's clothes into pants, but to his chagrin he long remained a head shorter than his sister. (The critics' later studies of his life and his aggressive masculinity have not paid as much attention to these early years as it seems they might have.)

Dr. Hemingway had never been altogether happy with his little son's upbringing and early began to pull him in the opposite direction by introducing him to the outdoor life, which he considered more appropriate. Before Ernest was old enough to say fish he had learned how to cast for one, and at four could give the Latin names of 250 North American birds. Shooting the birds came later.

But not so much later, for at ten he had his own 20-gauge shotgun and from then on guns were a large part of his life. "Treat a gun like a friend," his father always admonished him. "Keep it clean. Oil it, clean it after every use, but always remember it's an enemy if it's carelessly used."

Ernest, admiring his father unreservedly, was to emulate him in many and varied ways, and the passionate hunting and fishing to which he devoted entire years was an extension of his father's passion. Dr. Hemingway's physical courage similarly set a pattern. Once on a fishing expedition blood poisoning developed in his arm. Swollen to double its size, the arm had to be opened immediately if he was not to lose it, so, heating a knife red-hot, the doctor plunged it deep into his own infected flesh. The episode became a classic story of courage in the home, and years later Ernest performed his own version of it.

His early worship did not last throughout life, for too soon Ernest became unhappily aware of the husband's willingness to be bullied by the iron-willed wife, and then contempt and resentment followed. But the identification held always, to the very brink of the grave.

This emulation in no wise interfered with Ernest's consciousness even from babyhood of his own unique individuality. When he was no more than two his mother reported that, asked what he was afraid of, he would shout, " 'fraid o' nothing!" with great vehemence. And his sister Marcelline wrote of him later: "When Ernest was five his imaginative stories of things he had done or would do were so real to him that less understanding parents than ours might have punished him for telling lies. One day, after a particularly big exaggeration by Ernest—about how he had caught a runaway horse all by himself—Grandfather Hall turned to my mother and said in his soft, gentle way:

" 'Chumpy dear, this boy is going to be heard from some day. If he uses his imagination for good purposes, he'll be famous, but if he starts the wrong way, with all his energy, he'll end in jail, and it's up to you which way he goes.' My mother noted those words and often quoted them to my father in afteryears. I don't think she was reassured about which direction her older son was going until after he was married and started his newspaper career."

This perceptive grandparent had noted one of the major features of Hemingway's personality. The runaway imagination that made him a great fiction writer was given full scope in his everyday life as well. The tall tale designed to make him look brighter or tougher or richer or braver or more romantic than other people skipped off his tongue without a backward glance. If a lie would build him up he told it. In the face of indisputable evidence he denied having received any help from Scott Fitzgerald in writing *The Sun Also Rises,* and he recounted, claiming them as his own, glamorous experiences that had happened to other men. Conversely, he denied seamy episodes that were indisputably his.

These haphazard statements thrown out to fit the occasion have, to the student of his life, an effect beyond just adding color to a harlequin personality. Like a stone shattering a mirror, they break up the image so that basic facts about his life become unclear —for instance, after the break-up of his second marriage he said appalling things about the wife he had thrown over, yet many years later he told his brother that she was the best of all his four wives.

Still, Hemingway was a "true" writer. His careless attitude toward the truth did not extend to a situation *as he saw it.* That was all that he cared about—what *he saw.* Over and over he spoke of the struggle to write one completely true sentence, what you really felt, not what you ought to feel or had been taught to feel. The external facts were beside the point; writing "truly" meant giving the picture you saw bare and clean, and to that end he labored conscientiously all his life.

It is clear that this complex person, so long the only boy in the family, was the prize in a continuing tug-of-war between his parents. The massive, overpowering mother periodically given to "nerves" and the gentle father who at times might suddenly explode into righteous anger had separate goals for their son, though on one thing they agreed—strict moral and religious rectitude.

The rigidly high-toned atmosphere in Oak Park filled with music practice and females was annually exchanged for the more relaxed and masculine summers in the Michigan woods. There Windemere Cottage, standing beside Walloon Lake in a region populated by Ojibway Indians, was the center of the hunting and fishing life Ernest shared with his father. There the boy watched the doctor do emergency operations on the Indians. And there, though his father escaped this unhappy knowledge, the boy learned about drinking and girls.

These adolescent years, which he sometimes wrote about with loathing and sometimes with affection, were marked by several restless forays away from home, when he held odd jobs as a farm hand and dish washer and, having learned to box against his father's orders, occasionally as a sparring partner. Thus he managed to see a kind of life Oak Park never offered, and it was the Michigan woods rather than Oak Park that dominated his early fiction.

Having been nearly smothered by women in his home, this vigorous personality had to assert itself outside, and the two-year-old's boast " 'fraid o' nothing!" was the first of a thousand such boasts echoing through the years. Fiercely competitive, he had to be the fastest runner, the best shot, the bravest fighter anywhere around. Often, in fact, he was; but if he failed to be, his stories rarely conveyed the fact.

When he was sixteen, fate threw him a little male support in the shape of a baby brother. The little boy, though too young to be a companion, was very welcome anyway, for, as Leicester Hemingway wrote in his reminiscences, "He needed someone he could show off to as well as teach. He needed uncritical admiration. If the kid brother could show a little worshipful awe, that was a distinct aid in the relationship. I made a good kid brother when I was around."

The year 1917 brought America's entry into the World War and, simultaneously, Ernest's graduation from high school. His parents for some time had been worried not only by his braggadocio and insistence on being always first but, more serious, his careless attitude toward the truth and his irresponsible approach to life. Sports he worked hard at in order to build his body and beat his friends, and he showed an aptitude for writing and acting in school plays. But there were entirely too many scrapes. And when he was told to choose a college he fought off the whole idea. Higher education was the bunk.

The tension in the home tightened almost to breaking as he chafed under the rigid routine and the highly charged scenes with which his mother resolved any clash of wills. The parents' insistence on a college education was pitted against his own insistence on freedom. His first plan was to go to war, but for that seventeen-year-olds had to have their fathers' consent, so the next best escape route was newspapering somewhere. There the two sides rested, eyeball to eyeball.

The parents gave in, because they had to. A Kansas City relative provided an opening on that city's *Star,* and there he went, now a gangling six-footer, rosy-cheeked and dimpled, with an irresistible grin and the makings of extreme good looks. In *For Whom the Bell Tolls* he describes the farewell at the railroad station: "His father had kissed him goodby and said, 'May the Lord watch between me and thee while we are absent the one from the other.' His father had been a very religious man and he had said it simply and sincerely. But his moustache had been moist and his eyes were damp with emotion." The boy had been touched but at the same time embarrassed, glad to escape the display of sentiment.

On the *Star* Ernest managed to see the seamiest side of Kansas City life and always to get so near the action that on at least one occasion he got holes burned in his suit. He also got his first schooling in his profession, not only how to turn up the news but how to write it down. The *Star* style book was firm about that: "Write short declarative sentences. Avoid hackneyed adjectives. Use vigorous English. Strive for smoothness." It was a suitable primer for this learner, and he applied himself to it well.

His heart, however, was still on the battlefields of Europe, and on passing his eighteenth birthday he applied to every existing service, only to be rejected because of a bad eye. Finally he learned that the Red Cross was more broadminded about eyesight and he got himself assigned to its Ambulance Unit Four for Italy.

After taking three weeks off for trout fishing in the Michigan woods he reached Milan in June, 1918.

"Having a wonderful time!" he postcarded the *Star* on arrival. "Had my first baptism of fire my first day here when an entire munition factory exploded."

The jubilant tone was sheer bravado; at eighteen one did not admit to shock. But fourteen years later as a well-known writer he was still reliving the horror of gathering up the shattered bodies of the women workers and picking human fragments off a barbed wire fence. One could even write about it then. But at the time one passed it off lightly, as befitted a hardened newspaperman.

After this introductory incident there was nothing more to write home about for weeks. The ambulance corps was kept well back of the lines and soon Ernest became impatient. "I'm fed up," he growled to a colleague. "I'm going to get out of the ambulance section and see if I can't find out where the war is." The Red Cross maintained small canteens close to the lines, and at night men on bicycles carried cigarettes, candy, and postcards to the infantry at the front. So on the very black night of July 8 Hemingway pushed forward to a listening post on the bank of the Piave just where the river became a swamp. And "There," he said later, "I died."

Three Italian soldiers were standing beside him when the Austrians lobbed a mortar shell almost on top of them. Hemingway was knocked unconscious. "Then," he told his brother in after years, "I felt my soul or something coming right out of my body like you'd pull a silk handkerchief out of a pocket by one corner. It flew around and then came back and went in again, and I wasn't dead any more."

One of the Italians was really dead, his legs blown off, and the other, also legless, was screaming. Forcing himself to his feet, Ernest picked up the living soldier and carried him back toward the dugout. On the way an Austrian searchlight picked him out and a round of machine gun bullets ripped across his legs.

"I leaned over," he wrote, "and put my hand on my knee. My

knee wasn't there. My hand went in and my knee was down on my shin." Still, he struggled on somehow and brought his man to the dugout. By now he was dead and Hemingway blacked out again for a long time.

At the base hospital 227 pieces of shrapnel were removed from his legs. For a while he was not expected to live, and when a priest came through the ward he anointed Ernest along with the rest. This, Hemingway insisted later, had baptized him into the Catholic church.

This all but fatal wound was probably the most important experience of Hemingway's life, and for twenty or more years he observed its anniversary by rereading two of his favorite war books "to remind himself of what war was really like." But it was neither his first nor his last wound, for this life was an incredible succession of mishaps.

At the age of five he was running with a stick in his mouth when he fell and rammed the point into his tonsils. (Ever afterward he blamed this accident for his perennial bronchitis.) As a boy in Michigan he lodged a fishhook in his back and another time, boxing, got his handsome nose broken. After his World War leg wound he was gored by a bull while rescuing a friend in Spain, and in Paris a falling skylight split his head open. His car overturned in Wyoming, splintering his arm; an auto crash in London fractured his skull, and in Cuba, in another driving mishap, a rear-view mirror bracket was driven into his forehead. Firing at sharks in the Caribbean, he shot both his legs instead, and in Venice he nearly died of blood poisoning from a scratch on the eye. A hot-water heater exploded, cutting him with bits of flying metal; his chin was opened up in a horseback riding accident; he broke his toe angrily kicking open a gate and, slipping on a boat deck, cut his head open. Flying over Africa he sustained within a few days two plane crashes, in which he received severe internal injuries and a brain concussion, the last of seven. But still, that great wound on the banks on the Piave was the epoch-making, the unforgettable, the irreparable one.

It is not strange that for the rest of his life the period surrounding this event carried not only a special impact but a special glory. Only nineteen when it happened, he was the first American wounded in Italy, in itself a unique distinction. Lying in the hospital, so handsome, so somehow innocent and vulnerable in his youthfulness, he was visited and admired and petted. The tale was told over and over of his wounding, his rescue of his companion, his stoic endurance of pain, and especially his courage when—Dr. Hemingway's son!—he dug some shrapnel out of his own leg with a penknife.

Suddenly the tight mold into which his parents had sought to press him burst asunder, for from a youth with unthinking animal spirits he blossomed overnight into a hero brave and resourceful, decorated and respected.... And even modest. There was no need here for braggadocio, for in the hospital he had, unsought, all the attention he wanted, photographed for American newsreels and treated as an equal by superior officers who gathered around to laugh at his witty, free-flowing monologues. The ward was his private court where, lying covered with a bright-colored afghan, he reigned supreme. The older nurses adored and mothered him jealously while the younger ones reacted like steel filings to his newly discovered magnetism.

Inevitably love entered the ward. Agnes von Kurowsky was a young American nurse on her first foreign assignment, cheerful, sympathetic, with a mischievous sense of humor and a bright, attractive face. The fact that she was six years older than Ernest made no difference at first, and she cared for him, kidding and yet tender, as long as he was bedfast. When he graduated to crutches they walked in the lovely Italian countryside and went to the races in Milan, drinking aperitifs together. Soon Ernest was in love, but when he began talking of marriage Agnes held her age firmly in mind and, looking beyond the moment, rationed their love-making with care.

In November the war ended. He considered staying on in Europe to accept some of the luxurious hospitality offered by several women and men but she urged him to concentrate on getting back to work.

"Don't be a sponger or a bum," she pleaded. "It's wonderful to be alive in these stirring times, but only if we can do something good with our lives." If he went home and finished recuperating she might, just might, come over and visit him. This he took to mean she might marry him as well. In January, 1919, he sailed.

The newsreels had made him something of a celebrity, and on landing he was the only man aboard the troopship to be interviewed. The New York *Sun*'s reporter was under the impression that he had been actually fighting the Austrians, and he could not bear to disabuse him. Grinning modestly, he let the notion stand.

Oak Park too received him as a fighting hero. He came bearing manifold souvenirs—guns, bayonets, an unexploded hand grenade, a ring made of shrapnel from his leg, the bloodstained trousers worn the night of his wound. There were also two medals for bravery, one of silver presented by the Italian king.

Invited to speak all over Oak Park, he gave his audiences full measure, holding up the bloodstained trousers dramatically but at the same time minimizing his own exploits. Stunning in his uniform, polished boots, and Sam Browne belt, he was Britishly casual about the war, passing it off with easy modesty as "great sport." "It was a splendid triumph," observed his brother, "for the young man so recently regarded by his family as an irresponsible gray sheep who would not settle down."

But this poised and easy-going young warrior was not all there was to Hemingway. From an English officer he had learned some lines out of Shakespeare's *Henry IV:* "A man can die but once; we owe God a death . . . and let it go which way it will, he that dies this year is quit for the next." Death, he had written his father from the hospital, is a simple thing, a very little thing, nothing to fear at all. He had himself died once, there on the river, and he knew.

Familiarity, it is said, breeds contempt, and contempt minimizes fear. Hemingway was seeking to dispel his fear by staring it down. But he never succeeded. Though he denied hotly that his numberless accidents suggested a Freudian death wish, the fact is that he was hypnotized by death, enslaved and terrified by it all his life. (Alcohol, he said, was the giant-killer, and all his life he turned to it in crises.)

Fear began very young for Hemingway, if one can believe his own writings. His earliest stories were about a boy he called Nick Adams who lived "up in Michigan." Sometimes obliquely, sometimes directly, they give glimpses of a very observant, sensitive boy exposed to scenes of violence and horror.

In one tale he goes with his doctor-father to an Indian camp and watches him delivering a baby with a jackknife without benefit of anesthetic, while the woman's sick husband, unable to stand her screaming, slits his throat from ear to ear. Another story tells of riding the rods and being knocked off a moving train, when he has an unnerving encounter with two sinister prizefighters. In still another he suffers a wound on his spine. Later on going to war, he is badly wounded and depends on the giant-killer to numb his constant fear. But even the giant-killer cannot help him; he is unable to sleep for thinking about the night he nearly died. "If I could have a light I was not afraid to sleep," the man in the story says, "because I knew my soul would only go out of me if it were dark."

Subsequently this Nick Adams assumes other names—Jake Barnes in *The Sun Also Rises,* Lieutenant Frederic Henry in *A Farewell to Arms,* Robert Jordan in *For Whom the Bell Tolls,* Colonel Richard Cantwell in *Across the River and into the Trees.* In each case this man experiences more violence and endures more wounds. But, Leicester Hemingway writes, "Not all of Ernest's wounds were physical. Like hundreds of thousands of other soldiers before and since, he had received some psychic shock. He was plagued by insomnia and couldn't sleep unless he had a light in his room."

His parents perhaps did not fully understand the depth of Hemingway's sickness when he returned from war. It was disconcerting to them to see him lying about the house half the

day, clinging to the Red Cross afghan which he said kept
him from being so homesick for Italy. It was annoying that, having had his fling at adventure, he still would not settle down to
steady, sensible work. Soon their pride in his exploits simmered
down into indifference and they made no effort to hide their
impatience.

Only his sister Marcelline sensed something of his disquiet.
She would visit his room and find him strangely depressed. Once,
behind closed doors, he offered her a drink of kümmel. "Don't be
afraid of it," he told her. "There's great comfort in that little bottle." And then he said, "Don't be afraid to taste all the other things
in life that aren't here in Oak Park. . . . There's a whole big world
out there full of people who really feel things. . . . Taste everything,
Sis." Suddenly she realized that living in strait-laced Oak Park
must seem like "being shut in a box with the cover nailed down."
He could never settle down there.

All this winter Ernest had been waiting to hear from Agnes
about their marriage. Though her answers to his voluminous letters
had been shorter and more businesslike than his, nevertheless the
word he received in March was a severe shock. Agnes was planning to marry an Italian officer. On reading it, he went to bed,
turned his face to the wall, and lay for many days with a fever that
refused to respond to his father's ministrations.

Finally the fever left, and he recovered from the shock sufficiently to write another nurse at the hospital that he hoped Agnes
would fall down and "knock out all her front teeth." Within a
month he was dating another girl. And in time he so softened
toward his early love that she became the highly idealized heroine
of *A Farewell to Arms.*

The following year was devoted to breaking with his family.
His mother was growing ever more critical of his "drifting," and
he in turn was resentful of her plan to build herself a cottage as a
retreat from her family. She should, he complained, have used the
money for college for the younger kids. (Later, in a fit of self-pity,
he declared that he himself had been deprived of a Princeton

education because she appropriated the money for her own pleasure.)

All this time his family saw him constantly writing stories, but as he rarely sold anything they hardly counted that as work. At last, to escape their disapproval he took a job in Toronto as companion to a lame boy whose parents were wintering in Florida, and while there he managed to sell a dozen pieces to the Toronto *Star Weekly*. With spring, however, the Michigan woods and trout streams called.

Instead of returning to Windemere Cottage and doing the usual household chores—digging garbage holes, chopping wood, mending the roof, fetching ice from the icehouse—he stayed with friends and dropped in only at mealtimes accompanied by several young men. Finally he announced that four of them planned to work their way to Japan and his parents would please supply the railway fare to San Francisco.

Grace Hemingway, who was having her own emotional problems with growing old and corpulent and less able to cope as the mother of six, was more and more irked by all this irresponsibility. His father, sweating out the hot summer in Chicago, was equally displeased. Grace withheld her ire until Ernest's twenty-first birthday, but then, after putting together a ceremonial dinner at Windemere Cottage, she handed him an ultimatum: either pull himself together and get a job or leave home.

Here then was one more wound, no less painful because largely deserved. Hemingway was always given to self-pity, and this abrupt dismissal fractured the family relationship forever. From time to time thereafter he did go home; he did remain fond of his father always. But while he patched up his quarrel with his mother superficially and in the latter years accepted financial responsibility for her, he openly called her a bitch as long as he lived.

In the fall he made a complete break by moving into the apartment of two friends in Chicago and got a job on a fly-by-night house organ.

This was at the beginning of the decade when French-American currency exchange was so unbalanced that Americans could live in Paris for a song. Aspiring painters and writers were rushing over pell-mell to congregate on the Left Bank and enjoy *la vie Bohéme,* and Hemingway like the rest began saving for the passage.

Now occurred two events with significance for the future. Ernest met Sherwood Anderson, author of *Winesburg, Ohio,* who had already spent time in Paris and knew many of its famous expatriates. And he met a tall red-haired girl from St. Louis who was visiting in an apartment shared by a group of wild young intellectuals.

Hadley Richardson was an orphan with a small private income. Having nursed her dying mother through a long illness, she was now at loose ends, at twenty-eight looking forward somewhat apprehensively to spinsterhood. The Chicago group, all of them writing or doing something interesting, all a little crazy with the joy of being alive, brought her a breath of new life and she gulped down the winey atmosphere joyously. Ernest Hemingway, with his good looks, bursting energy, and ready laugh, was the most exhilarating of the lot.

His reaction to her was equally positive. "The moment she entered the room," he told a friend, "an intense feeling came over me. I knew she was the girl I was going to marry."

Her love moved forward unchecked, no doubts assailing it, and life was suddenly all one great, exciting Christmas Eve. But Ernest, despite his immediate attraction, was less certain. From thoughts of marriage his eyes turned back longingly to the freedom of the Michigan woods, and he regarded the seven years' difference in their ages with some questioning. When she went home he wrote her that he "hoped" he would go on loving her "for a little while at least."

His wavering tone caught her ear and she wrote anxiously that if he was any less sure of his love than she of hers he was to tell her at once. But the attraction was very strong. And Ernest not only loved but admired her. Having hurt her foot just before she was due to go with him to a football game, she limped along gamely in a red felt bedroom slipper. "Anybody else would have been embarrassed," he said approvingly. "But she went along as though nothing had happened. That girl's a real sport." This, throughout the next thirty years, she was to prove many times.

For once Ernest's parents approved of his plans. Married to a nice girl, surely he would settle down, write if that was what he wanted but at any rate stick to something steady and constructive. They gave the couple a large wedding at the lake and lent them Windemere Cottage for the honeymoon.

Paris was now the goal for both of them to save for. With Hadley's income for a base and Ernest's occasional sales to the *Star* for trimmings, they could just make it. Sherwood Anderson came through with a number of flattering introductions to his famous friends—Gertrude Stein, the nucleus of a galaxy of painters and writers; Sylvia Beach, the owner of the bookshop Shakespeare and Company and publisher of James Joyce's *Ulysses;* and Ezra Pound, poet, famous in London, Paris, and New York. All received word of the "quite wonderful newspaper man with extraordinary talent," the "writer instinctively in touch with everything worth while" who would soon be among them. In a burst of gratitude Ernest filled a haversack with the canned goods he and Hadley would no longer be needing and carried it up several flights of stairs to Anderson's apartment.

As they stood on the train's back platform waving good-bye Marcelline noticed that Hadley's hands were bare and red with cold. Pulling off her gray wool gloves, she tossed them to her. One of Ernest's friends likewise donated his wool muffler. So, warmed by their friends, they left for Paris, arriving at Christmas, 1921.

Sherwood Anderson had correctly noted Ernest Hemingway's instinct for being where everything worth while was going on. Paris just then was certainly that place, and perhaps no other point in both time and space has ever furnished so many romantic reminiscences. Ezra Pound, Gertrude Stein, Lewis Galantière, Scott Fitzgerald, Morley Callaghan, John Dos Passos, Sherwood Ander-

son, Max Eastman, Caresse Crosby, Paul Scott Mowrer, Thomas
Wolfe, Ford Madox Ford, James Joyce, Lincoln Steffens, Edmund
Wilson, John Peale Bishop, Kay Boyle, William Carlos Williams,
Archibald MacLeish, Janet Flanner, Josephine Herbst, Donald
Ogden Stewart, George Plimpton, Calvin Tomkins, Malcolm Cow-
ley, and Vincent Sheean—all published memoirs of this magic time
when the franc was cheap and French wine better than Prohibi-
tion gin.

Since most of this colony was not overburdened with money,
the Hemingways' poverty did not set them apart, and soon they
were at the hub of the excitement. Their first flat was up four
flights of stairs, two dirty, smelly, noisy rooms whose huge gilded
bed nearly filled the bedroom. There was a toilet in the hall and
for bathing a bowl and pitcher in a closet. But the Paris scenery
from their windows was breathtaking, and Paris living was un-
believably cheap—five cents for breakfast and sixty cents for a full
dinner.

Paris winters being what they were, Ernest wrote in bed with
chattering teeth, pounding the portable on his knees. Later, for
quiet and solitude, he took a tiny room nearby, burning bundles of
twigs for warmth, or went to his favorite cafe, the Closerie des
Lilas, where he could write for hours undisturbed. But wherever
he went he carried a rabbit's foot worn bare by fingering in his
pocket. He needed all the luck he could get, for writing was hard
work.

For the first time he was in it up to his eyelids. He had written
reams before, but those stories had been largely invented. Now,
starting afresh, he resolved to take things he knew firsthand, things
that had happened to a boy, say, in Michigan, a boy he would call
Nick Adams. Stripping them down to essentials, he would tell what
he knew with a new truth and simplicity—short, direct sentences,
plain words, no adjectives or embroidery. All one had to do, he told
himself, was write one true sentence, the truest sentence anyone
could think of. Then, if that one went right, he could write another
one, and so go on from there. When he had got to a certain place

in a story, the point where he knew exactly what was to come next, he would stop for the day, going out to walk and observe and drink and talk and listen, meanwhile leaving the story for his subconscious to follow up.

He liked to sit with Hadley in cafes and listen, but when the other expatriates began talking loftily of art and artists he exploded with impatience. Annoyed by pretentiousness, he was not fond of talking about his work to people he did not trust, but when he finally took Hadley to see Gertrude Stein and her companion Alice B. Toklas, then things were different.

Stocky and mannish and old enough to be his mother, Gertrude Stein was enchanted with the handsome young man and his pretty wife, and in her big warm apartment crammed with great paintings the young couple were fed and treated like attractive, bright children. He thought Miss Stein and her friend were somehow resentful of their frank love for each other but forgave them humorously, and the friendship grew and prospered. Ernest showed Gertrude his poems and stories. She liked some and disapproved of others, and he listened gratefully, thinking her "always right."

In return for her kindness he copied out and proofread fifty pages of her *The Making of Americans* and was later able to get it published. Being rich she did not need the royalties but she wanted to be published anyway, and this was a great favor he did her. (Later there was a famous quarrel, each side claiming to have taught the other all he knew. Certainly there is a similarity of style —the simple, spare sentences, the repetition, the small, sharp words, the violence told in a cold objective tone. She had been working that vein for many years and published the famous "Melanctha" in 1909, so the priority was evidently hers. But the style is only part of Hemingway's innovative genius and even without it the importance of his influence on subsequent writers would have been profound.)

Since nobody was buying his stories he had to keep feeding at the Toronto *Star*'s trough. In April, 1922, he covered an international conference in Genoa, and after that traveled ten thousand miles to assignments all over Europe and the Near East. Taking Hadley with him when he could, he revisited the Piave to show her the scene of his wounding. But the trip was a disappointment. The spot where he had fallen was overgrown with weeds, the rubble and shattered houses were all cleaned up, and the dugout he had carried his soldier to was gone. In four years his past had been all but obliterated and he was wistful. But in a few more years he would recreate it out of his memory.

In due course, when he went to Spain, he found not his past but part of his future. The bullfighting there fascinated him. "A great art," he called it, "a beautiful dance involving death." He wanted to test his courage as a picador in the ring but was prevented by the bullfighters' union. Nevertheless he vowed to return; many times he would come back and back to tell the world about this graceful art.

All this time there seemed to be a solid wall set up against his fiction. Finally he managed to make a crack in it by selling a few "somewhat obscene" poems to a German magazine and he thought the spell was broken thereby. And so it might have been. But that will never be known, for here occurred one of those nightmare accidents that haunt one until death. Ernest was in Switzerland in early December covering the 1922 Lausanne Peace Conference and, feeling bored, he wired Hadley to join him for skiing. Thinking to please him, she took along his manuscripts to work on in the Christmas recess.

Everything he had written in his year in Paris went into the suitcase, eighteen stories and the first draft of a novel. Only two stories were left out, "Up in Michigan," which Gertrude had said was not worth bothering with, and "My Old Man," which Lincoln Steffens had helpfully sent off to *Cosmopolitan* magazine. During the few minutes while Hadley's luggage was being carried to the train, the suitcase was stolen.

So pitiable was her condition when Ernest met her at the train that he had to be kind. And actually he was not too much disturbed, because of course she hadn't put in the carbons as well. She wouldn't, she just *couldn't* have done that. However, he had better go to Paris and make sure.

"It was true all right," he wrote later, "and I remember what I did in the night after I let myself into the flat and found it was true." What he did he never told, but the following day he rushed to the Stein abode in a state of hysteria.

Never, he moaned, never would he be able to write again. This was the end of life. And when he went back to Hadley he was indeed numb and hopeless. However, in the midst of his despair he met the editor Edward O'Brien, who was putting together his anthology *The Best Short Stories of 1923.* "My Old Man" had been returned by *Cosmopolitan,* and like one showing a lock of a dead child's hair Hemingway showed him the story.

Customarily this anthology contained only stories already published. But now O'Brien announced to an incredulous Hemingway that he intended to include this unpublished one. This exhilarating event made writing easier to get back to, and he produced a third story, "Out of Season," about a young man who has quarreled with his wife. Writing as he did out of experience, it had a certain ominous significance.

A friend of Ezra Pound's took a fancy to Hemingway's stories and published them along with some poems in an edition limited to three hundred copies. Thus *Three Stories and Ten Poems* was Ernest Hemingway's first book. He sent a copy to Marcelline, but when she read "Up in Michigan" she was so shocked, not only by the "vulgar, sordid" story but by his use of friends' real names, that she never told her parents of its existence.

The quarrel pictured in "Out of Season" was not the first nor the last difference between Ernest and Hadley. He was self-centered and demanding and she was overprone to tears. Still, they were deeply in love, and Hadley's pliancy made her an ideal "playmate." Whatever Ernest enjoyed Hadley enjoyed—skiing, shooting, fishing, camping, mountain climbing, watching bullfights, most of all going to bed. He wrote lyrically of their pleasures together, rejoicing in the free-wheeling irresponsibility of their life.

But suddenly a blight fell on it. Hadley was pregnant. Ernest went moaning to Gertrude Stein; he was too young, they would be tied down and have no more fun together. But what was done was done, and so, sighing heavily, he moved Hadley to Toronto and took a steady job with the *Star.*

John Hadley Nicanor Hemingway (named in part for a Spanish matador and immediately nicknamed Bumby) was born in October, 1923. Ernest's parents were delighted with this settling influence on their son; Hadley was delighted with the baby's beauty; and Ernest, while hardly delighted, found the child more interesting than he had anticipated. In time he even wrote Gertrude that he was getting "quite fond" of him. But he hated Toronto and the *Star,* hated its editor, and was only waiting for an excuse to get back to Paris.

This excuse came via Edward O'Brien, whose *Best Short Stories* contained "My Old Man." O'Brien, astonishingly, had dedicated the entire volume to the unknown young writer (incidentally misspelling the writer's name Hemenway). This gave him the courage he needed. After writing a blistering letter of resignation to the editor he enlisted his friends to carry their belongings from the apartment one by one. Then while the landlord was not looking they slipped out and sailed back to France.

There they presented the baby to Gertrude, whom Ernest appointed his godmother. Hadley wrote Grace Hemingway reassuringly about the baby's care: Miss Stein, who was really Dr. Stein and visited Bumby every day or so, had been an obstetrical surgeon at Johns Hopkins and knew all about babies.

Ernest's decision to throw over his steady salary left them both feeling somewhat breathless, for bad investments had cut Hadley's income to the bone. Times now were very hard, and Ernest found domesticity puzzling and worrisome. Rising at dawn, he boiled the bottles and rubber nipples, made the formula, and gave Bumby his bottle, after which he could write at the dining table until Hadley's housekeeping noises drove him out of the house. The writing moreover went badly, nothing sold, and he would beat the bed pillows at night in a helpless rage. Though later descriptions of his hunger were an exaggeration—"belly-empty, hollow-hungry"—there were in fact times when what they ate was the pigeons from the park, and he made his love of boxing support them by sparring in a gym.

Nevertheless he worked faithfully, and in the seven months after Toronto turned out nine powerful stories. Two of the current expatriates, John Dos Passos and Donald Ogden Stewart, encouraged him to try for American publication, and a third, Harold Loeb, went further, sending a collection of the stories to his own publisher, Horace Liveright. Loeb's girl, Kitty Cannell, having heard Hemingway make a number of anti-Semitic remarks, warned Loeb to beware of him, but like many others Loeb was spellbound by this man who wore genius on him like a headlight, and persisted in urging Hemingway on Liveright. Early in 1925 came a cable: *In Our Time* was accepted.

Hadley had always been aware of the threadbare ties between Ernest and his family and had tried to be the ideal daughter-in-law, writing long friendly letters and unostentatiously picturing their life in its best light. Now, with this impending publication, she wrote that the three of them were terrifically happy, that the baby was so handsome it hurt and so smart he could talk in three languages. And wasn't it wonderful how well Hem was doing—not only Boni and Liveright bringing out his book, but the story "Big Two-Hearted River" coming out in *This Quarter* and some stories sold to a German magazine. He had actually received $200 advance from Liveright and they were saving it up for a trip to Spain.

This trip was a long-planned project. Ernest, as an old bullfight expert, had gathered a group of friends to indoctrinate them into the beauty and grandeur of the art, and chattering knowingly of *veronicas, muletas,* and *recibiendos,* he pointed out the spot between the bull's shoulderblades where the sword entered at the moment of truth.

One morning he decided to prove his courage in the amateur free-for-alls held each day, and did it so spectacularly that Donald Stewart, somewhat intoxicated and inspired by Hemingway's bravery, undertook to leap onto the bull's back and blow smoke into its eyes. The irritated bull lifted him on his horns and tossed him into the air, breaking two of his ribs. Hemingway rushed to the rescue and was also slightly gored. The horns, however, had been padded in anticipation of such an accident and both men survived.

The episode went into the Hemingway dossier in the States and made headlines in some Chicago papers, which the family read with amazement. They were gradually becoming inured to their unpredictable relative, and these flattering comments were agreeably soothing after the shock sustained on receiving six copies of *In Our Time*. When that package came the doctor had given one horrified glance through it and shot it back to the publisher.

The following year Ernest and Hadley returned to Pamplona bringing with them some truly exotic friends. They had come to watch the performance of a remarkable nineteen-year-old matador, Ordoñez, whom Hemingway had discovered the previous year. Lady Duff Twysden, a striking Englishwoman with unbridled appetites, had come to keep an eye on Hemingway, whom *she* had discovered the previous winter. Harold Loeb, who had recently discovered that lady's irresistible charm, had come to keep an eye on her. One Pat Guthrie, the lady's sometime lover, was keeping an eye on her and Loeb combined. Hadley, who was not really enjoying herself but was trying to keep in the spirit of the party, was casting a mildly flirtatious eye on Ordoñez. And that young matador did his part by giving her the ear of his first bull.

Hemingway himself was having a glorious time. The central, fixed star around whom swirled a veritable galaxy of emotions, he reveled in the turmoil he had instigated. And he himself was not altogether uninvolved. Lady Duff Twysden, beside herself with passion, was laying desperate siege to him, but with a lingering loyalty to Hadley he could not quite make up his mind to be unfaithful. At the same time, enjoying his power, he drove Duff distracted by rejecting her himself but making an unconscionable scene when she turned in desperation to Loeb. Altogether it was a spirited and bracing time.

Out of it, naturally, came a book. Ernest, his head swimming with the hot Spanish fiesta, the bullfighting, and the intoxicating sexual complications, decided on a novel about the young matador. Very shortly this switched to the more dynamic Duff Twysden and her friends, and once finding its groove, the manuscript moved ahead effortlessly.

Some months later, when Harold Loeb and Kitty Cannell were back together, they joined the Hemingways for dinner. Loeb and Kitty had long been urging Hem to write a novel and now, as he and Kitty followed Hadley and Loeb to the restaurant, he said to her, "I'm doing what you said. I'm writing a novel full of plot and drama." He pointed to the two in front. "I'm putting everyone in, and that kike Loeb is the villain. But you're a wonderful girl, Kitty, and I wouldn't do anything to annoy you."

Kitty said nothing, though her heart had stopped momentarily, and the evening passed without comment. Already, as a genius, he was being allowed special privileges.

Five days after Hemingway had accepted Liveright's offer for *In Our Time* he received a letter from Maxwell Perkins, eminent editor of Scribner's in New York. Perkins had been alerted to Hemingway's stories by one of his authors living in Paris, Scott Fitzgerald, and he wondered if Mr. Hemingway had a novel he would care to let him read.

Replying, Mr. Hemingway told him regretfully about the Liveright contract, which included options for his next three books. He was terribly sorry, he would certainly have liked to be with Scribner's.

Later Fitzgerald, recognizing him in a bar, introduced himself and told him at great length what an absolutely great writer he was. Hemingway, unaccustomed to authors who praised other writers' work, was embarrassed and suspicious, but he finally decided Fitz was a really "nonconceited writer." He noted approvingly that he was also an accomplished drinker, and they spent many an evening killing a bottle together.

Scott and Ernest were both friends of the wealthy American couple, the Murphys, who lived on the Riviera and collected talented young writers. Gerald and Sara Murphy had welcomed the Hemingways into their circle and shared their luxurious life with them. And for a while the impoverished young couple, fresh from the traditional artist's garret in Paris, reveled in expensive restaurants, chauffered cars, and breakfasts in bed.

But inevitably Hemingway turned against them. Many years later he decided that he had been betrayed by "the rich." In *A Moveable Feast,* the bitter book he wrote near the end of his life, he tells, without names, of the corruption of an innocent young writer: "When you have two people," he writes, "who love each other, are happy and gay and really good work is being done by one or both of them, people are drawn to them as surely as migrating birds are drawn at night to a powerful beacon. . . . Those who attract people by their happiness and their performance are usually inexperienced. They do not know how not to be overrun and how to go away. . . . That every day should be a fiesta seemed to me a marvelous discovery. I even read aloud the part of the novel that I had rewritten, which is about as low as a writer can get."

Translated, this is a regretful look back at his loss of innocence, which he dated from about this time. Integrity in a writer, he once said, was like virginity in a woman—once lost never regained—and he was remembering how admirably he had acted before he had lost his. He was just making a name for himself and the Hearst organization had offered him a contract that would have meant a great deal of money and security. But, fearing to lose his integrity, he had refused it and gone on "starving." Then later, having tasted the Murphys' luxury, he had let himself be seduced. He had never forgiven either himself or them.

The publication of *In Our Time* had brought fine reviews, which was gratifying; but too many of them had noted a resemblance to Sherwood Anderson, and that was annoying. The book, furthermore, made him no money. So Ernest, hearing from Fitzgerald of Scribner's generous terms and regarding his new novel as far too fine for Liveright, was doubly anxious to switch publishers. The only obstacle was Liveright's option on his next books. At last, however, he thought of a plan to kill two birds, Anderson and Liveright, with one stone.

The magic ingredient in his plan was the fact that Liveright was Anderson's publisher. Quickly he dashed off an amusing parody of Anderson's recent novel, *Dark Laughter,* which made the book seem suddenly ridiculous. Liveright, he knew, could never afford to bring out a book so damaging to one of his own important authors; he would have to reject it, and Hemingway's contract would thereby be voided.

Fitzgerald and the Murphys thought the book funny and brilliant. Dos Passos on the other hand called the whole idea a snide attack on an aging champion. Hadley detested it—after all, hadn't Sherwood sponsored them and introduced them to his best friends? Gertrude Stein was furious.

The magic worked, however, and Hemingway was freed. The book proved him the master rather than the disciple of the other man; and Perkins, anxious to acquire him at any price, snapped up *The Torrents of Spring.* A few months later he got Hemingway's second book, which was what he really wanted.

The Sun Also Rises confirmed Hemingway's assertion that he had put everyone in. Cocktail hour conversation in Paris the fall of 1926 flourished on the guessing game of Who was Who. Brett Ashley was Duff Twysden, naturally, and Romero the young matador Ordoñez. Robert Cohn had to be Harold Loeb—and how could poor Harold *bear* it? No wonder he had threatened to kill Hem. And poor Kitty Cannell—having to go to bed for three days, so sick with shame for herself and Harold. Duff Twysden, of course, was acting typically: so like Duff to say she didn't give a damn. And she really did have a marvelous, deadpan sense of humor—after all the men she'd slept with, to be so literal about *not* having slept with the little bullfighter.

Gossip swirled around the book's Jake Barnes, the American who had been wounded in such an unfortunate and embarrassing way in the war. Was it Hem or not? Jake had much the same background—Midwest U.S., newspaper job, wounded on the Italian front, and all that. But the part about Jake's wound couldn't be true of Hem, because Hem had a child. What *was* the story there?

Had these Parisians been able to survey Hemingway's entire literary output they would have recognized Jake's wound as only one in a long succession of wounds, some visible, some invisible, but all the same hallmark of a Hemingway hero.

The Sun did not require a guessing game to stimulate its sales in the United States. A flood of rave reviews sent it roaring down the best-seller path, and very soon it became one of those literary phenomena that leave a permanent imprint on a culture. College girls began modeling themselves after Lady Brett, and a critic reported that "bright young men from the Middle West were trying to be Hemingway heroes, talking in tough understatements from the sides of their mouths."

His parents could not conceal their distress and alarm. His father hoped for "healthier" books in the future, while his mother "could not keep silence any longer." Had he utterly forgotten loyalty, nobility, honor? Did he know no words other than *damn* and *bitch?* However, she loved him still and believed he would one day do something worth while.

He replied angrily that he could use a little family loyalty himself. Didn't she understand that he needed tranquillity to write, particularly at this time?

There was no explanation of the significance of "this time," but gradually one appeared. Some months earlier he had once or twice mentioned going to mass, which had mystified his Protestant parents. Now, very casually, he reported that he had ordered all his royalties paid to Hadley and Bumby as he and Hadley had been living apart for six months. The relationship of the two facts was not clear at once to the shocked parents, but all too soon it was clarified.

The year before, Ernest and Hadley had met Pauline Pfeiffer, daughter of a wealthy landowner in Pigott, Arkansas, who was in Paris working for *Vogue*. Younger than Hadley but four years older than Ernest, she was tiny and chic and, in contrast to Hadley, very expensively dressed. She took an immediate interest in the couple and soon moved into a close friendship with Hadley. When the Hemingways went to Austria to ski she went along, making Hem promise to teach her the art of skiing. And there, in a romantic snow-covered village, having come and seen, she made up her mind to conquer.

The next months had a strange, unreal quality. One of the trio had by this time a clear knowledge of what she was doing. One, living in a bemused trance, was enjoying it so much he refused to wake up. And one, as yet, was innocently unaware. Many years later, in that same reflective mood in which Hemingway describes his seduction by the Gerald Murphys, he looks back on his seduction by "another rich."

"The oldest trick there is," he writes in *A Moveable Feast*, ". . . is that an unmarried young woman becomes the temporary best friend of another young woman who is married, goes to live with the husband and wife and unknowingly, innocently and unrelentingly sets out to marry the husband. . . . The arrangement has advantages until you know how it works out. The husband has two attractive girls around when he has finished work. One is new and strange and if he has bad luck he gets to love them both. Then instead of the two of them and their child there are three of them. First it is stimulating and fun. . . . You lie and hate it and it destroys you and every day is more dangerous, but you live day by day as in a war."

This was at the time he was switching from Liveright to Scribner's, and he had to go to New York to complete the deal. Away from Pauline, he came out of his trance, but passing through Paris on his way back to Austria, he saw her again and "did not take the first train or the second or the third."

On the Schruns railroad platform Hadley was waiting for him. "When I saw my wife again . . . I wished I had died before I ever loved anyone but her. She was smiling, the sun on her lovely face tanned by the snow and sun . . . and Mr. Bumby standing with her . . . . I loved her and I loved no one else . . .and it wasn't until we were out of the mountains in late spring and back in Paris that the other thing started again. . . . Paris was never to be the same again."

His remorse was terrible. Having withstood the importunate Duff Twysden, he had succumbed to this new attraction. But, as he confessed many years afterward, there was a fundamental difference between the two situations. Pauline was rich. And he had learned from the Murphys the pleasures and power of wealth.

But he still loved Hadley, and "double-crossing" her drove him to meditations on suicide. "Probably the best way, unless you could arrange to die some way while asleep, would be to go off a liner. . . . There would be only the moment of taking the jump."

The difficulty was that Pauline wanted not just a love affair but marriage. She was a rigorous Catholic and had taken him to mass a number of times, and this tended to complicate the marriage question. But he recalled being anointed by the priest in the Italian hospital and this, he declared, had made him a Catholic too. And if he had been a Catholic when he married Hadley, why then, since that was a Protestant ceremony, he had never been married at all. Thus this problem was cleared up.

By now of course Hadley knew the whole story. They put the situation up to her then, and after crying a little (or perhaps a lot, in private) she agreed to give Ernest a divorce. Only, just to make sure that he really wanted it, she stipulated that he and Pauline should stay entirely apart for a hundred days. If they were still of the same mind at the end, she would go ahead. She wrote out an agreement and signed her name.

Sick with remorse, Ernest wrote her that she was being brave, unselfish, and generous, and that since she had supported him while he wrote his early books he was now not only making over all his royalties to her but writing a new will leaving everything to Bumby. The boy's best luck, he said, was having her for a mother, with her straight thinking, her good head and heart, and her lovely hands. She was the best, truest, and loveliest person he had ever known.

During the months of probation Ernest wandered about Paris alone acting as if he had lost his best friend. But it was not Pauline he was mourning for. Over many years, during accidents, disasters, and broken marriages, his mind kept turning back to Hadley for consolation; the more he saw of other women, he wrote her on his fortieth birthday, the more he admired her.

Pauline, who had gone to Arkansas for her probation period, now returned to Paris, and the wedding took place in May, 1927. The Pfeiffer family, including a benevolent Uncle Gus, head of a large cosmetic firm, sent handsome checks and off they went for a three-week honeymoon of fishing, swimming, and writing. Hemingway never knew poverty or hunger again.

It was during this year that *Jimmy Breen,* the first of Hemingway's unpublished novels, was begun. But after twenty chapters he lost interest and stopped; it would never do to follow a smash hit with something anticlimactic, and he put the manuscript aside. (This, along with much other unpublished work over the years, went into storage in the Ritz basement, in Sloppy Joe's Bar in Key West, and in Cuban bank vaults. After his death four novels, thirty-three poems, nineteen short stories, and eleven works of nonfiction—nearly 20,000 pages in all—were opened, read, and in 1969 inventoried.)

What did follow *The Sun Also Rises* was a collection of the short stories he had been writing at intervals for some years. *Men Without Women* dwelt again on the Nick Adams of his youth. Selling well on the strength of his former success, it brought him praise for his brilliance but a general murmur of regret for his obsession with "bullfighters, bruisers, touts, gunmen, professional soldiers, prostitutes, hard drinkers and dope-fiends." He declared angrily that the critics were trying to "put him out of business" and vowed never to read their comments again.

During 1927 a great change came in his life. Pauline became pregnant and, a little apprehensive about having a first baby at thirty-two, she yearned for American doctors. So the six glorious years of youthful struggle in Paris came to an end. They sailed for the States and drove down to Florida in a yellow coupé donated by Uncle Gus and settled in a house in Key West, also donated by Uncle Gus.

Once established in their new home, Ernest shook down into a routine of writing in the early morning, wandering about town gossiping for an hour or so, then fishing the rest of the day. During this period literally thousands of marlin, kingfish, barracudas, amberjacks, snappers, grunts, groupers, whip rays, sharks, and tarpon gave up their lives, and probably a good half of his daylight hours were spent on the water. (Any apparent hiatus in his story for the next thirty years may be assumed to be similarly filled with hunting or fishing.) At this time he was actually selling enough of his catch to pay for bait and gasoline; *Men Without Women* was doing satisfactorily, but the extra money he earned made him feel better about Uncle Gus' generosity.

In June, 1928, young Patrick Hemingway was born after eighteen grueling hours that were finally terminated by a Caesarean operation. The experience frightened everybody, and Pauline's doctor ordered her not to have another child for at least three years. For conscientious Catholics at this time this was a dismaying prospect demanding more self-control than Hemingway was accustomed to exercise, and years later, after the marriage had disintegrated, he told someone the whole sex business had got just too complicated.

His comments on the new baby, "built like a bull and bellows like one," were disenchanted. Why, he wondered aloud, did people want to have children anyway? Three years after, however, there was another one. He had comforted himself with the possibility that this one might be a girl, for he had a tender feeling for

small girls and made friends with them well. But the baby was
another boy, and they named him Gregory.

Ernest's parents had never been able to accept his divorce
and remarriage, and there had been an almost complete estrangement between them. But now they were in Florida on business; the
doctor, having invested heavily in real estate in the twenties, had
come down now that the boom had evaporated to see what could
be salvaged. They met by accident and at once the hard feelings
were swept away in one noisy embrace. Hemingway took them
home to meet the pregnant Pauline and the situation was finally
healed.

But Dr. Hemingway himself was more in need of healing. His
real estate holdings had proved worthless. And when he returned
home he discovered that he had diabetes, with all its tiresome
diet-watching. Then he developed angina pectoris, a painful heart
ailment. His physical anxiety, compounded by his financial worries, deepened into severe depression, and from an active, cheerful man he turned to one suspicious of stranger and relative alike.
Distressed in body and mind, he took to shutting himself up in his
room alone. Finally one day, after burning some personal papers
in the basement, he returned to his room, locked the door, and shot
himself in the head.

Ernest hurried to Oak Park to see to the funeral and take
charge of his mother and Leicester, the only members of the
family still at home. He was grim and businesslike, the grief of
losing the man he loved and revered mingled with shock at that
man's "cowardice" and dislike of that man's wife. He adjured
Leicester to honor their father and pray for his soul and, as a
keepsake, to send him his father's ancient Smith and Wesson revolver.

When he went home he wrote his mother that he and Pauline
had agreed to look after her financially. But the letter carried
a not very subtle threat: though he had never written a novel
about the family, not wanting to hurt anybody's feelings, now
that the man he loved had died, all bets were off and he

just might feel it necessary to write such a book.

His mother, deadpan, ignored the threat and shortly there-after a large crate arrived in Key West. Ernest let it lie around awhile, knowing it contained some pictures his mother had painted and wanted him to sell. Finally he opened it. There indeed were the paintings. There also was a large moldy chocolate cake. And there at the bottom of the crate lay the grim keepsake.

Soon after settling in Key West Ernest had begun a new novel. His father's death had been profoundly unsettling, but with the help of his favorite sister Madelaine, whom he invited back to Key West with him to act as his secretary, he brought it to completion.

A Farewell to Arms detailed the further development of the young man hitherto called Nick Adams and then Jake Barnes. This time, under the name Lieutenant Frederic Henry, he was an American fighting in Italy, the same physical and psychic war casualty as before. In *The Sun Also Rises* the aimless hedonism of Jake Barnes and his friends had epitomized a certain faltering purposelessness typical of the America of the Roaring Twenties. Now, in Lieutenant Henry's evolution from enthusiastic involve-ment in the war to embitterment and disassociation—his "private peace" and desertion—Hemingway was describing the general revulsion against war's carnage. "I was always embarrassed by the words sacred, glorious, and sacrifice and the expression in vain," says the disgusted lieutenant, speaking not only for a certain group of men but for the times themselves. "I had seen nothing sacred, and the things that were glorious had no glory and the sacrifices were like the stockyards of Chicago."

The critic Clifton Fadiman called *A Farewell to Arms* "the very apotheosis of a kind of modernism," and with its tough yet touching love story and a kind of deadpan majesty of prose, it soon reached the top of the best-seller list, sharing the spotlight with another unromanticized account of the same war, *All Quiet on the Western Front.*

With this success Hemingway was well into one of the most spectacular fiction careers of the century, a career built honestly on hard work. He did not often write quickly or easily, and much labor went into that spare, uncomplicated style. Nevertheless he was blessed with several helpful idiosyncrasies: he had almost total recall, which eliminated all laborious note-taking, for if the facts had not stuck in the first place they were not worth remembering. He could write anywhere, which saved shopping around for the perfect studio or the perfect atmosphere. He loved to read on almost any subject, which supplied him with a mountain of foreground and background material painlessly acquired. And last, his concentration was like a spotlight in the dark, trained on one small point and conscious of nothing else anywhere.

Since a writer deals in human beings, a feel for them is indispensable, and here Hemingway was outstandingly endowed. He attracted all kinds of people, all classes, all sexes and ages. The young were charmed by his combination of fatherliness and boyishness and flattered by his interest in them, which was touched with a graceful deference. To those people he respected he was thoughtful, gentle, almost diffident in manner, and in spite of his abounding egocentricity he had a kind of clairvoyance about others. "In a group of people," said one friend, "if two of them were antagonistic to each other, Ernest felt it at once, as accurately as if they wore printed placards."

Now that money was coming in, a latent generosity manifested itself. Knowing the dread of hunger at first hand, he saved many another writer and painter from the same anxiety, and by the end of his life is said to have had several hundred more or less regular dependents. And during the period when his fame attracted a horde of importunate reporters seeking interviews, more than once he refused them angrily, only to soften at the appeal, "I need the money."

Other kinds of generosity came a little harder. All his life he had pitted himself against his friends, determined to outshine them in everything, and as a writer he could not tolerate rivals. Fragile beginners who were no threat to his standing received lavish help, money as well as patient criticism and suggestions, and he was generous with introductions to editors and publishers. But any writer who was big enough to challenge him was sooner or later cut to shreds.

As in writing, so in sports: jealousy was a malignant disease that ate away the good in him. Once on an African safari he had set his heart on getting a giant kudu, a rare kind of large antelope. He and the professional hunters with him had all bagged a few specimens but Ernest was determined to get one better and bigger than anyone else's. Hearing of fresh kudu tracks beside a nearby salt lick, he boasted, "I'll kill you two tomorrow on that lick." And he did get two noble bulls, their horns rising in great dark spirals that would, he knew, look magnificent in the photographs. But when he got back to camp he found that the pros had been out too. And there, propped up in the firelight, was "the biggest, widest, darkest, longest-curling, heaviest, most unbelievable pair of kudu horns in the world."

Raw fury boiled up within him; the rest of the men lowered their eyes in embarrassment, and it was morning before he could speak civilly. However, then so visible was his effort to be gracious that they had to forgive him. His friends generally did forgive him, for his charm was very great.

He did not take criticism well. After *A Farewell to Arms,* which had catapulted him to international fame, he wasted some years turning out very minor nonfiction. The critics were disappointed and said so. And the bullfighting book, *Death in the Afternoon,* was called by some morbid in its preoccupation with death, while others regretted his "he-mannish" posturing. Max Eastman commented quizzically on Hemingway's insistence on his red-blooded masculinity and on his literary habit of "wearing false hair on his chest." All these men, he was convinced, had "ganged up on him," and Eastman's gibe rankled in his flesh for four years. Then he ran into him in Perkins' office, where after some words he ripped open his own shirt to exhibit a chest convincingly hairy and then ripped open Eastman's for comparison. A fight ensued that delighted the gossip columnists for weeks.

It has been noticed that one becomes especially sensitive to that in others which unconsciously he recognizes in himself. So it was with Hemingway; he took to scolding several of his writing friends for "selling out to the rich" (that is, taking a soft job with the Luce or the Hearst organization or writing for the movies) just about the time that *A Farewell to Arms* as novel, play, and movie put him in the lap of the rich himself.

He had glimpsed this enticing world with the Murphys, but at that time he was merely standing on its fringes. Now he had won his own place there, and with his usual zest he plunged in over his head. In 1933, while America was struggling through the Great Depression, he and Pauline made a seven-month safari in Africa hunting big game, part of whose $25,000 cost was a wedding gift from Uncle Gus and part was fees from *Esquire* magazine.

Already known to his intimates as Papa Hemingway, he delighted in tutoring young Alfred Vanderbilt and other gilt-edged youths in the fine points of hunting, and a casual reading of *The Green Hills of Africa,* his account of the expedition, suggests unalloyed enjoyment. But some readers have wondered at his somewhat truculent insistence that this was his own life and he would live it any damn way he chose. Was it, they wondered, his own conscience he was shouting down?

In any case, the expedition, in the intervals between highballs and kudu hunts and attacks of dysentery, had provided him with time for thinking. So had his return to Key West and the rich there, with their yachting and drinking. One feels gradually coming over him a revulsion, a turning of the stomach as he regards himself in the unproductive environment he has let himself enter. Two famous short stories point up this revulsion. Neither is literal autobiography like the Nick Adams stories, but both picture Hemingway struggling with a certain misery within, and both show him living with a woman he sees as destroying him.

The stories come out of Africa and the safari with Pauline and their white hunter. "The Short Happy Life of Francis Macomber" is about a husband who is a coward. He disgraces himself by running away from a charging lion and his wife contemptuously humiliates him by having a blatant affair with the hunter. Then suddenly, strangely, in a moment too quick for thinking, his fear has gone "like an operation." Having wounded a buffalo without killing it, he risks his life by pursuing the dangerous beast into the bush to put it out of its pain. The wife, seeing him now grown strong enough to resist her domination, shoots him dead while pretending to aim at the wounded animal. Hemingway, who all his life had been afraid of being afraid, here symbolically conquered fear and asserted his male domination—even if only for one happy moment. And even if the wife must destroy him for it.

In "The Snows of Kilimanjaro" Hemingway presents a sour picture of a writer who has "destroyed his talent by not using it, by betrayals of himself and what he believed in, by drinking so much . . . by laziness, by sloth, and by snobbery, by pride and by prejudice." He is dying of a loathsome disease, alone on the African plain with a cold woman he dislikes almost as much as he dislikes himself. In death he dreams he is escaping to the mountain heights where he may find freedom and immortality.

Hemingway was indeed sick of a loathsome disease. After writing "truly and purely" and achieving a beautiful book, he had frittered away good years doing stupid things with stupid people, meanwhile grinding out trivia for slick magazines. Now, in disgust, he produced a novel, *To Have and Have Not,* about the Key West–Bimini yachting set in which he parodied the Haves so specifically that his publisher consulted lawyers about the danger of libel suits. For hero he had chosen a Have Not and, signaling the conversion of his conscience, introduced a somewhat forced social message. But the critics were unconvinced and unimpressed, and again he felt himself the victim of a vendetta.

He was unhappy and unsettled. Back in the Paris days with Hadley and Bumby, though he was poor and unrecognized he had walked with certainty, the ground firm underfoot. Now there were tremblings and rumblings and his feet were unsure as they might be before an earthquake. He had expected *To Have and Have Not* to put him back at the top of the fiction field and it had failed him.

Contributing to his unease about his work was an ever-growing rumble of disapproval among his colleagues about Hemingway the man. Not only had he gone globe-trotting in luxury while Americans were starving, but now Spain, a country he loved, was in trouble, on the point of civil war, and he was doing nothing about it.

He was not the only one to notice his dis-ease. An article about him by a Russian critic, a translator of his work, described his state of mind by paraphrasing the Latin term "a sound mind in a sound body." Hemingway, said this Ivan Kashkeen, was a case of "a sick mind in a sound body." And Scott Fitzgerald, who had always admired him beyond reason, saw something wrong too. Fitzgerald had recently written a magazine article about his own nervous breakdown and been castigated scornfully by Hemingway for it. Reacting to Hemingway's attack, Fitzgerald told Max Perkins that Ernest was "'as nervously broken down" as himself. Only, he said, "his inclination is toward megalomania, and mine toward melancholy."

Perhaps the greatest upheaval underfoot, as yet subterranean but already throwing him off balance, was the presence of a tall blond girl named Martha Gellhorn. Handsome, sleek, and an ambitious writer of novels and magazine stories, she had met him in Sloppy Joe's bar in Key West and interviewed him for a magazine article. The friendship had moved rapidly forward from there.

In an odd repetition of Pauline's seduction technique, Martha hastened to establish a close friendship with Ernest's wife and was soon spending so much time at the Hemingways' that she became, as she laughed apologetically, "almost a fixture there, like a kudu head." She and Hemingway talked endlessly about the Spanish war. It was, she felt, a must from a journalist's point of view, and as soon as she got back to New York she was going to arrange for an assignment overseas.

After several weeks she dragged herself away, stopping in St. Louis to visit her mother on the way. While there she wrote Pauline complimenting her on her "lovely guy, Ernestino."

Ernestino himself left Key West almost immediately and went straight to New York. There the two met. But now this was not the Hemingway who had hung about Key West glooming indecisively. The upheaval had shaken him out of his torpor and he was losing no time in getting into "the Spanish thing."

Once he had made his commitment the black cloud lifted. He had recently told Archibald MacLeish that he loved life so much that it would be a "big disgust" when the time came for him to shoot himself. But now there was no talk of suicide; all was bustle and activity. He signed a contract with a newspaper syndicate, he purchased some ambulances for the Loyalist forces, he helped write a propaganda film and made a fund-raising speech. Altogether he made four separate trips to Spain and they yielded plenty of rich fruit—a play, many articles, and one of his major novels.

Now revitalized by all these delightful activities, he seemed the epitome of mental and physical soundness. "His chest," wrote a young reporter, "bulged through his coat like a parapet." With his ruddy skin, black moustache, ingratiating grin, he looked the image of youthful vitality, always, like a prizefighter, bouncing on the balls of his feet and holding his fist waist-high as if ready for a jab.

Arriving in Madrid in the spring of 1937, he was joined by Martha, who came looking for him one night in the restaurant where he was eating. "I knew you'd get here, daughter," he beamed, looking up. "I fixed it so you could."

Together they visited the front by jeep, by chauffered limousine, and on horseback. They endured the bombardment of Madrid (inadvertently revealing their relationship when a bomb landed on the hotel and everyone rushed out of whatever bedroom he was occupying). And during the cold fall days they took along a sleeping bag which, after publication of *For Whom the Bell Tolls,* became probably the most-discussed sleeping bag in all history.

Anyone as public as Hemingway could not hope to keep his

activities secret, and Pauline had long ago heard about the blond lady in Spain. At Christmastime, wearing a long bob as much like Martha's as possible, she came to Paris hoping to win him back. But all that her efforts achieved was a husband whose conscience was scratching him like a burr and making him unbearable to live with. To her reproaches he replied bluntly that "those who live by the sword must die by the sword," and though the separation was not official at this time, she knew she had had her day.

By the time the Spanish Civil War was over Hemingway had written a large collection of stories. He had also written a play about a correspondent who joins the Loyalists, has the same night horrors as other Hemingway heroes, and loves a tall blond college girl who is also a correspondent. *The Fifth Column* was eventually produced by the Theatre Guild but created no great stir. It was his first and last brush with the theater, the numerous rewrites and producers' indecisions convincing him that the written word was a more manageable tool.

While revising the play and thinking deeply about Spain, Ernest let the treachery, courage, and sacrifice he had seen there wash over him. There must be, he thought, a novel in it all. But he was through with politics and propaganda; now he would simply take the place and its sturdy, obscene gypsies, a new hero Robert Jordan, and a lovely new girl Maria.

Over the years Hemingway had concerned himself chiefly with two types of women. At one extreme was the bitch of "The Short Happy Life," of *To Have and Have Not,* and many short stories. In them Hemingway was pillorying his mother, the domineering woman who he said had driven his father to suicide. At the other extreme was his wish-woman, submissive, passionate, and devoted to her man. Catherine Barkly of *A Farewell to Arms* had been such a woman. And now Hemingway created for himself such another, Maria of the sleeping bag and the cruelly cropped hair.

The manuscript started out packed with obscenities, and Max Perkins, a New England gentleman of the old school, entreated

Ernest to cut out some of them. Challenged to specify which ones, Perkins could not bring himself to say the words but scribbled them on a paper and shoved it across the table. Hemingway argued that clean speech was impossible for these rough peasants, so finally as a compromise the offending words were replaced by the figleaf "obscenity." An arresting trick, it was irritating at first and then, as the reader accepted the device, somehow curiously effective.

Here again is the troubled hero who cannot sleep for thinking, who is superstitious about signs, who has had terrifying experiences in early life that damaged him irrevocably, who drinks himself numb to kill the giant Fear, and who is haunted by something that until now he has shoved down inside and never faced.

But here at last he faces it; here the hero talks about his father's suicide. Though he is still scarred, the scars are toughened now. This is at least a step toward greater strength. Therefore, unlike Jake Barnes and Frederic Henry, Robert Jordan, though he is destroyed in the end, accomplishes something positive first.

For Whom the Bell Tolls was dedicated boldly to Martha, the affair being by now generally accepted. And finally, after living three years in "contented sin" on an estate called Finca Vigia (Lookout Farm) near Havana, he was given a divorce by Pauline. The wedding took place in November, 1940, and the book having brought the highest price yet paid for a movie, Hemingway bought his wife the Finca Vigia for a Christmas present.

Now that they were "legal" he hoped Martha would give him a daughter. But in this, as in some other matters, she disappointed him. Hadley and Pauline, women without much personal ambition, had been willing to "tag along" with Hemingway and enjoy whatever bizarre activity he engaged in. But Martha had been a working writer before marriage and she had no plans now for dropping her profession. *Collier's* magazine offered her an assignment in China, and since, as her husband grumpily remarked, her idea of a honeymoon was covering the war on the Burma Road, he agreed to take on a similar assignment to be with her. It was a switch from the usual order and he did not enjoy it.

Later on several occasions she went off on junkets alone, leaving him with his sons at the Finca to brood longingly about Hadley. During the years 1942 to 1944, meanwhile, he and a group of rich adventurers operated the "Crook Factory," a melodramatic scheme for the destruction of German submarines. They outfitted his boat, the *Pilar*, with radio equipment and high-powered ammunition and cruised about the Caribbean with the idea of getting hailed by a U boat; when it closed in on them they were to blow it up. Though none was ever caught, Hemingway was credited with locating one or two, and so was given an A for Effort by the U.S. ambassador to Cuba.

Martha meanwhile made several trips to the European war zone, and with each return she was more crisply impatient with Ernest and his Crook Factory. It was, she contended, outrageous for him to fiddle with this silly scheme while the whole civilized world was fighting and dying, and she wondered if it wasn't just a dodge to get rationed gasoline so the group could go on with their fishing. There were hideous fights at the Finca from which their guests retreated to the swimming pool and distant points, the effect on him being a heightened defensiveness characterized by constant boasting, scolding, and showing off. The omniscient father, he knew everything and told everyone all about it. An indulgent, smiling "Yes, Papa" was the catchword going around the bars at this time.

By May, 1944, Martha had worn him down and he flew to England for *Collier's,* she to follow by boat. And as in 1936, his curious reluctance to go to war was succeeded, once he got there, by an absolute ecstasy of enjoyment.

According to the Geneva Convention, correspondents were prohibited from bearing arms; nevertheless after the Normandy invasion he got into the thick of the action attached to a regiment that subsequently lost eighty percent of its men. In his eagerness he rushed sixty miles ahead of the entire First Army, sending back information and calling for tank support in order to hold out.

On another occasion he rounded up two hundred French irregulars, set up headquarters in a hotel, and carried on his private operation, guarding roads, dispatching patrols, and ordering out civilians on bicycles to spy out enemy positions. Finally, at the liberation of Paris, he made a grand entrance at the head of his personal army, driving in style down the Champs Elysées. At the Place Vendôme he and his men "liberated" the Ritz Hotel and enjoyed a magnificent celebration on fine old liberated wine.

At war's end he came close to being severely disciplined under suspicion of having violated the Geneva Convention. But numerous colleagues were rounded up who swore solemnly they had never seen him with a weapon in his hands, and he ended by being awarded the Bronze Star instead.

A good many of these men who had lied for him would probably have done much more if called on, for officers and men alike admired him extravagantly for having deliberately chosen to go under fire. Nosy correspondents and thrill-seeking celebrities were never welcome at the front, and when Hemingway was shown into Colonel Charles Lanham's operations map room the Colonel prepared to give him short shrift. But Ernest respected soldiers, and Lanham found him "simple, direct, gentle and unaffected," asking intelligent, almost professional questions in a softly deferential voice. And later, the man who had constantly worried about his courage proved it, if not for himself, at least for a good many others.

He was eating dinner with a group of officers and visitors close to the German lines when an 88 crashed through the wall. Every man threw himself flat, grabbing for his helmet for protection. Every man but one, that is. When the candles were relighted there was Hemingway still sitting at the table, bareheaded, alone, quietly eating his dinner.

His success with the soldiers was hardly matched by that with his wife. Having flown to London while she took a boat, he had got there some days ahead of her. On arrival she had started looking for him and had found him in a hospital, having been out on an all-night party that ended in a car crash. Fifty-seven stitches had been taken in his head and he had sustained a concussion that caused him severe headaches for months. When she walked in he was sitting up in bed, his head swathed in bandages like a turban and his beard half covering his chest. Somewhat tactlessly she burst out laughing.

Her "silly inhumanity" rankled for months. Perhaps, he complained, the break-up of his first two marriages might have been his fault—in fact he would gladly admit it. But Martha was a woman like his mother and no man could live with a woman like that.

By this time he had met the kind of woman he could live with. Mary Welsh was a small blond newspaperwoman from Minnesota who was working for Time-Life. She had long admired Hemingway and his work. Hemingway, on sight of her, admired her and her figure just as sincerely. Quickly they fell in love.

Her attentiveness during his hospitalization pointed up Martha's cavalier attitude, and he wrote her an eight-page poem about love and death which he read aloud at a party with great success. Since Martha was more than agreeable to divorce they had an informal troth-plighting in the fall of 1944, the formal ceremony being held two years later.

Once again, with a different woman Hemingway's life changed sharply. After four years he began to think about serious writing again. He told Colonel Lanham that he would miss the war sadly, but he had three sons who had grown up in their mothers' care and it was time now that he did something about them. He would return to Cuba, fix up the Finca for Mary and the boys, and get himself back in shape for writing. In the last analysis, writing was what he had to do. Retirement was the filthiest word in the language, and to retire from what one did best was to back up into the grave.

The Finca was put in shape and equipped with a Chinese cook, a butler, a maid, a chauffeur, four gardeners, two small boys to run errands, and twenty-seven cats. But he was disturbed to find that his body was not so easily put in shape. To a doctor he described various disquieting physical and psychological symptoms and the doctor prescribed, along with other remedies, less liquor. But Ernest, convinced that he had a private arrangement with fate permanently immunizing him from any ill effects from alcohol, consented merely to wait until noon for his first drink.

The unpleasant symptoms declined for a while after Mary arrived, and he did get started on a new novel. But *The Garden of Eden* was doomed to go unfinished into the Havana bank vault. He worked on it half-heartedly for two years. And then, as had happened before, an idea seized him by the elbow and walked off with him.

It happened when he and Mary went to Italy, back to the historic scene of his wounding on the riverbank. Pacing off the precise spot, he carefully dug a small hole in the ground and forced into it a thousand-lire note as a symbol of all he had given to Italy. Shortly thereafter he nearly died from an infection on his face, his life being saved only by massive doses of penicillin.

The coincidence of these two brushes with death having occurred at the same place had some compelling significance for him. So, putting aside his long novel, he wrote a book about a soldier of fifty—his own age—who after many painful war wounds is about to die.

It would seem that, forever thinking and planning for his own death, he was now writing out the scenario for this greatest of dramas. Certainly Colonel Cantwell's experiences closely approximate his own. And he gave the script his favorite kind of heroine, a nineteen-year-old Italian countess who is as loving and compliant as were Catherine and Maria before her.

In drawing this portrait he started with a real person, Adriana Ivancich, who was the carefully chaperoned daughter of an aristocratic Venetian family with whom he had fallen in love. He had first caught her attention when, hearing her say she had lost her comb, he sprang like Walter Raleigh to her aid, breaking his own comb and giving her a half. But conscious of her strict respectability, his own age, and the proximity of his wife, he was always meticulously paternal in his manner, calling her Daughter and never attempting to be alone with her. Still, that did not stop his dreaming; she was his renewal and his inspiration, the freshness, innocence, and idealism of the youth he had lost.

In *Across the River and into the Trees* the girl's name is Renata, which means *reborn*. And in the story she loves him, all her innocence and youth dedicated to the adoration of Colonal Cantwell. Hemingway believed the book, because it meant so much to him, to be a great one, and he boasted to Scribner's that it was going to be a better one that any other son of a bitch alive or dead was able to write.

But that too was part of the dream; the love story was false, and even the style, that famous Hemingway magic with words, at times sounded like a parody of its former self. The critics wanted to like it but few succeeded.

Later, however, Adriana inspired him to write another book that made up for everything. After returning to Havana he moped for her miserably, persuading himself that it was quite natural to love two women at once—that in fact it contributed to one's creativity. Mary had to have considerable forbearance during this period, for his behavior swung wildly between a sweet docility in which he even accepted the honorary presidency of the local PTA, and a manic abusiveness laced with sulks and tantrums. She was privately worried; these extremes were too wide even for him. At last, displaying surely the apogee of indulgence, she invited Adriana and her mother to Key West for a visit.

When the two women arrived Ernest's heart went soaring; life was all an April morning, bright and new. To perserve it unspoiled he did what he knew he must, maintained an iron self-control, made no sign of his feelings, avoided going near the guest house where Adriana slept with her mother, did not even dance with her. Mary was being maternal and patient but wary. And the two innocent women, trotting all unknowing over a terrain spiked with mines, had the time of their lives, exploring fascinating places,

doing fascinating things, and meeting celebrities from society, the
stage, and the movies.

Despite Hemingway's belief in the inspirational force of love,
he had often said that too much actual lovemaking sapped a writer's powers. And so now that he was in love but doing no love-
making his writing ability fairly exploded into bloom. He had long
planned three books about the sea and, filled with the exaltation
of love and genius combined, he worked "like a bulldozer" to
finish one section of that project.

Then, still hot with excitement, he tackled a story he had been
pondering for sixteen years. He had never quite dared to tackle it
before, but now, with a speed and facility that amazed him, he
charged forward headlong. Proudly he wrote his editor that while
at twenty-six it had taken him six weeks to write the first draft of
The Sun Also Rises and he had had to rewrite the whole thing after
that, now at fifty he had done *The Old Man and the Sea* in eight
with not a word to be changed.

Could a medical chart have been made of Hemingway's writing career it would have marked him suffering from some psychic
undulant fever, for every depression was followed by a peak,
which in turn went into another depression. *The Torrents of
Spring*, a low point, was followed by the peaking *The Sun Also
Rises*. After that came *Jimmy Breen*, a book not even worthy of
publication, and then *A Farewell to Arms*. The unimportant *To
Have and Have Not* was succeeded by *For Whom the Bell Tolls*.
And after the depressing *Across the River and into the Trees* came
the small, simple story that made everyone happy and won back
every friend he had lost. *The Old Man and the Sea* brought him
not only a Pulitzer Prize but, in 1954, the Nobel Prize in recognition of his "powerful, style-making mastery of the art of modern
narration."

But unfortunately the fever chart continued on its erratic
course. After the heights of *The Old Man* one could wish his career
had ended in this warm, humane glow. But in the late fifties two
cracked old trunks were found in the storage basement of the Paris

Ritz. Opened, they yielded a few books, a few dirty sweatshirts and sandals, and several penciled notebooks. These were the basis of *A Moveable Feast,* the retrospective book about Paris that was published after his death.

These sketches of his early days have been called vintage Hemingway for the immediacy of his impressions and the liveliness of the language. And it is true that they are clearly the product of a twenty-six-year-old savoring Paris with all the ardor and intensity of first love. But more than one reader, concerned for his total image, has wished that they had never been published.

For the raw young pugilist ready to take on the world had grown in thirty years into a weary old man. And in rewriting his original sketches this man's bitterness had turned them into malicious attacks on old friends and rivals.

True, in looking back, he had not spared himself either, for his account of replacing a poor first wife by a rich second one, and of letting the Murphys' wealth seduce him is corrodingly unadorned.

This misanthropic retelling of his early days took place in the last years of Hemingway's life and doubtless reflects his general deterioration. No one knows exactly when that began, probably many years before. Certainly Mary had long been witnessing behavior so irrational that at times she was almost driven to leaving him. (That she had stuck proved the depth of her love. But then, too, life with Hemingway was always high drama.)

In 1959, homesick for bull fighting, he went back to Spain. Twice he covered the fights in Pamplona, the scene of *The Sun Also Rises.* And there on his sixtieth birthday Mary set up a tremendous party that took a month to arrange. But it was not altogether a success, for his drinking sometimes drove him into an almost lethal rage. Mary refused to nag. "He didn't marry a policeman," she said, having learned her way about by now.

A major disruption occurred in 1960 when the Hemingways were suddenly and shockingly forced to leave their home in Cuba. They had tried to remain aloof from local politics by keeping friendly relations with all regimes. But with Fidel Castro in power it finally became unwise to stay any longer and they slipped out, leaving manuscripts, personal possessions, even a pile of unopened letters. They never went back, though much later Mary was permitted to take away his manuscripts in return for the deed to the Finca, which the Castro regime set up as a museum.

By now the bold figure had shrunk, the lively eyes were full of nameless terrors. He was surrounded by enemies, the police were spying on him, he had lost all his money, strangers were trying to kill him. Eventually he was taken to a hospital, where his condition was carefully disguised in the reports given to the papers. "He was suffering from high blood pressure, but was working steadily."

He did write, desperately, through the final winter, working on *A Moveable Feast.* But in February, 1961, even the writing deserted him. Then he knew that the end had come.

Many years ago Hemingway had quoted the Biblical phrase to Pauline, "He who lives by the sword must die by the sword." Always he had lived by the gun. And so, on August 1, 1961, in the way he had chosen long ago, in the way his father had chosen, he died by the gun.

Bibliography

I.   W. SOMERSET MAUGHAM

The Summing Up, W. Somerset Maugham. Garden City, New
York: Doubleday, Doran & Co., 1938.

A Writer's Notebook, W. Somerset Maugham. Garden City, New
York: Doubleday & Co., 1949.

Of Human Bondage, W. Somerset Maugham. Garden City, New
York: Doubleday, Doran & Co., 1915.

Somerset and All the Maughams, Robin Maugham. New York: The
New American Library, 1966.

Somerset Maugham: A Biographical and Critical Study, Richard
Cordell. Bloomington, Indiana: Indiana University Press,
1961.

Remembering Mr. Maugham, Garson Kanin. New York:
Atheneum, 1966.

The World of Somerset Maugham, Klaus Jonas. Bristol, England: St.
Stephen's Bristol Press, Ltd., 1959.

The Maugham Engima: An Anthology, Klaus Jonas, ed. New York:
British Book Centre, 1959.

A Case of Human Bondage, Beverley Nichols. London: Martin
Secker and Warburg, Ltd., 1966.

The Two Worlds of Somerset Maugham, Wilmon Menard. Los
Angeles, California: Sherburne Press, 1965.

II   SINCLAIR LEWIS

Sinclair Lewis: An American Life, Mark Schorer. New York: McGraw-Hill Book Co., 1961.

With Love From Gracie: Sinclair Lewis; 1912–1925, Grace Hegger Lewis. New York: Harcourt, Brace & Co., 1956.

Dorothy and Red, Vincent Sheean. Boston, Houghton Mifflin Co., 1963.

III   WILLA CATHER

Willa Cather, Elizabeth Sergeant. Philadelphia: J. B. Lippincott Co., 1953.

The World of Willa Cather, Mildred R. Bennett. New York: Dodd, Mead & Co., 1951.

Willa Cather Living: A Personal Record, Edith Lewis. New York: Alfred A. Knopf, 1953.

Willa Cather: A Critical Biography, E. K. Brown (Completed by Leon Edel). New York: Alfred A. Knopf, 1953.

Willa Cather and Her Critics, James Schroeter, ed. Ithaca, New York: Cornell University Press, 1967.

The Landscape and the Looking Glass, John H. Randall III. Boston: Houghton Mifflin Co., 1960.

IV   EUGENE O'NEILL

O'Neill, Arthur and Barbara Gelb. New York: Harper and Brothers, 1962.

Part of a Long Story, Agnes Boulton. Garden City, New York: Doubleday & Co., 1958.

The Tempering of Eugene O'Neill, Doris Alexander. New York: Harcourt, Brace & World, 1962.

The Curse of The Misbegotten; A Tale of the House of O'Neill,

Croswell Bowen (with Shane O'Neill), New York: McGraw-Hill Book Co., 1959.

O'Neill, Son and Playwright, Louis Sheaffer. Boston: Little, Brown & Co., 1968.

V THOMAS WOLFE

Letters to His Mother, Thomas Wolfe, edited, with an introduction, by John Skally Terry. New York: Charles Scribner's Sons, 1943.

The Notebooks of Thomas Wolfe, 2 vols., Richard S. Kennedy and Paschal Reeves, eds. Chapel Hill: University of North Carolina Press, 1970.

Thomas Wolfe, Andrew Turnbull. New York: Charles Scribner's Sons, 1967.

Thomas Wolfe. A Biography, Elizabeth Nowell. Garden City, New York: Doubleday & Co., 1960.

The Journey Down, Aline Bernstein. New York: Alfred A. Knopf, 1938.

The Marble Man's Wife: Thomas Wolfe's Mother, Hayden Norwood. New York: Charles Scribner's Sons, 1947.

Writers in Crisis: The American Novel, Maxwell D. Geismar. Boston: Houghton Mifflin Co., 1963.

VI F. SCOTT FITZGERALD

Letters, F. Scott Fitzgerald, Andrew Turnbull, ed. New York: Charles Scribner's Sons, 1963.

Scott Fitzgerald, Andrew Turnbull. New York: Charles Scribner's Sons, 1962.

The Far Side of Paradise; A Biography of F. Scott Fitzgerald (Sentry edition), Arthur Mizener. Boston: Houghton Mifflin Co., 1965.

The Crack-Up, F. Scott Fitzgerald, edited by Edmund Wilson. New York: New Directions, 1945.

Beloved Infidel; The Education of a Woman, Sheilah Graham.

New York: Henry Holt & Co., 1958.

The Rest of the Story, Sheilah Graham. New York: Coward-McCann, 1964.

Zelda, A Biography. Nancy Milford. New York: Harper & Row, 1970.

VII   ERNEST HEMINGWAY

A Moveable Feast, Ernest Hemingway. New York: Charles Scribner's Sons, 1964.

The Green Hills of Africa, Ernest Hemingway. New York: Charles Scribner's Sons, 1935.

Ernest Hemingway. A Reconsideration, Philip Young. New York: Harcourt, Brace & World, 1966.

Ernest Hemingway. A Life Story, Carlos Baker. New York: Charles Scribner's Sons, 1969.

At the Hemingways. A Family Portrait, Marcelline Hemingway Sanford. Boston: Little, Brown & Co., 1961.

My Brother, Ernest Hemingway, Leicester Hemingway. Cleveland and New York: The World Publishing Company, 1962.

The Best Times. An Informal Memoir, John Dos Passos. New York: The New American Library, 1966.

Papa Hemingway. A Personal Memoir, A. E. Hotchner. New York: Random House, 1955.

Being Geniuses Together, 1920–1930, Robert McAlmon and Kay Boyle. Garden City, New York: Doubleday & Co., 1968.